# CRUISING GUIDE TO THE CHANNEL ISLANDS

# *Cruising Guide to the*

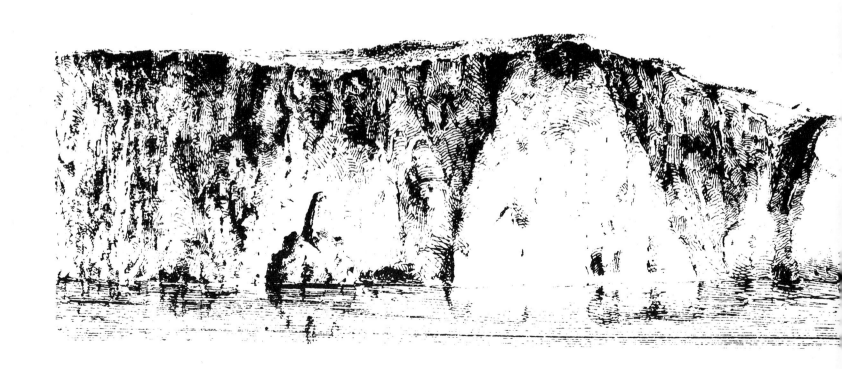

# *Channel Islands*

Text: Brian Fagan     Photography: Graham Pomeroy

*Published by*
CAPRA PRESS *and* PACIFIC SKIPPER
Santa Barbara *and* Newport Beach

1979

LIBRARY OF CONGRESS CATALOGING IN PUBLICATION DATA

Fagan, Brian M
  Cruising guide to the Channel Islands.

  1.  Boats and boating—California—Channel Islands—Guide-books.
2.  Channel Islands, Calif.—Description and travel—Guide-books.
I. Pomeroy, Graham, joint author.  II.  Title.
GV776.C22C424          917.94'9          79-85
ISBN 0-88496-093-5

Published for the book trade by
**CAPRA PRESS**
P.O. Box 2068
Santa Barbara, California 93120
with the cooperation of
**PACIFIC SKIPPER**
P.O. Box 1698
Newport Beach, California 92663

# PREFACE

This Cruising Guide is an attempt to provide a definitive account of the anchorages and harbors of the Santa Barbara Channel. It has been compiled from official and unofficial sources, and is not designed as a substitute for charts. You should use them in conjunction with the appropriate N.O.A.A. charts for the Santa Barbara Channel. We list these at intervals in the text.

We have used the following sources in writing this book:

— U.S. Coast Pilot 7 for 1977 and earlier editions, back to 1858,

— N.O.A.A. (and earlier) official charts for the area and charts dating back to 1853,

— *Local Notices to Mariners* and *Weekly Notices to Mariners,*

— Army Corps of Engineers, *Small Craft Ports and Anchorages,* 1949,

— *Chart Guides for Southern California and Catalina,* Edmund Winlend, 1975, 1977.

— Leland R. Lewis and Peter E. Ebeling, *Sea Guide, Volume One: Southern California,* Sea Publications, Newport Beach, 3rd ed., 1973,

— William Berssen (ed.), *1978 Pacific Boating Almanac, Southern California Edition,* Western Marine Enterprises, Ventura, 1978.

— Articles in *Sea* magazine and other periodicals,

— Most important of all, our own experience of the Santa Barbara Channel and its many ports and anchorages, obtained during a period of over ten years.

The first part of the book covers general problems of cruising in the Santa Barbara Channel, while the rest of the volume consists of detailed sailing directions for the area between Point Arguello and Point Mugu. Two concluding chapters give information on Santa Barbara Island and on Santa Catalina, San Nicolas and San Clemente. We felt that some mention of these islands was worth making, as they are often used as staging posts for a cruise of the Channel. However, we also feel that Catalina is too well-known and developed to need detailed description here, while the military control the other two and inhibit regular visits by pleasure craft.

The sailing directions have been written unashamedly from the perspective of a sailing vessel, inevitably so because we are sailors ourselves and used a 32-foot sailboat for much of the research. We did, however, take a number of trips along the mainland and to the islands in fast motorboats, which enabled us to examine the anchorages from a powerboating perspective. Most of the sailing directions can be used either under sail or power, for, after all, the same basic principles of careful seamanship apply to both.

Readers should also be aware that we are based in Santa Barbara, so at times the sailing directions may have a flavor oriented in that direction. Our coverage of Santa Barbara is particularly complete, simply because the entrance of this popular harbor can be tricky, especially in winter. We have also paid detailed attention to the western portions of the Channel, which are less well-known to pleasure craft. An important feature of the book are the unique Tables of Weather Data and Refuge Anchorages compiled by Peter Howorth, which you are likely to refer to constantly.

The research for the *Cruising Guide* revealed an astonishing mass of recorded and unrecorded information about the Santa Barbara Channel. We delved not only into modern sources but into nineteenth century charts and pilot books for useful data. The manuscript was reviewed by a number of expert cruising people and commercial fishermen, who generously gave us the benefit of their knowledge. While we are satisfied that this book is accurate at time of publication, we are conscious that conditions in the Channel are changing constantly and that, despite every care, some errors or inaccuracies have crept into this book. Interested skippers are encouraged, nay urged, to bring changes and errors to our attention, care of Department of Anthropology, University of California, Santa Barbara, California 93106.

---

*IMPORTANT WARNING*

This book expresses numerous opinions about the many anchorages in the Santa Barbara Channel and about cruising conditions in the area generally. If anything, these opinions are on the conservative side. Realize that these are opinions of the authors, and that your judgment as to whether to use an anchorage, make a passage, or pursue some other course of action may differ according to weather and other conditions at the time.

*In the final analysis, safe cruising comes down to sound judgments on the spot — and we cannot make these for you.*

---

*Santa Barbara, California*      Brian M. Fagan
*January, 1978*                  Graham Pomeroy

## CONVENTIONS

Certain arbitrary choices had to be made when writing this book, basic conventions that are carried right through the text. You should be aware of these as you use the volume.

*Points of the compass and directions* are not all written out in full, i.e., North, South, Northwest, etc., but often given in letters: NW, SSW, etc., *except* when referring to a landmark (Northwest Anchorage) or a weather phenomenon (southeaster).

*Bearings* in the *Guide* are given in degrees magnetic (1978). Although normal convention is to use true bearings, we felt that a magnetic bearing would be less trouble for small craft fitted with magnetic compasses. Check the variation for the year you use this book, and remember to convert true bearings from other publications, where appropriate.

*Distances* are given in nautical miles (2000 yards), *even land distances,* or yards and feet.

*Depths:* We give depths in feet, and usually give a range, i.e., 25-30 feet. *All soundings are given to mean lower low water.* In other words, calculate your tidal depths from our base line soundings. Note that U.S. charts sometimes give depths in fathoms (one fathom equals six feet).

*Lights and radio beacons:* Although every effort has been made to make this book relatively timeless, we have given light and radio beacon characteristics as they were on *August 1, 1978. Check later editions of charts and Local Notices to Mariners for corrections.*

Light characteristics are given typically as follows: Gp. Fl. W.R. 5 sec. 200 ft. 10 miles.
(Group flashing white and red every five seconds, light exhibited 200 feet above high tide, visible (theoretically) for 10 miles.) Light characteristics used are those used on U.S. charts, as explained in HO Chart Number 1, Chart Symbols.

*Anchorage and landmark names* do not always conform to those on the charts, in cases where we know the official source is wrong. These have been identified in the text, also some changes of name in the last century.

*Services* in the major ports are listed at the end of harbor descriptions, and make no pretensions to being complete. You should consult the Yellow Pages or local people for more information. *The listing of a company or service in this book in no way represents our endorsement.*

Although some historical and other background information is given in this book, we have designed it as a practical tool to be used at sea. You should consult your local bookstore or public library for background data of this type.

Finally, some of the anchorages described in this book may be unsuitable for larger vessels or deep draft yachts. There is an important distinction between safe anchorages for fast motorboats and even 25-foot yachts. We have been conservative in our descriptions and deliberately omitted small anchorages in such difficult areas as inside Talcott Shoals or the NW coast of San Miguel Island. We feel that these, and some other locations, are more the preserve of commercial fishermen than pleasure craft.

---

### DISCLAIMER

This book has been compiled from both official and private sources of information, as well as the authors' practical experience of the area. Any opinions expressed are those of the authors and not of the U.S. Coast Guard or other government agencies. And, while every effort has been made to ensure the accuracy of this publication, neither the publisher nor the authors can assume any responsibility for errors in charts, pilotage, sailing directions, soundings, or other information in this volume.

---

# Acknowledgements

Dozens of cruising people, commercial fishermen, and navigational experts have contributed to the compilation of this book, so many that we can't hope to acknowledge everyone individually. But we owe a particular debt of gratitude to:

— Nancy Barron, Travis Hudson, Mike and Debby Pyzel, John and Randi Sanger, and Dan Secord, who read through all, or parts of the manuscript and suggested dozens of useful changes.

— Peter and Jane Howorth, who not only made detailed comments on the manuscript, but provided us with photographs, unique weather and navigational information from their vast experience, and took us on a memorable trip up to Point Arguello in their fast motorboat.

— Alan Hur and Rick Gutierrez, who accompanied us to the islands on several vital photographic trips. We benefited greatly from their detailed knowledge of the Channel.

— Ernest Gabbard, who flew Graham over the Channel on several photographic safaris.

— Dr. Carey Stanton, who generously placed his unrivaled knowledge of Santa Cruz Island at our disposal, and reviewed Chapters 7 and 8 for accuracy.

— Elyse Mintey of Sea magazine for help with back numbers.

— Noel Young and our other friends at Capra Press, who not only published this work, but made the process of writing, research, and production a joyous experience.

— Last, but not least, everyone with whom we had casual conversations about the Channel and who have answered our dozens of questions. We hope that their collective knowledge is reflected in the pages which follow. And we're deeply grateful to those good friends who have cruised with us and tolerated our cameras, bearing compasses and strange maneuvers.

# CONTENTS

Preface

# Cruising Guide to the Channel Islands

# Part I:

# Introductory

The first four chapters introduce the area and describe some of the problems you may encounter in the Santa Barbara Channel. We describe the history of the Channel, weather patterns, equipment, and many other topics that are a logical introduction to the detailed sailing directions in Part Two.

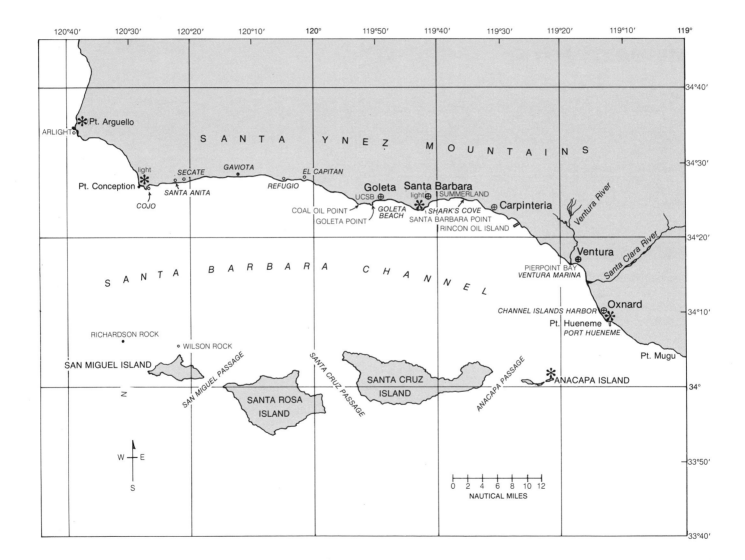

120°40'  120°30'  120°20'  120°10'  120°  119°50'  119°40'  119°30'  119°20'  119°10'  119°

34°40'

Pt. Arguello
ARLIGHT
S A N T A   Y N E Z   M O U N T A I N S
34°30'
light  SECATE  GAVIOTA  EL CAPITAN
Pt. Conception  SANTA ANITA  REFUGIO
COJO
Goleta  Santa Barbara  SUMMERLAND
UCSB  light  Carpinteria
COAL OIL POINT  SHARK'S COVE
GOLETA POINT  GOLETA BEACH  SANTA BARBARA POINT
RINCON OIL ISLAND
Ventura River
Santa Clara River
34°20'
Ventura
S A N T A   B A R B A R A   C H A N N E L  PIERPOINT BAY
VENTURA MARINA
CHANNEL ISLANDS HARBOR  Oxnard
34°10'
Pt. Hueneme
PORT HUENEME
RICHARDSON ROCK
WILSON ROCK  Pt. Mugu
SAN MIGUEL ISLAND  SAN MIGUEL PASSAGE  SANTA CRUZ PASSAGE  ANACAPA ISLAND
34°
N  SANTA CRUZ ISLAND  ANACAPA PASSAGE
SANTA ROSA ISLAND

W — E

S
33°50'

0  2  4  6  8  10  12
NAUTICAL MILES

33°40'

4

# CHAPTER *1*

# *Channel of Many Winds*

The California coast between Point Conception and Point Dume is one of the most popular cruising grounds in the United States. It includes desolate anchorages, quiet coves, and magnificent offshore islands that have attracted explorers, missionaries, settlers, and tourists for centuries. This superb area, centered around the Santa Barbara Channel is entered from the west between rugged Point Conception and San Miguel Island (Fig. 1.1). This desolate and often windy part of our cruising area is less frequented than the quieter anchorages and harbors within the Channel itself. From Point Conception, the mainland turns east and SE in a series of bights. The Santa Ynez Mountains form an impressive backdrop to the coastal plain with their steep canyons and low cliffs.

The coastline west of Goleta and Santa Barbara is sparsely populated, except for the constant traffic on U.S. 101 between San Francisco and Los Angeles. This major artery hugs the coast most of the way between Gaviota and Ventura, and the constant roar of passing traffic can be heard far offshore on still days. The University of California at Santa Barbara lies on the coast just west of Goleta. Its conspicuous high-rise buildings and bell tower can be sighted from a long distance off. Red-roofed buildings and other urban landmarks mark the coastline past Goleta, Santa Barbara, Montecito and Summerland with its distinctive steep, yellow sandstone cliff. Southern Pacific freight trains can be seen hauling their huge loads past the foot of this cliff. The tracks parallel the freeway most of the way between Gaviota and Ventura. East of Summerland and Carpinteria, a small resort town that boasts of the "safest beach in the world," the mountains crowd the coastline as the freeway and railroad hug close to the breakers. Artificial oil islands add a blaze of light to parts of the coast at night and can confuse the navigator. The coastal range dips at Ventura, where the river of that name empties into the Pacific. The low lying sandy beach turns sharply SE close to downtown Ventura, at the mouth of the Santa Clara River. Oxnard and Port Hueneme lie on this flat, intensely cultivated floodplain that forms the east end of the Santa Barbara Channel. At Point Hueneme, the coastline again turns more to the east. The flat, sandy plain gives way to rugged cliffs at Point Mugu. From there to Point Dume, the westernmost promontory of Santa Monica Bay, the coast is relatively inhospitable, although busy with road traffic on U.S. Highway 1.

The Santa Barbara Channel is sheltered by four offshore islands, the westernmost being San Miguel, 22 miles SSE of Point Conception. San Miguel is a desolate and fascinating place, with its herds of sea lions and sweeping winds. In recent years, San Miguel has been a ranch and naval gunnery range. It is now controlled by the National Park Service and is open to the public on a controlled access basis. But its wild, rocky anchorages have a unique fascination, and San Miguel's reputation for strong winds is fully justified. There are times when it feels like the end of the earth, with all normal sounds in its anchorages blotted out by the scream of the wind in the rigging. Santa Rosa, its neighbor, is also relatively inhospitable, although it is a prosperous cattle ranch. Landing is by permit only. There are useful anchorages on the south and east sides of the island, while most people avoid the west end. The winds can blow hard off Santa Rosa as well, especially down the island canyons, and in the passages separating Santa Rosa from San Miguel and Santa Cruz.

Santa Cruz Island is 20.5 miles long and 5.5 miles across at its widest point. The island itself is partly private and partly under Nature Conservancy ownership. Landing rights (by permit only) are jealously guarded. Its deeply indented coastline offers dozens of anchorages to the discerning seaman. Some coves are secure in any weather, others are merely fine weather picnic spots. Although the winds can blow hard off Santa Cruz Island, its weather seems more predictable than that of its more remote neighbors. The biggest dangers are strong nocturnal canyon winds and very

occasional NE storms. But, most of the time, the weather is benign and the anchorages are secure. A Santa Cruz anchorage is a world of its own. The bustle and traffic roar of the mainland is exchanged for the peaceful roll of waves on placid beaches, the barking of sea lions and the bleating of feral sheep high on the steep cliffs that enclose the anchorages. Santa Cruz offers a momentary glance at another, less hasty world, miraculously intact in a much polluted twentieth century world. Long may it offer such a contrast!

Anacapa Island offers few secure anchorages for small vessels, but an abundance of good fishing (Fig. 1.2). Its kelp beds and steep coastline are much frequented by excursion boats and small outboard fishing craft. Anacapa appears like a camel's hump from a distance, but the low lying east end of the island comes into view as one nears the 11-mile passage that separates the island from the mainland at Point Hueneme. A conspicuous lighthouse lies at the east end of Anacapa, which marks the east limits of the Channel. It is now automated, although once manned by Coast Guard crews who lived in the white houses that can be seen clustered near the light. Anacapa is now controlled by the National Park Service. It is possible to land and camp on the island.

Santa Barbara Island lies much further offshore, 39 miles SE of Santa Cruz, 23 miles west of Catalina. The National Park Service controls the island as a wildlife sanctuary, but you can land there. Normally this rocky islet is uninhabited except for sea lions, birds, and occasional parties of naturalists. There is an anchorage of sorts on the south side of the island, as well as a precarious landing in quiet weather. Perhaps it is best to visit this island in the spring, when its wild flowers, especially the Giant Coreopsis (Coreopsis gigantea), are a blaze of yellow.

Catalina Island is the most frequented of all the offshore islands, lying just 26 miles off metropolitan Los Angeles. Avalon is a major tourist resort, and many of the island's best anchorages are congested with private moorings. But the island countryside with its

Fig. 1.2 — *Anacapa Island*

quiet hills and grazing buffalo is essentially unspoiled, a logical stepping off point for a cruise west to the Santa Barbara Channel. It is for this reason that we have included it here.

The diverse cruising ground offers not only contrasting scenery and both urban and rural environments, but the advantage of having relatively predictable weather. The weather is ideal for sailing most afternoons, whereas the mornings are often calm and foggy. Winter storms bring occasional SE blows and hard NW winds that can reach 40 knots or more. Perhaps most dangerous of all are the Santa Ana and local canyon winds that can sweep down on coastal waters in sudden windstorms that can exceed 50 knots. These unpredictable winds are dangerous, for they can blow without warning. But, in general, provided normal seaman-like precautions are taken, you can cruise this fascinating area in complete safety. Many people serve their cruising apprenticeship here before venturing to Mexico, to San Francisco, or even further afield.

## Prehistory and History

People have been exploiting the coasts and fishing grounds of the Santa Barbara Channel for thousands of years. When Juan Rodriguez Cabrillo sailed to California from the west coast of Mexico in 1542, he hoped to find a new route to China and to explore the unknown frontiers of New Spain. He encountered California Indians at San Diego and Santa Catalina Island, then passed through the Santa Barbara Channel in October and November, 1542. He returned to spend the winter among the Channel Islands. The expedition stayed three months, but Cabrillo himself died while his ships were wintering at San Miguel Island. The navigator, Bartolome Ferrel, returned to Mexico to write an account of these remote islands.

Ferrel and his shipmates had ample leisure to study the local inhabitants. The Chumash Indians were friendly and intelligent people, skilled navigators and expert fishermen. They were capable of navigating long distances over open water in their remarkable frameless, planked canoes. These canoes were used for hunting sea mammals (except for whales), fishing, and transporting cargo and people around the offshore islands and along the mainland coast. The average canoe was about 25 feet long, propelled by three or four men with double-ended paddles (Fig. 1.3). Each plank was carefully shaped and fitted with stone and shell tools, then secured in place with a mixture of hard asphalt and pine pitch, called *yop*. The plank was allowed to harden in place before being sewn to its neighbor with vegetable fiber. In spite of the asphalt

Fig. 1.3 — *Brooks Institute photo*

caulking, the canoes leaked. But this effective caulking material made it possible for the Chumash to take their frail craft far offshore in settled weather, with a bailer who sat in the middle of the boat and kept her dry. Certainly the Indians of Santa Cruz had regular contact with their neighbors on the mainland, except in October which they considered a dangerous month, when canoes were put ashore for repair.

The mainland Chumash were described by one early Spanish missionary as "well formed and of good body, although not very corpulent." Neither men nor women wore many clothes. The men normally went naked except for a deerskin, bird feather, or fur cape in cold weather. They often carried a wooden-handled stone knife in their hair. The women wore knee-length, two-piece aprons of tule, deerskin, or sea otter pelts, and occasionally covered their upper bodies with animal skin cloaks. They wore basketry caps to prevent chafing from the weight of the heavy loads. The Chumash made much use of body paint, the various designs serving to distinguish one village from another. They pierced their ears and wore necklaces of shell and stone. The men perforated their nasal septums.

Chumash villages consisted of well-built, dome-shaped houses made of a pole frame, many of them housing extended families of several dozen people. The houses were arranged in well-organized, clean rows. The occupants slept on sleeping platforms arranged in tiers along the walls. Mats were hung to give some privacy. Each village had one or two sweat houses, the larger ones semi-subterranean ceremonial lodges that were entered through the roof. Village cemeteries enclosed by stockades were situated close to the settlement, the graves marked by painted poles. Some Chumash settlements in the Santa Barbara Channel area housed up to a thousand people, centers for important ceremonies, trading activities, legal matters, and so on. Such larger settlements were political capitals over provinces or villages. The islands were one such province, the capital, *Liyam*, on Santa Cruz.

Each province was ruled by a hereditary chief *(wot)* and his assistant. *Wots* served as war leaders and patrons of ceremonial village feasts. They were the only Chumash allowed to have more than one wife. Apparently groups of villages were organized into loose political confederations that covered a wider area, but the details of this aspect of Chumash life are uncertain.

Chumash villages and provinces were constantly quarreling with one another over food supplies and territory. Probably the most common cause of warfare was squabbling over food resources on the borders of provinces. But disputes over wives, social insults to chiefs (like non-attendance at ceremonial banquets), even witchcraft, were common causes of bloody feuding. Marriage ties were probably along wealth and status lines. The principal Chumash gods were Earth and Sun, which they worshipped in rich ceremonies held in the fall and at the winter solstice respectively.

People from hundreds of miles away would flock to the coastal villages for these ceremonies. The planets, stars, and moon had important religious significance. Some plants and animals were believed to have supernatural powers, also.

Although most people believe that the Chumash lived entirely off the ocean, they did in fact utilize an astonishing range of wild vegetables and game animals. The relative importance of different foods varied regionally and seasonally, but in general, the most important resources were fish, shellfish, acorns and deer meat. On the mainland, the Chumash hunted mule deer year-round, especially in the late summer, stalking them near streams where lush feeding was found. They hunted and trapped every type of small animal, even rats, squirrels and skunks. They dried seaweed and ate it in considerable quantities. "It may be said that for them, the entire day is one continuous meal," wrote one missionary.

Below Point Conception and on the Channel Islands, fishing was the main Chumash activity. The early Spanish pioneers often remarked on the incredibly rich marine life in the Santa Barbara Channel. In 1769, Pedro Fages of the famous Gaspar de Portola expedition that prospected for mission sites, wrote that "the fishing is so good, and so great is the variety of fish, known in other seas, that this industry alone would suffice to provide sustenance to all the settlers which this vast stretch of country would receive." The Chumash were able to catch large quantities of fish throughout the year. Their planked canoes enabled them to venture offshore in search of sardines, tuna, marlin, swordfish and other species. They hunted barracuda and giant black sea bass with harpoons. Much offshore fishing depended on the seasonal appearance of the tuna. Tuna are warm water fish and the waters of the Channel are only warm enough for them in mid-summer and fall. They leave the Channel by late November or early December most years. Tuna feed on spawning sardines, also on the abundant phytoplankton in the Channel. Off Point Conception, a hydrographic phenomenon known as upwelling enriches the fertility of the marine environment and constantly replenishes the surface layers of the Pacific with nutrients that foster plant growth and cause microscopic unicellular algae — phytoplankton — to flourish. This process of upwelling is caused by the prevailing NW winds that blow parallel to our coast. They tend to push surface water away from the coastline. The warmer surface layers are replaced by colder water from several hundred feet below surface, especially south of major headlands and along steep coasts. Upwelling is most intense during the summer months. A submerged peninsula which extends SE from Point Conception, and includes Santa Rosa and San Nicholas Islands, intensifies the process of upwelling near the Channel. In spring, billions of spawning sardines feed on the nutrients and zooplankton that lie near the surface west of the islands. The sardines move inshore in the summer. Larger fish and pelicans feed on the sardines and other small fish. The Chumash literally harvested these various fish in their abundance with hooks, with nets, and spears, taking advantage of this unique oceanographic condition. This regular food supply enabled them to settle in far more sedentary villages than many of their neighbors.

Everyone who sails in Southern California has cursed the dense tentacles of kelp that catch one's rudder in the middle of a critical race or while on passage. Kelp beds consist of great forests of marine algae that form in shallow water nearer shore, normally in depths from 30 to 70 feet. Much Santa Barbara Channel kelp grows in depths of 40 to 50 feet. Kelp depends on light as a source of energy, flourishes within easy reach of the shore. It enriches the biological environment. At least 125 species of fish, some 22 percent of the known California fish population, occur in the kelp. Bass, halibut, ling cod, sea perch, and sheepshead are but a few of the common species that the Indians were able to catch from small canoes. The kelp fish populations included many smaller species such as sardines and mackerel. Seals and sea lions abounded. Sea otters flourished in

the marine forest. It is no coincidence that the densest concentrations of Indian archaeological sites are to be found close to the greatest densities of kelp beds, even if the shoreline itself — like the NW coast of San Miguel — is relatively exposed. The Chumash, and their southern neighbors, the Gabrieliño of Catalina, harvested the ocean for much of their protein.

Marine mammals and shellfish were also major food sources. Two species of true seals and four of eared seals occur in the Channel. The Indians hunted them for their pelts and meat, stalking and clubbing the herds as they lay sleeping on land. Sea otters were taken in the kelp with ingenious snares and shot with arrows from canoes. Father Luis Sales described their techniques in the late eighteenth century:

*He (the hunter) has provided a club and a long cord with two hooks, and when he discovers an otter he draws near it. The otter ordinarily swims carrying its young ones, teaching them to paddle with their little paws. Seeing the canoe, she dives under the water and leaves her young on the surface. The Indian comes up immediately and ties the cord to a leg of the little otter so that one hook lies close to the foot and the other a span away. This done, the Indian retires with his canoe, paying out the cord, and when a little way off jerks the cord so as to hurt the otter, and it cries out because of the pain. At its call, the mother comes and sees the Indian is far away, she approaches it, clasps it and tries to take it away, but since the Indian holds tightly to the cord, she cannot. Then the big otter tries by kicking its feet to get the cord off its baby and usually gets entangled with one of the hooks. Now that it is caught, the Indian comes up in his canoe with a club in his hand, gives it a blow on the head, and it is his. I have seen how much this operation requires of the poor Indians; sometimes in a whole day, they get none, sometimes only one, and sometimes they lose all to a sudden surge of sea and are drowned. They also hunt them when they are asleep on the water or when they come upon the beach to rest.*

Eight species of whales visited the Channel seasonally. The Chumash did not hunt whales from their canoes, but took advantage of whale strandings, when they feasted on the meat from the carcass. People would come from afar to share in the unexpected bounty.

Everyone is familiar with the huge, grey accumulations of abandoned marine shells left by the Indians at places where they had camped and foraged for food among the rocks. These "shell middens" can be seen from miles at sea because of the stunted vegetation that grows on them, and their light grey color. They sometimes serve as landmarks for entering small coves which are otherwise inconspicuous. No one knows exactly how important shellfish were to the Indians. Mussels are known to have been used as fish bait. Clams, abalone, octopuses, lobsters, and large bivalves were commonly devoured, perhaps at lean times of the year when few other food supplies were available. Some marine shells were traded far into the mainland interior, for they were widely prized as ornaments.

Plant foods provided a significant part of Chumash diet. Many Chumash archaeological sites are littered with broken pestles, mortars and grinder. Acorns were a staple once the poison was removed, useful because they could be stored in huge quantities. California live oaks abounded on the coastal plains and in the foothills. The Chumash ate many other seeds as well, including walnuts, pine nuts, yucca and various roots. As is true of all Indian groups, the Chumash possessed an encyclopaedic knowledge of the animal and vegetable resources of their environment. As a result, they enjoyed a normally plentiful food supply and continued to live in the same general localities for generations.

The Chumash are most famous for their planked canoes, a replica of which was beautifully constructed by Peter Howorth in 1976 and paddled at speeds of up to seven knots (Fig. 1.3). Their tool kit was simple but skillfully manufactured. They had no metals, but were able to split wood with whale bone wedges and to work steatite and granite into cooking vessels and mortars. The Chumash used sinew-backed bows and cane arrows and clubs against birds and game. Snares, nets and harpoons were commonplace, while Chumash baskets are justly famous. Storage baskets held acorns and dried meat. Shallow basketry trays were used to parch seeds by roasting them with hot embers or pebbles, also for gambling, a favorite Chumash pastime. Chumash wooden bowls, made entirely with stone and shell tools and smoothed with shark skin and rushes, were greatly admired by the Spanish, who thought they had been turned on a lathe.

For thousands of years, the Chumash lived on a regular food schedule. During the rainy season, from November to March, the Indians lived off dried meat and stored vegetable foods, collected shellfish and relied on kelp bed fishing. The spring brought fresh plant growth and the Chumash ranged afield for fresh roots and other plant remains. Fishing improved at the islands, the season reaching its peak at the end of summer and in early fall, when huge schools of tuna and other fish could be harvested. Pine nuts and acorns were gathered in the fall, huge supplies being laid away for use in the lean winter months when the bountiful environment was less productive.

How many Chumash lived on the mainland and Channel Islands? Early Spanish records are vague on the subject, but anthropologists estimate that some 15,000 Chumash were scattered over Santa Barbara and Ventura Counties. The densest populations were concentrated in villages along the Santa Barbara coastline, where perhaps as many as 1000 people lived in the major permanent settlements. These figures may be conservative. The offshore islands had a lower population, where impoverished villages relied heavily on fish, shellfish, and sea mammals for their diet, but did trade food stuffs and raw materials from the mainland. Although the islanders gathered vegetable foods, these resources were soon exhausted by the fishing villages. The island people were concentrated on San Miguel, Santa Rosa and Santa Cruz. They visited Anacapa and Santa Barbara Islands in calm weather to collect shells, pebbles and other objects.

Geographer Sherburn Cook once estimated the Chumash population of the offshore islands at 1000 souls. Current estimates are about 2000 souls for Santa Cruz, 1000 for Santa Rosa. These conservative estimates are far smaller than those for the mainland population.

Juan Rodriguez Cabrillo was the first European to record sailing into the Santa Barbara Channel. On October 10, 1542, his tiny squadron of two caravels anchored off what is now the Rincon near Carpinteria. A large Chumash village known as Shuku lay close to the shore, consisting of circular, thatched huts that held as many as 40 or 50 people each. Cabrillo marveled at the Chumash canoes which skimmed over the calm waters between the shore and his caravels in only a few minutes. His seamen named Shuku the Pueblo de las Canoas which means "canoes" in Spanish. The village site itself lies partly under U.S. 101. Cabrillo explored north of Point Conception but returned to winter at the islands.

The Spanish expeditions which visited the Channel intermittently after 1542 brought back a patchwork of observations of Indian customs with them. After the discovery of a return route to the New World from the Philippines in 1565, Spanish ships regularly sailed south along the California coast after making landfall on the Northern California shore. Two centuries later the Gaspar Portola Expedition explored the coastline between San Diego and San Francisco Bay in late summer, 1769, and winter, 1770. These Spaniards spent several weeks among the Chumash. Father Juan Crespi, a priest accompanying the expedition, was careful to set down his observations of the local people. He visited not only the Pueblo de las Canoas, which he called La Rinconada, but also another large village known as Syuhtun, at the site of modern Santa Barbara. Syuhtun contained 60 well-built houses. Seven canoes were fishing off the surf. "A good arroyo of running water" flowed into the Pacific near Syuhtun. The soil seemed fertile. Crespi and his superiors decided it would be an admirable place for a mission. Five missions were founded in the Santa Barbara area in the next quarter

century. San Buenaventura Mission was built in 1782, and a Royal Presidio established a short distance from Syuhtun in the same year. Four years later, the Santa Barbara Mission was established close to this Presidio. A small Spanish settlement soon stood where Syuhtun had once flourished.

Each mission was responsible for converting the surrounding Indians to Christianity. They were to be civilized by teaching them agriculture, Spanish, and new religious beliefs. The scattered Indians were to live in communities governed by Spanish social and political institutions. The celebrated British explorer, George Vancouver, anchored off Santa Barbara and Ventura in 1793 and witnessed reduction in progress. The Chumash were little influenced by the Spanish until the "reduction" program began. Although the mission system did not last long, the Chumash were dramatically affected. Crowded together at the missions and exposed to strange European diseases, the Indian population was rapidly decimated. As Mexicanization of the Chumash accelerated, more and more of them intermarried with settlers and soldiers. Traditional Chumash lifeways and beliefs were gradually submerged by an overwhelming Spanish-Mexican culture, although the missions experienced considerable difficulty in preventing the Chumash from reverting to their old ways. The mission fathers had brought the last inhabitants of the islands to the mainland in the early nineteenth century, leaving their canoe ports for the seal, sea otter and whale hunters who flocked to the offshore islands in succeeding years. Many Chumash became ranch hands or drifted into pueblos like Los Angeles. By the early twentieth century, few Chumash remembered mission life. The last traditional ceremonies were held in the 1870s. By the turn of the century, few Indians could recall these rituals and their meaning.

Fortunately, a few local settlers took an interest in Chumash culture and interviewed surviving Indians about their culture. The Santa Barbara Museum of Natural History has thousands of pages of notes compiled by the anthropologist John Peabody Harrington, who studied the Chumash at intervals between 1912 and 1961. His records — in English, German, Spanish and Chumash itself — will take years to unravel. But they are slowly revolutionizing our knowledge of the nearly extinct, indigenous inhabitants of the shores of the Santa Barbara Channel.

In the early 1800s, Russian sealers began venturing into the Channel in search of sea otter, found by the thousands on the offshore islands. Their ruthless hunting methods practically wiped out the sea otter population in a few years. The Chumash were humiliated at the hands of the sealers, who were constantly in search of women. New Bedford whalers followed the sealers, for the Channel was an ideal place to hunt grey whale as they migrated along the California coast. The whalers based themselves on Cojo anchorage under the lee of Point Conception and at Goleta, as well as on Santa Cruz Island. They moved directly out from shore in their long boats. Harpooned whales were towed to shore, the carcasses rendered to whale oil in huge iron cauldrons which remained on the beaches long after the whalers finally left the area.

There were even pirates in the Channel! In 1818, the French brigand Hypolyte Blanchard sacked the city of Monterey and then sailed into the Channel to plunder the wealthy Ortega Ranch near Refugio. Fortunately, Ortega had been forewarned of the attack and was able to move his household and valuables to safety inland. Three of Blanchard's men were ambushed by a small party of soldiers from the Santa Barbara Presidio and clapped in prison. Blanchard burned the ranch buildings and killed all the livestock in retaliation. Two days later, he anchored off Santa Barbara. His 300 men vastly outnumbered the 50 defenders of the Presidio. Fortunately, the Spanish commander was a resourceful man. He marched his small garrison round and round a thicket on the beach, changing their clothes each time they came into view. Blanchard watched closely through his telescope, figured he was outnumbered, and decided to negotiate. The three

prisoners were quickly returned and Blanchard slipped away toward San Diego. These were the last pirates in the Channel.

The nineteenth century saw the beginnings of a brisk coastal trade. Richard Henry Dana wrote an immortal account of his experience of the California sailing trade in the brig *Pilgrim* in his *Two Years Before the Mast,* in which he described the Spanish settlement at Santa Barbara, the long sandy beaches of Point Hueneme, and the SE storms that bring violent winds in their wake. He complained in particular of the long swells that rolled onto the beach every winter.

Southern California was a prime hide-producing region in those days. Dana describes the backbreaking work of trading hides by boat, the Spanish grandees and occasional Americans who lived in this remote land. He left an account of a Santa Barbara wedding between the youngest daughter of Don Antonio Nonejo, a local gentleman, and the *Pilgrim's* agent, Mr. Albert Robinson. He described the bride's father's house with a large courtyard in front, "upon which a large tent was built." Nearly everyone in town had crowded into the courtyard to take part in the dancing and other festivities which lasted three days. The El Paseo shopping center off State Street is the site of this famous wedding.

Twenty-four years later, in 1859, Richard Henry Dana returned to California, this time by steamer. He was strongly moved by the sight of the familiar landmarks of the Channel, by Santa Cruz and Santa Rosa Islands, and Santa Barbara "on its plain, with its amphitheater of high hills and distant mountains. There is the old mission with its belfries, and there is the town, with its one-story adobe houses, with here and there a two-story wooden house of later build," he wrote nostalgically. "Yet little is it altered," Dana continues, "the same repose in the golden sunlight and glorious climate, sheltered by its hills; and then . . . there roars and tumbles upon the beach the same grand surf of the great Pacific." He called on the local worthies and *Pilgrim's* former agent, remembered the harsh,

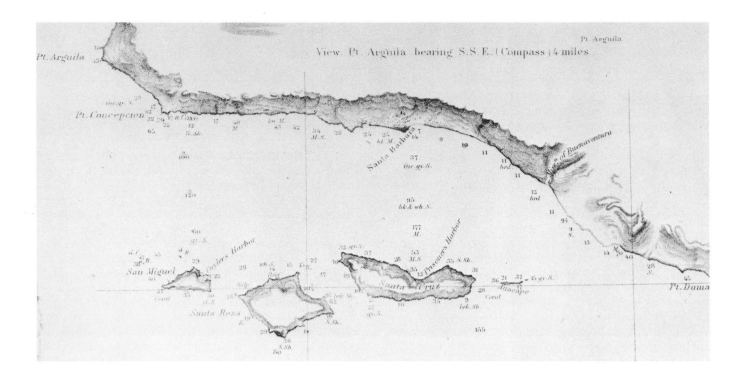

View. Pt. Arguila bearing S.S.E. (Compass) 4 miles

monotonous routine of loading hides. Santa Barbarans were making just enough from sheep, wine, and olives to keep the town going. Dana found one major difference, however. The weather seemed more predictable, for ships were able to lie safely off the town inside the kelp all year-round.

The pace of American settlement accelerated dramatically after the Gold Rush of 1849, and with the opening of the transcontinental railroad. Coastal trade picked up momentum, as numerous sailing vessels and, later, steamers plied between the various settlements carrying hides, tallow, lumber, hardware and passengers. Santa Barbara gradually became a winter resort for wealthy easterners. Stearn's Wharf was built out from the beach in 1872 and provided a convenient staging

post for the coastal steamers. Even Chinese junks traded in the Channel, hunting sea mammals and collecting abalone shells for far-off markets.

Despite the efforts of Sebastian Vizcaino and other pioneers, the California coast was virtually uncharted until the 1850s. In 1783, Juan Pantoja's chart of the Channel showed Cojo and mapped soundings off the entrance to Goleta Slough. After the Gold Rush, the United States Coast Survey began a long-term mapping project on the West Coast. The Federal Government started lighting the coast, too.

In 1885, George Davidson, at that time an assistant in the Coast Survey, and later an eminent surveyor and geographer, published his *Directory for the Pacific Coast of the United States*. This set of informal sailing directions was designed to amplify the new surveys completed by the government and published in the Annual Reports of the Coast Survey from the early 1850s onwards (Fig. 1.4). Davidson's *Directory* was seized upon with avidity by seamen unfamiliar with California. Within a decade, the *Directory* had become the first edition of the *U.S. Coast Pilot* for the West Coast, also under Davidson's authorship. By 1889, the fourth edition was 700 pages long, a monumental compendium of navigational information and interesting historical data. Seamen referred to it as "Davidson's Bible." Today's *U.S. Coast Pilot* is derived from Davidson's pioneer work, stripped of much of its historical information to become a strictly utilitarian work for large ships. Much of Davidson's information is still valid today. We have drawn on his Pilots and on the original charts of the Santa Barbara Channel in compiling this work. Certainly the quality of the engraving on the charts probably will never be bettered.

In 1887, the Southern Pacific Railroad reached Ventura and Santa Barbara. Slowly the coastal trade began to decline as the railroad and, later, trucks, took over load carrying from steamers. But the Channel was still a relatively unspoiled and remote place, a favorite winter resort for the wealthy and famous. Santa Barbara boasted of its own film industry in the early years of silent movies. In 1929, Major Fleischmann paid for the erection of a rock breakwater to protect the anchorage west of Stearn's Wharf. The stone came from Fry's Harbor on the north coast of Santa Cruz. Even so, there were only a few yachts in the Channel, mostly large vessels. But the Santa Barbara Yacht Club was founded in 1872. The great expansion of sailing in the Channel has come since the Second World War and especially in the last two decades as mass-produced yachts have become widely available. So the quiet coves of the offshore islands are now used by pleasure craft of all sizes, rather than the Chumash canoes, American and Russian sealers and Chinese junks of earlier centuries. And the deserted anchorages of Santa Barbara and Ventura now shelter hundreds of yachts and fishing boats of every shape and size behind protective breakwaters.

The offshore islands have enjoyed as colorful a history as the mainland. The Cabrillo Expedition anchored off Anacapa Island in October, 1542, and spent some time at the three larger islands. It was on San Miguel Island that Cabrillo fell and broke a limb. He died in Cuyler's Harbor on January 3, 1543. Cabrillo named the islands "Islas de San Lucas," but the label never stuck. When Juan Perez, captain of Portola's supply ship, visited the largest island in 1769, he renamed it Santa Cruz, while Santa Rosa Island received its name from the same source. George Vancouver, an English voyager in these waters in 1793, obtained a Spanish chart that perpetuated the present names. Soon they appeared on British Admiralty charts.

After about 1816, few Indians lived on the islands. For a while sea otter hunters and sealers inhabited the remote coves of the islands, rapidly decimating the wildlife population.

In 1850, a local sealing captain named George Nidever settled on San Miguel. He imported cattle and sheep and ran a ranch on the island until 1870 when he sold out. The island became sheep-grazing land until 1892 when Captain James Waters leased the island for eight years. He claimed San Miguel was still in Mexican territory and refused for a while to let U.S. coast surveyors land on the island. Waters' stance was overridden by an order signed by President Cleveland himself. His greatest claim to fame was the construction of a remarkable house built from driftwood and shipwrecks. New Englander Herbert Lester and his family were the last ranchers on San Miguel. They arrived on the island in the late 1920s and had but sporadic contact with the mainland by boat and private plane. The Lesters' two daughters were educated in a tiny schoolhouse complete with two desks, using books and curricula supplied by Santa Barbara's Board of Education. Herbert Lester committed suicide when he learned that the Navy was to take over San Miguel and the family would have to evacuate.

Santa Rosa was awarded as a Mexican land grant to Carlos and Jose Antonio Carrillo in 1834. By the 1850s, the island was on its way to becoming a prosperous sheep ranch. The island passed into the hands of L. Vickers and J.V. Vail in 1902. The same company still runs one of California's largest cattle ranches there. The U.S. Air Force maintained a small base on the south coast of the island by Johnson's Lee in the 1950s, which is now abandoned.

Santa Cruz Island, once known as San Lucas, was so named by Portola's supply ship captain, Juan Perez, in 1769. The origin of the name is uncertain, but may be connected with either the Feast of the Holy Cross (May 3) or the Feast of the Exaltation of the Holy Cross (September 14). Another legend states that the name commemorates the Indians' return of a lost crucifix. The island first appeared on British Admiralty charts after George Vancouver recorded the name in the late eighteenth century. Sea otter, seal, and sea lion hunters, as well as fishermen and contraband traders, used its coves during the early nineteenth century. In 1839, Mexican Governor Juan Alvarado granted Santa Cruz Island to Spanish-Mexican Andres Castillero, who probably kept cattle, sheep and pigs. Castillero sold the island to William E. Barron, an Englishman in the Mexico/California trade, in 1857. But the land title was contested before the Land Claims Commission after the annexation of California in 1852. It was not until 1859 that the Santa Cruz Island case was settled by a judgment of the U.S. Supreme Court signed by the celebrated Justice Roger Taney.

Barron sold Santa Cruz Island in 1869. A group of 10 investors connected with the so-called French Bank in San Francisco purchased the property. But the bank fell on evil times. So an assayer and hardware merchant named Justinian Caire paid off the debts of his fellow partners in exchange for control of the Santa Cruz Island Company they had incorporated in 1869. Caire himself never visited the island until 1880, but he developed an old style family ranch there, staffed by Italian immigrants and local Barbareño Vaqueros. Caire's wife was Genoese, so he used these connections to recruit farmhands who worked off their passages on the island. The ranch prospered as Santa Cruz wines became popular on the mainland. Caire grew almonds,

olives, and kept cattle and sheep as well. After 1880, he took to spending some months each year on the island. A network of ranch dwellings through the island kept track of cattle, sheep and crops. In 1891, Caire built a Roman Catholic chapel in the central valley. This chapel was reconsecrated in recent years and is now part of the Parish of Buenaventura.

Caire died in 1898. His family and descendants quarreled among themselves and entered into prolonged and expensive litigation over ownership of the land. The ranch fell on bad times as a result of Prohibition and the Depression. In 1937, Edwin Stanton purchased approximately 90 percent of the acreage of Santa Cruz Island, while the Gherini family, descendants of Justinian Caire, retained the remaining 10 percent. Stanton maintained a cattle ranch on his acreage until his death in 1963. His son, Dr. Carey Stanton, incorporated a new Santa Cruz Island Company in the following year. In 1978, the Nature Conservancy acquired the Stanton acreage, thus ensuring the continued protection of the property, while allowing controlled public access. The Conservancy has the double challenge of preservation of Santa Cruz Island's unique environment, and of operating the magnificent nineteenth century style ranch operated by the Stanton family with such care for many years.

Anacapa Island is named after an Indian word 'anyapah,' meaning mirage. This precipitous island has rarely been settled except by government personnel. On December 2, 1853, the 225-foot side wheel steamer *Winfield Scott* struck the rocks near the present Anacapa lighthouse in a dense fog. All the passengers and $800,000 of gold bullion from San Francisco were rescued safely. The following year the federal government sent a survey party to look for a lighthouse site. A young man named James Whistler accompanied the survey and made a sketch of the island for publication (Fig. 1.5). Later, he went on to international fame as an artist. In 1912, 56 years after the original request to Congress, an automatic light was finally built on Anacapa. The original pyramidal skeleton tower was replaced by a lighthouse with resident keepers in 1932. The operators lived in four white, red-tiled houses near the light. These buildings and the water reservoir can be seen from a considerable distance away. The light was recently automated for a second time. The Coast Guard now controls its operation from Port Hueneme on the mainland. Anacapa and Santa Barbara Islands became the Channel Island National Monument in 1938.

Santa Barbara Island has never been settled permanently, despite sporadic attempts to grow cereal crops there. In 1938, President Franklin Roosevelt declared the island, with Anacapa, as a National Monument. The U.S. Navy used it as an aircraft early warning outpost in World War II.

The military has a large investment in San Nicolas and San Clemente Islands. San Nicolas has been government property since 1848. Several sheep ranches flourished on San Clemente earlier this century, but the sheep and hundreds of goats ate the vegetational cover and denuded the soil. The island passed into government hands before the Second World War.

Santa Catalina was visited by Cabrillo in 1542, when he named it La Victoria. When Vizcaino visited the island in 1602, he found it densely populated by a people described by George Davidson "as very ingenious, particularly in pilfering and concealing." The Indians had long vanished when Catalina was granted to a sea captain, Tomas Robbins, in 1846. After passing through several hands, Catalina came under the ownership of the Santa Catalina Island Company, which controls it today. Catalina is now an important Southern California resort, much more developed than the other islands.

The Santa Barbara Channel is now a major sailing center, rather than a remote corner of the New World inhabited by quiet Indian fishermen for thousands of years. Despite the inroads of real estate developers, the oil industry, and the military, it is a tribute to the owners of the offshore islands that so much of the Santa Barbara Channel remains unspoiled for everyone.

*A fierce Santa Ana wind in Avalon Harbor, Catalina.   Photo: Gene's Rock and Gem Shop, Avalon.*

CHAPTER **2**

# *Wind and Weather*

The coastal area between Point Conception and Catalina Island enjoys a relatively favorable climate, that enables one to cruise safely throughout the year — provided one observes the weather and follows the forecasts closely. The weather and seasons may seem monotonous to outsiders, but sometimes startling changes in sea and wind conditions can surprise even the most experienced crew. This unpredictability makes some understanding of local meteorology essential to anyone who ventures offshore. This chapter summarizes the major features of coastal weather between Point Conception and the Mexican border. But you should remember that local conditions can often create radically different sea and wind conditions in a small area. Examples are strong winds that can funnel through the channels between the offshore islands, and the fresh offshore breezes that blow over the Oxnard plain on many fine mornings.

## Weather Forecasts

Public weather forecasts available to cruising vessels in this area are usually rather generalized. Everyone is familiar with the classic "Point Conception to the Mexican border, winds light and variable morning hours, westerlies 10-18 knots in the afternoon" routine so belabored by disc jockeys. It is up to the individual skipper to interpret the forecasts and to become familiar with local weather signs in the area. The following are the major sources of forecasts (for further information — see Table 2.1).

1. *VHF.* Continuous broadcast of weather forecasts from the Los Angeles National Weather Service office are heard on Channel WX-1 and WX-2.

2. *Coast Guard Weather Broadcasts.* These cover a broad area, and serve large ships as well as small. Coast Guard Long Beach Radio (NMQ 2670 Kc), San Pedro (KOU 2466 Kc) broadcast at scheduled times.

3. *Telephone.* Weather forecasts can be obtained from the National Weather Service in Los Angeles and Santa Maria (see Table 2.1).

4. *TV, Commercial Radio Stations, Newspapers.* Newspaper forecasts can be useful, especially if they include a weather map. The *Los Angeles Times* is particularly good. TV newscast reports can be effective, but have to cover too much in a short time. Some are becoming increasingly "folksy" and less useful. Commercial radio spots are superficial, and often out of date. Station KNX in Los Angeles (1070 AM) broadcasts accurate harbor weather reports at intervals through the U.S.C. Sea Grant Program. But they cover only one harbor at a time.

### TABLE 2.1
#### WEATHER INFORMATION
*National Weather Service Marine Weather Forecasts*
*Telephone*

Los Angeles  (213) 479-6779  24-hour recorded message
             (213) 824-7211  Mon-Fri 0800-1630
Santa Maria  (805) 925-0246  0630-2200 daily

*Radio*

Los Angeles
    WX 1   162.55 MHz   Continuous broadcast
Santa Barbara
    WX 2   162.40 MHz   Continuous broadcast
These stations cover Point Conception to the Mexican border. Tapes are updated every two or three hours, and include weather warnings in effect.

*Coast Guard Marine Information Broadcasts*

These cover coastal weather reports and also important information about changes in navigational conditions. The frequency of Coast Guard Long Beach Radio (NMQ) is 2670 KHz, and broadcasts of information and/or weather are made at 0633, 0800, 1503, 2000, 2103 PST.

*Commercial Broadcasts*

Consult local newspapers for precise schedules, but here are some major AM stations in our cruising area:

| 0725 | KUHL | Santa Maria | 1440 KHz | Mon-Sat |
| 0800 | KTMS | Santa Barbara | 1250 KHz | Mon-Fri |
| 0825 | KUHL | Santa Maria | 1440 KHz | Mon-Sat |
| 1215 | KUHL | Santa Maria | 1440 KHz | Mon-Sat |
| 1215 | KSMA | Santa Maria | 1240 KHz | Mon-Fri |
| 1600 | KUHL | Santa Maria | 1440 KHz | Mon-Fri |

*Storm Warnings are Displayed at:*

Port Hueneme Chief Wharfinger's office
Channel Islands Harbormaster's Office
Ventura Marina Harbormaster's Office
Santa Barbara Harbormaster's Office

5. *Bulletin Boards, Local Officials.* All Harbormaster's offices display weather forecasts and, even more useful, reports of prevailing conditions at key coastal stations in the region as well. You can usually learn local weather conditions by calling your Harbormaster, or a port near your destination. This is the best way to learn about prevailing swell conditions at Ventura and elsewhere.

6. *Direct radio communication* with vessels in the area you plan to visit can give you invaluable insights into developing weather conditions.

By combining forecast reports with your own observations of local conditions, you should have enough information to go on. There are, however, two golden rules:

**Never go to the islands or near Point Conception without checking the weather forecasts.**

**Monitor weather forecasts periodically in the channel and at the islands.**

The abundant forecast information available is, however, almost useless unless combined with the ability to interpret local weather types.

## Major Weather Conditions

The coastal climate of Southern California is noticeably cooler than areas inland. Banks of rolling, grey fog and cool sea breezes keep the shoreline at a lower temperature throughout the day. Coastal fogs pose a continual complication in the navigation of small craft, but the conditions that create fog also encourage predictable westerlies in the afternoons.

### Marine Layers and Inversions

Weather conditions on the California coast are radically affected by high and low pressure systems offshore and in the interior. The most common conditions occur when a long-lived high-pressure area sits off the California coast while a low-pressure area lies over southern Nevada and the California deserts. These conditions create a pressure difference that maintains an air flow in from the Pacific across our cruising ground and over the coast.

As this air passes over the cool waters along the coast, a relatively cool layer known as the "marine layer" is formed. Cooling effects of the ocean create this marine layer that contrast sharply with the mass of warmer air at higher altitudes. The transition zone between the marine layer and the warmer air above is called the "inversion layer."

The inversion layer can vary in intensity and lie close to the surface or several thousand feet above sea level. Its intensity depends on the temperature differences between the cool and warm air. Pressure differences between high and low centers vary. The inversion tends to weaken if low pressure lies to the north, NE, or east. Cooler temperatures above the inversion layer tend to weaken it. If warm air sinks down from higher altitudes, the inversion tends to strengthen (Fig. 2.1).

The inversion layer serves as a lid that suppresses vertical air movement. As the inversion strengthens, the lid becomes tighter. Cooler air tends to stay in the layer as it is too dense to rise into the warmer zones. As the lower layers pass over coastal waters, they pick up moisture from the Pacific, which becomes fog and low, grey, stratus clouds. These vary in thickness with the altitude of the marine layer. Haze and smog accumulate

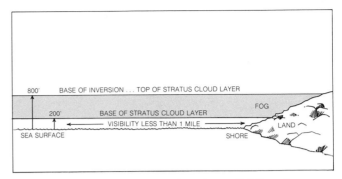

Inversion layers over Southern California
Fig. 2.1a — *When the inversion is lower than 800 feet, the chance of dense fog over coastal waters increases.*

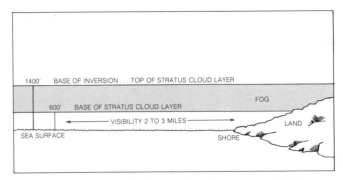

Fig. 2.1b — *When the inversion is around 1400 feet, low clouds rather than fog form over coastal waters.*

below the inversion, too, for they are unable to escape to the upper atmosphere.

Coastal fog and low clouds are at their thickest during night and morning hours. As the air near the land surface warms up during the day, the lower air layers reach a similar temperature as the air above the inversion, which then dissipates. Fog and clouds disperse and we enjoy afternoon hazy sunshine before the inversion reforms and visibility drops down again.

Fig. 2.2 — *Fog whirls at Crook Point, San Miguel Island. —Photograph by Bob Evans*

### Fog and Low Clouds

Fog and low clouds occur when inversion conditions exist. Fog and low clouds are frequent between May and August. Or, many summer days, a dense layer of grey stratus clouds will lie several hundred feet above the surface, presenting no particular hazard for careful navigation, for the visibility will be at least several hundred yards. Dense fogs, when clouds lie on the surface, are more common in late fall and early winter. The difference between fog and low clouds is hard to discern, but is determined by the thickness of the inversion layer.

Fog and low clouds tend to clear in the afternoons, only to reform as evening cooling sets in. As cooling proceeds, the layer of clouds thickens toward the surface. According to the National Weather Service, if the layer of clouds is less than 600 feet above sea level, the chances of fog rather than low clouds are much higher. If the dense haze associated with the low clouds

persists near the coast, then the inversion layer is intense, and dense fog may be possible in the evening. Sometimes banks of fog will linger offshore and then be swept inshore by the sea breeze. These fog belts can be very dense and should, if possible, be avoided, even though sailing from dense fog into bright sunlight and into fog again is dramatic and unusual (Fig. 2.2). Very often, the wind will be strongest along the fog line, a useful racing tip.

Because fog conditions change constantly, they are difficult to predict accurately. You must rely on your own judgment to decide whether a particular passage is safe under prevailing conditions.

### Land and Sea Breezes

When high and low pressure systems lie some distance off the Southern California coast or are of weak intensity, then they have only a minor effect on cloud cover or winds near the mainland. At times like these, the land and sea breeze cycle becomes a dominant factor in our weather pattern (Fig. 2.3).

After the sun sets, the land cools, the cooling air sinks to lower levels. This air will first move down north and east-facing slopes that lose the sun first, then down the south and west-facing slopes. As this breeze moves downslope and reaches the coast, it gains momentum. The downslope wind will blow in a direction determined by the slope of the land and by the headlands and bays that indent the shoreline. Once it fans out over the water, the land breeze loses velocity rapidly and rarely extends more than five or ten miles offshore.

Nighttime cooling is most pronounced on long winter nights with clear skies. Land breezes tend, therefore, to be more prevalent in winter, can persist all night, but often blow strongest about sunrise. As the land begins to warm up, they die rapidly.

The sea breeze is a reverse process to that of the land breeze. Air over the warming land tends to move upslope as it also warms on hilly coastlines. But air over the ocean remains cooler, and tends to move inshore to replace the rising warm air over the land. As this sea breeze approaches the coast, it will change direction toward the easiest shoreward path. It bends around hills, cliffs and headlands, leaving a zone of confused winds in the lee of the land. Sea breezes are strongest in the summer months when the Southern California desert and inland valleys warm up rapidly. Their greatest influence is felt within five or ten miles of the coast, although winds further offshore can be affected by a strong sea breeze, the former changing flow in the same general direction. Sea breezes blow most strongly between June and September, are nearly equal in force in spring and fall, and are weakest from late November to March. These should not be confused, however, with the strong and persistent NW winds of mid-March and mid-May.

### Catalina Eddy

The so-called North Pacific High dominates the weather map off the California coast most of the

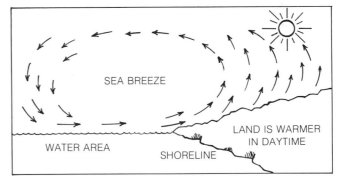

Fig. 2.3 — *The circulation of air during Sea and Land Breeze conditions near the coast.*

summer. As we have shown, the pressure gradient between the high and low zones of the SW United States dominates the weather patterns over the coast and ensures a prevailing NW air stream parallel to most of the California coastline. This wind blows almost parallel to the coast until it reaches Point Arguello, where the shoreline turns east. A wind of 25 to 35 knots inshore at Point Arguello now fans out both offshore toward San Nicolas Island 60 miles off Port Hueneme,

23

and also inshore along the east-west mainland coastline. This counterclockwise swirl of air is known as the Catalina Eddy.

If the Eddy is blowing, winds at Point Arguello will come from the north or NW at 20-30 knots, and at slightly less velocity from the same direction off San Nicolas Island. Winds in the Santa Barbara Channel will blow more south than usual — SE in the night and early morning, and SSW to SW in the afternoons. The increased south component of the winds is a good sign that Eddy conditions are in effect. Very often the Eddy will bring more fog and low clouds.

The Eddy can be modified by sea and land breeze conditions. Sometimes a persistent land breeze will deflect air currents from the Eddy to the north, forcing a south or SW breeze. But the sea breeze increases the tendency for the morning SE winds to veer west. Forecasters normally predict the Eddy by using small variations in pressure not normally available to small craft skippers. But they say as a general rule, when San Nicolas Island has NW winds of less than 10 knots, then Eddy conditions are absent. The Catalina Eddy is most common in spring, summer and early fall, when the Pacific High is well established.

### Lows and Weather Fronts

Winter months bring more unsettled weather to Southern California. The Pacific High wards off constant low pressure systems that cross the Pacific from California during the summer. But when the High weakens, Pacific lows and associated weather fronts reach the Southern California coast at least 10 to 15 times a year. These low pressure systems are tracked carefully by weather forecasts as they move toward the coast. The circulation of air around the low center is such that leading edges, or "fronts," between warm and cold air masses are formed. Clouds, shifting winds, and rain develop along these fronts, caused by mixing and turbulence. "Warm" fronts are the leading edge of a warm air mass, cold the opposite. Clouds form most densely east of a weather front, which is why our winter storms are often preceded by 24-36 hours of cloudy weather.

Most low pressure systems move inland north of Southern California. Our storms are caused by the trailing portion of the front as it crosses the coast. Position of the Pacific High pressure area helps determine the directions from which lows approach the California coast.

Lows that approach from SW bring some of our heaviest rainstorms that may last between 36 and 48 hours. Massive cloud layers herald the approach of rain from SW. SE winds between 10 and 20 knots veer to SW, 15-25 knots as the low approaches the islands and coast. Clouds and rain clear more slowly, and temperatures remain relatively constant.

Lows from the NW are cooler than those from SW, and move SE from the Gulf of Alaska toward the California coast. They bring unstable, cold air with them, their rain is often short-lived, and gusty winds are associated with their fronts. Skies clear rapidly as the front passes, the south or SE winds in advance of the front will veer round to west and blow from 15-35 knots out of a clear blue sky.

Lows that approach from the west are often associated with a broad area of low pressure extending over the middle latitudes of the east Pacific. This area can direct a wide series of lows toward Northern California, and we enjoy several days of rain as a result.

Winter storms and the cold fronts associated with them will normally yield the following sequence of phenomena:

a. About 24-36 hours ahead of the front, a low cloud layer will form, often a thickening of coastal fog.

b. The wind will fill in from SE, initially at 10-20 knots, increasing to 20-30 knots about six hours before cold frontal passage.

c. As the front passes overhead, the winds become more gusty, with heavy rain, and a sudden wind shift to SW may be experienced.

d. Some six hours after frontal passage, the wind may continue to veer west to NW and blow from a clearing sky at speeds of 20-40 knots, with locally stronger gusts. The roughest sea conditions in the Channel are likely to occur between 12-36 hours after frontal passage.

Sometimes a vigorous front will leave a period of blustery weather with squalls behind it. Unstable cold air may extend up to 20,000 feet, the turbulent air causing squalls and heavy rain showers. Gusts up to 35-40 knots are not uncommon in the Channel. The movements of these squalls can sometimes be detected by watching the direction in which cumulus clouds lean, or the curtains of rain associated with them.

Occasionally waterspouts form in unstable conditions over the ocean. Several are spotted in the Santa Barbara Channel each year. Since severe, circulating winds gust to 60 knots around the visible vortex of a waterspout, do everything you can to avoid them.

*Santa Ana Winds*

Everyone is familiar with the notorious Santa Ana winds of Southern California, so named from the river valley of that name, down which they can blow with great velocity. The term "Santa Ana" is, however, used to describe almost any dry NE wind that blows offshore in the coastal area between Point Conception and the Mexican border. Forecasters often speak of "local NE winds 20-35 knots below coastal canyons." These gusty NE winds can reach much higher velocities and invariably blow out of clear skies, often at sundown, whence their common nickname "sundowners."

Strong NE winds sweep into Southern California when barometric pressures over Nevada and Utah are higher than those in Southern California. These winds often occur when a front has moved inland through Northern California, and is followed by high pressure that builds up over the Pacific Northwest and the Great Basin. The difference in pressure between Nevada and Utah and the Southern California coast, sometimes as great as 25 millibars, will determine the strength of the Santa Ana winds.

As these strong winds move into Southern California, they climb over the coastal mountains before descending to the coast. As they spill over these summits via mountain passes, the winds are heated at the rate of about 5.5 degrees F./thousand feet by compression. The Santa Anas then sweep seaward over the coastal plain.

If the descending, heated air is cooler than the air overlying the coastal plain, it will push coastal marine air out to sea and sweep over the entire coastal plain with great velocity. These "cold" Santa Anas are destructive ones. If the descending air is warmer than the marine air, the "warm" Santa Anas will remain confined to the passes and coastal canyons where they began. "Warm" Santa Anas are less intense and less destructive.

Santa Anas and strong offshore winds commonly occur between September and January, although similar conditions can form at any time of the year when high pressure conditions in the interior bring dry NE winds of lesser strength and very high temperatures to the coast. Santa Ana conditions usually last from four to six days. As the high weakens, the marine layers reform and coastal low cloud and fog returns to Southern California.

Obviously it is difficult to forecast a Santa Ana or equivalent offshore winds. They can form when dry fronts or rapidly clearing frontal weather move over the coast. If high pressure then moves into the Pacific Northwest, a Santa Ana condition is likely. High pressure in Nevada and Utah, or higher pressure in the Mojave Desert as opposed to Los Angeles, may also lead to a Santa Ana. Strong north jet streams are often associated with vigorous Santa Anas, a condition often mentioned in FAA forecasts.

Santa Anas can be extremely dangerous to small craft, especially in the first two or three days of a Santa Ana condition. Figure 2.4 shows the major areas of our region affected by Santa Anas. These are the Palmdale, Point Mugu, Anacapa, east Santa Cruz Island area, and the east shores of Catalina, as well as Santa Barbara Island. Although these are the windiest areas, local offshore winds of great velocity can develop west of the Oxnard-Ventura area and down inland canyons at any time of the year when conditions are right. There is little advance warning, especially at the islands. Within a few hours, a heavy swell and steep wind waves will sweep into normally safe anchorages on the east and north coasts of Santa Cruz, rendering them treacherous for yachts. The only advance warning may be a new swell from the NE that rocks your boat in the anchorage just before the wind gets up. Visibility will normally be crystal clear, too. Since the winds come up with extraordinary rapidity, you should leave anchorage at once if you suspect such a condition is about to threaten your safety.

Very strong down-canyon gusts can be experienced even under normal conditions off Gaviota and Point Conception. Be prepared to reef in a hurry in these areas even if conditions a few miles away are flat calm. In the Santa Barbara Channel, offshore winds are very localized, often of great fury, and should, by virtue of their very unpredictability, be treated with great respect.

## Weather Conditions Through the Year

We are fortunate in being able to sail all year. The various weather conditions mentioned above form enough of a consistent pattern that we can provide here a broad outline of seasonal conditions, keeping in mind that the "average year" is in fact a rare phenomenon.

*January to March.* The first three months of the year are often the wettest. Active weather fronts pass through

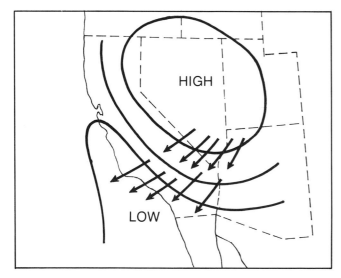

Fig. 2.4 — *Santa Ana conditions*
*a. Typical pressure pattern associated with Santa Ana conditions.*

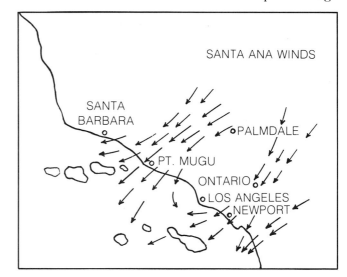

*b. Favored courses of Santa Ana winds between Newport Beach and Santa Barbara.*
(National Weather Service, *Southern California Weather for Small Boaters,* 1971)

Southern California with varying frequency during these months, giving us four to six rainy periods a month in an average year. These periods of rain can last as long as a week if a close succession of fronts passes overhead. SE winds are associated with these fronts, the wind veering to west or NW as the front passes over, and frequently blowing between 25-35 knots out of a clear sky. Santa Ana conditions may develop once or twice a month after frontal passage with occasional strong winds and often NW breezes. Fog is relatively infrequent, but four to six foot swells and high surf generated by intense Pacific storms from far offshore are not uncommon.

*April to May.* Coastal fog and low clouds are more frequent in the spring as frontal activity dies down. The usual frontal weather pattern occurs once or twice, normally in April, when strong west to NW winds blow in the Channel. Santa Anas are rare, three to five foot swells from far offshore not uncommon. Frequent, strong NW winds will be experienced west of Gaviota and Santa Cruz Island.

*June to September.* Frontal weather is rare, except occasionally in mid- to late September. But few of these bring rain to our area. Fog and coastal low clouds are frequent as coastal inversion becomes stronger, most commonly from mid-May to July. Drizzle is not uncommon and low cloud conditions can persist all day. The afternoon sea breeze can reach 15-20 knots, especially near the offshore islands, where it can reach 30 knots when the Catalina Eddy is present. This wind is so predictable that Richard Henry Dana called it "California trade winds." Generally, weather conditions are very settled during the summer, although tropical air can move in from the SE, bringing warm, humid conditions and sometimes rain or thunderstorms with them. Sometimes four to six days of very high temperatures and low humidity in the late summer provide magnificent visibility and very high fire danger. Santa Anas begin in September, too. Seas are generally calm, causing few problems for small craft. Tropical storms off the Mexican coast can, however, generate long southerly swells that make south facing anchorages uncomfortable.

*October to December.* Our old friend the weather front appears more frequently from October onwards, bringing several days of rain and strong winds in the Channel. In October and November, downslope winds often develop after weather fronts have passed through, generating periods of very strong offshore winds (30-40 knots) below coastal canyons. Short periods of very warm, brilliantly clear "Indian Summer" type weather are not uncommon in October and November. By December weather fronts are often more frequent, with some form of Santa Ana conditions on four to six days in the month. Coastal fog and low clouds are of shorter duration, but can occur on six to eight days in December.

Weather patterns in the Santa Barbara Channel follow a fairly regular annual cycle, despite major variations in the amount of rainfall and its concentration — in 1969, for example, Santa Barbara had 16 inches of rain in four days. It is perfectly possible to enjoy a week or more of glorious, almost fall-like warmth in January, days when the air feels like crisp champagne, and small boats are the only possible lifestyle!

## Weather Signs

It takes time to understand the subtle signs given by our weather, and everyone works out their own indicators. Here are some common general observations which may help you amplify radio broadcasts and weather maps.

— Fog and low clouds with hazy sunshine in the afternoons is normally a sign of settled conditions, especially in the summer. You will normally experience afternoon westerlies.

— Dew in the morning tends to indicate settled

Fig. 2.5 — *Cloud cap at the west end of Santa Cruz Island. —Photograph by Bob Evans*

weather. In the west parts of the Channel, dew may indicate NW winds.

— Good visibility associated with hard grey profiles of the offshore islands and approaching frontal cloud is a sign of rain. A SE swell can indicate the approach of a rainstorm.

— If you can see the offshore islands with sharp clarity from the mainland, you can probably expect stronger winds, often at the islands themselves. Smog near coastal canyons spreading seaward indicates NE (Santa Ana) conditions.

— Cloud trailing from the mountain tops on Santa Cruz Island indicates the presence of strong winds offshore (Fig. 2.5).

— A low layer of white, sea-level haze at Santa Cruz with the mountain peaks clearly visible above is sometimes a sign of strong winds close to the north shore and in the island passages.

— Cumulo-nimbus clouds over the mountains, or turbulent clouds in the same area — south or SW showers and squalls or thunderstorms are likely (mainly summer).

— Clear, cool weather with snow on the mountain peaks can be a sign of cold NE conditions.

— When at the islands, dry decks, clear visibility, and a swell from NE when the wind is calm can warn you of impending strong offshore winds from the mainland. If in doubt, leave your anchorage, fast. Stay offshore, or make for home.

— Stratus or layer clouds on the summits of the Santa Ynez Mountains indicate that strong NW winds are imminent.

Few people rely on the barometer for weather forecasting in our area. The passage of fronts can be detected by the fluctuations in barometer readings, while the movement of the prevailing high pressure systems can be monitored in general terms. But beyond measuring the passage of lows and fronts, the barometer is less use than it is, say, in the Pacific Northwest or in Maine. Nevertheless, barometers are useful tools, and you should learn how to use one from any weather forecasting manual.

We have listed but a few of the signs people use to amplify official forecasts. As you become more familiar with local conditions, you'll add your own. Table 2.2 describes some detailed indicators for the offshore islands and western Channel developed by Peter

Howorth, which amplify our general information. We are very grateful for his permission to reproduce them here. Our weather can be your greatest asset when sailing, *provided* you monitor forecasts and keep a constant watch for impending changes. They can be upon you almost without warning. This very unpredictability of weather conditions makes the Santa Barbara Channel a fascinating cruising ground (Fig. 2.6).

---

**TABLE 2.2**
## *CHANNEL WEATHER SIGNS*
Peter Howorth has spent many years diving and fishing in the west parts of the Santa Barbara Channel and as far north as Morro Bay. He very kindly provided us with details of natural weather indicators he has found useful in predicting Channel weather. This is a unique source of hitherto unpublished weather information.

This table should be used in conjunction with *Table 5.1 Refuge Anchorages.*

### NW CONDITIONS
NW winds, usually strongest from mid-March to mid-May, are highly predictable through careful observation of natural weather indicators. Foremost are veil clouds, often called cloud caps. These cling tightly to coastal mountain passes and to the west ends of the offshore islands. These white cloud masses are usually seen in the morning and at dusk. As winds increase during the day, cloud caps often break into whirling round cotton balls dubbed puffers or puff clouds.

Puffers flying low to the land or islands indicate strong NW winds, while high-fliers indicate moderate west to SW winds from Santa Cruz Island east, including the eastern offshore islands and excepting San Nicolas.

When other clouds are visible also, NW winds will last only half a day or a day. If other clouds disappear and cloud caps and puffers remain, NW winds will usually persist for three or four days.

By observing the location and magnitude of cloud phenomena, surprisingly accurate estimates of wind velocities may be determined for each area:

*Early morning cloud cap* at Gaviota Pass and San Miguel Island, and puff clouds over Santa Rosa, indicate *afternoon* NW winds 15-25 knots from Arguello to Gaviota and from the west half of Santa Rosa to San Miguel. Winds for east half of Santa Rosa will be west to NW 5-15 knots with stronger gusts likely at Becher's in afternoon and evening. Winds at Santa Cruz west to SW 5-15 knots except locally stronger westerlies at the Potato Patch. Anacapa SW to west 5-10 knots. Wind will blow offshore along the mainland coast from Gaviota to Conception in the morning, slack off late morning, blow onshore in afternoon, calm about sundown, offshore again at night. Wind will blow from 5-15 knots in morning, 10-20 knots afternoon, 5-15 knots offshore until midnight.

*Early morning cloud cap* at Gaviota Pass, Refugio Pass, San Miguel, Santa Rosa, occasional puff clouds at Santa Cruz: north to NE winds 15-25 knots offshore in the mornings from Cojo to Arguello, switching in the afternoons 15-30 knots north to NW. From Cojo to Gaviota: offshore 10-20 knots morning, changing to 15-20 knots NW in afternoon. San Miguel 15-30 knots NW, stronger gusts in Cuyler and Tyler, particularly in afternoon and evening. Santa Rosa 15-25 knots NW, locally stronger gusts at Becher's in the afternoon and evening. Santa Cruz 10-20 knots NW to SW from Coches Prietos to Gull Island and from Fry's to West Point. West Point to Gull Island, NW or west, 15-25 knots with locally stronger gusts near Fraser Point. Wind from Fry's to San Pedro Point, west to NW, 5-15 knots in the afternoons. From Albert's to San Pedro Point, calm or moderate in the mornings, shifting to SW 5-15 knots in the afternoon, west to NW, 10-20 knots in the evenings. Anacapa 5-15 knots SW.

*Early morning cloud cap* at Gaviota Pass, Refugio Pass, San Marcos Pass, San Miguel, Santa Rosa, west end of Santa Cruz: afternoon west to NW winds, 20-35 knots from Point Arguello to Goleta, generally offshore winds 15-30 knots in the morning. San Miguel NW 20-45 knots, Santa Rosa NW 15-35 knots. From Gull Island to Fraser Point, 15-35 knots, more in the Potato Patch. From West Point to San Pedro Point, NW 15-30 knots. From Gull Island to Coches Prietos, 15-30 knots. Albert's to Smuggler's, offshore 10-25 knots mornings, 15-30 knots in the afternoons.

## NE CONDITIONS

NE winds are quite predictable also, although they often strike with less advance warning. Watch the sky and sea carefully. Northeasters generally hit in the evening and moderate by the following morning. They are most common from September through November.

Natural indicators include warm, dry weather, particularly in the evenings. Smog, low in horizon, frequently spreads offshore from the canyon at Point Mugu; sky otherwise clear or with high cirrus. A spreading dark blue line on an otherwise glassy horizon often heralds a northeaster. NE swell of two to four feet at east end of Santa Cruz indicates NE wind 15-30 knots imminent. NE swell four to six feet at the same place indicates 30-45 knot NE wind imminent. NE six feet plus indicates 50 knots or more of NE wind imminent.*

Wind blows offshore from coastal canyons, swings into Santa Barbara from SE, same sky conditions. Two to three feet swell in Santa Barbara means NE wind outside 25-35 knots. Three to five feet means 35-45 knots. Five feet plus means 50 knots plus.* Excellent San Miguel weather if swell is three to four feet or more, for NE winds are rare there.

If puff clouds are visible over San Miguel and/or Santa Rosa, but NE swell and smog are visible, expect localized SW to NW winds 15-25 knots at Santa Rosa and San Miguel.

## SE CONDITIONS

Southeasters, which bring winter rain, usually begin during the day, start blowing at night and by the next morning are in full swing. They may occur from October through April, although the peak months are December through March.

Natural indicators are: frequent wind changes, gathering dark clouds, stillness in air. Often the sea has a strange leaden appearance and the water close to shore becomes quite clear, particularly early in the season before much runoff has occurred. Some people can even *smell* the rain coming. The cloud cover spreads, has peculiar, gently wavy, grey undersides. SE swell arrives, normal west swell disappears or moderates. SE swell of two to four feet indicates 15-25 knot southeaster imminent. Four to five feet, 25-35 knots, five to seven feet, 35-50 knots. During a fast moving front, it often takes a few hours more for the chop to build in proportion to the wind velocity.

Watch for clearing in west, followed by cloud caps developing at mountain passes and west ends of islands. This indicates shift to NW winds.

## SW CONDITIONS

Since this summer wind is usually relatively moderate, most protected anchorages will suffice during this condition. Natural indicators generally include high, white cumulus behind the coastal range and sometimes beyond the islands extending toward the coast at Arguello.

---

*Note: If wind rises exceptionally fast, the preceding chop will give less warning. Often the swell will be relatively small until wind has been blowing a few hours.

Fig. 2.6 — *"Our weather can be your greatest asset when sailing,* provided *you monitor forecasts and keep a constant watch for impending changes. They can be upon you almost without warning. This very unpredictability of weather conditions makes the Santa Barbara Channel a fascinating cruising ground."*

# CHAPTER **3**

# *Equipping Your Boat Right*

Although the Santa Barbara Channel lacks the intricate navigational challenges of the Pacific Northwest or the boiling tides of San Francisco Bay, its sometimes unpredictable weather conditions and long stretches of open water can easily trap the unwary into a fatal sense of security. Every year the Coast Guard is called to rescue small boat sailors in trouble off the mainland or at the islands. Every year a few people die in boat accidents which could have been prevented by a few sensible precautions. The Channel can be misleading, for its waters are often placid and blue, the wind light. Yet, within a few hours, six-foot swells and 30-knot winds may make the entrance to Ventura Harbor a mass of broken water, or the approach to Pelican Bay at Santa Cruz Island a squall-swept nightmare. Despite frequent warnings, people still do incredibly stupid things. We have seen small outboard runabouts off the bumpy west end of Santa Cruz Island, racing dinghies sheltering in Scorpion after a 25-mile crossing from the mainland

without escort. Such people are neither brave nor clever, they are foolhardy. What happens if your outboard fails or you capsize and are unable to right your dinghy? At best, you will be rescued by the Coast Guard which costs the taxpayers, or by some other yacht which might involve you in a salvage claim. At worst, you drown. The stakes are high, yet time and time again one sees people at the islands in unsuitable craft, without adequate safety gear, or anchored with toy ground tackle that would barely hold a rubber raft. It's a wonder there are not more fatalities in the Channel. Perhaps our reaction seems harsh, but the sea is a harsh teacher.

While many of these foolhardy people are simply inexperienced, often cruising people with many seasons behind them become careless and run into trouble through inadequate planning or foresight.

The single most important safety item aboard any boat is in fact intangible. Knowledge of seamanship is the sailor's most valuable tool. The would-be small boat sailor who lacks the mental preparedness necessary for cruising is most likely to forget or neglect the other essentials discussed in this chapter. Ignorance is not bliss when you find yourself faced with an emergency at sea: man overboard, a sudden gale, fire on board, an injured crewman. If you are a beginner, Southern California is fortunate in having available a wide range of courses in sailing technique, seamanship, first aid, navigation. Take advantage of these opportunities. Then sail with more experienced friends until you gain your own sea-sense.

## Suitable Vessels

Fierce controversy surrounds the thorny topic of choosing a boat for island and Channel crossing. While the Chumash crossed the Channel in 25-foot open plank canoes, you can be sure they chose their weather carefully, and that a number of canoes were lost every year. An old lady in an open bathtub could cross the Channel on a few days of the year. That's not the point. A Chumash canoe can become a death trap when the wind rises to even 15 knots off Santa Cruz on a typical summer afternoon, especially when manned by inexperienced paddlers. The same applies to small yachts. While many tiny pleasure vessels are perfectly seaworthy off Oxnard on a calm summer's day, they are not designed to cope with more rugged conditions offshore. Therefore, they should not be taken to the islands. When choosing a vessel, whether power or sail, for island cruising, you should, in our judgment, select one with the following basic features:

a. Adequate waterline and overall length to handle swells of up to eight feet and winds of up to 40 knots in an emergency, with a family crew aboard. Sailing experts of prehensile strength may be able to bring an 18-foot shoal cruiser safely through 30 knots of wind. Your average family crew will find it much harder. Never venture to the islands short-handed without an expert crew.

b. Covered decks and adequate sleeping and cooking accommodations for an overnight stay, whether voluntary or involuntary, are essential. The cockpit should be deep enough to give some shelter in rough water and have large-sized drains. Your interior should be designed for safety and seaworthiness first, comfort at anchor second, comfort in the marina third.

c. The rig should be adequately stayed, with running gear in good condition. An effective reefing gear and at least one foresail smaller than a working jib is essential.

d. If you select a sailing vessel, make sure you have a reliable system of auxiliary propulsion of adequate power. While this may be a sweep on a 20-foot trailer boat, an outboard or inboard engine is vital in a larger boat. The ideal on a larger vessel is a diesel, which is both safer and cheaper to run than gas. With today's congested anchorages, auxiliary power of some type is an essential safety factor. Remember the Channel enjoys long periods of calm, especially at night and in foggy conditions. Auxiliary power can get you to port and out of busy shipping lanes. *However, you should also be able to sail out of anchorage if your engine fails.*

e. Your vessel should have adequate means of sealing off the cabins, well-designed ventilation, and a portable or built-in bilge pump, operable from the cockpit.

f. The deck should be protected with fore and aft pulpits and permanent lifelines.

No two skippers will agree on the ideal sailing yacht for Channel waters. Some experienced sailors cruise extensively round the islands in 20-footers or small trailer yachts. But they pick their weather carefully and rarely venture to Santa Rosa or San Miguel Islands. The size of your boat depends on the depth of your pocket, your experience and long-term cruising plans, as well as available crew (Fig. 3.1). Many people spend considerable periods of time at the islands in fine 40-foot ketches that one day may take them further afield. Many have bought their yachts with such long-term plans firmly in mind. This is a sensible area to test your ambitions and skills. We feel the ideal overall length for serious Channel cruising is between 25 and 35 feet. Vessels of this size are small enough for two people to handle even in rough weather, yet large enough to accommodate the average family or a group of up to six friends for a sociable weekend. Most local yachts are fiberglass, although one can often admire beautiful, older, wooden yachts in marinas and anchorages, glowing testimony to the tender care their hardworking owners lavish upon them.

So, choose a size of yacht that fits both your pocketbook and your family needs, but a boat capable of handling boisterous conditions offshore with safety and minimal anxiety for the crew. If you are a beginner, start with a smaller yacht and become familiar with the area before trading up to a larger vessel that requires more careful handling in congested anchorages.

## Equipment and Safety

The Santa Barbara Channel must, for planning purposes, be regarded as exposed ocean waters (Fig. 3.2). The safety gear you would have on your boat on an inland lake or estuary, or even on a day sail off the harbor must be regarded as inadequate for a cruise to the islands.

## Safety Gear

A well-equipped sailing vessel should carry the following safety gear (we consider Coast Guard requirements the barest minimum):

— Adequate ground tackle, including two anchors, of sufficient weight to hold your boat in a wind in excess of 40 knots (see Anchoring, Chapter 4).

— Navigation lights and an anchor light that satisfy Coast Guard regulations.

— Life jackets for every member of the crew, U.S. Coast Guard approved, equipped with lights and whistles.

— A life ring, either round or preferably U-shaped, mounted on a carrier on the aft pulpit, equipped with a Xenon Man Overboard light, drogue, whistle and die canister.

Fig. 3.1 — *"The size of your boat depends on the depth of your purse, your experience and long-term cruising plans, as well as available crew."*

— A "Transpac Pole" attached to the life ring.
— Deck safety harnesses for every crew member.
— A radar reflector mounted either permanently or of a collapsible type.
— A set of day and night flares.

Fig. 3.2 — *"The Santa Barbara Channel must, for planning purposes, be regarded as exposed ocean waters."*

— At least two fire extinguishers, one near the galley/engine room, the other in a cockpit locker.
— At least two flashlights, one of a searchlight type, capable of throwing a long beam.
— An inflatable life raft or dinghy that can be inflated in rough seas under emergency conditions. A good fiberglass dinghy is an excellent alternative, provided it has adequate flotation tanks.
— A foghorn, either Freon compressed air type or mouth blower.
— A compass, mounted permanently on the boat, corrected for deviation.
— First aid kit.
— A set of charts for the Santa Barbara Channel.
— A sharp knife accessible from the cockpit, also a pair of bolt cutters for cutting wire shrouds.
— A heaving line and spare warps sufficient to allow emergency towing and rescue operations.
— Wooden plugs for emergency repairs to through-hull fittings.
— Radio receiver and transmitter.
— Some form of depth sounder or a lead and line.

The following safety gear is desirable but not essential:

*VHF Radio.* Most yachts of any size seem to fit a VHF transmitter as a matter of course these days. Although relatively expensive, they do allow you to monitor weather forecasts and emergency frequencies. They are invaluable for locating your friends' yachts and a host of other mundane purposes. Make sure you fit crystals that suit your requirements. Some useful channels are shown in Table 3.1.

If you plan extensive cruising in the future, it is probably best to fit a 55-channel set. As stern anchors are commonly used at the islands, we recommend you mount the antenna at the masthead, where reception is better and the antenna is out of the way.

*Emergency Locator Beacon.* More and more yachts are mounting ELBs on a convenient bulkhead. These are emergency, battery-operated transmitters originally developed for light aircraft that are tuned to the commercial air search and rescue frequency. When activated, they will pinpoint your position accurately to passing commercial and military aircraft. Time and time again ELBs have saved not only the lives of pilots but increasing numbers of offshore sailors as well. If you can afford it, fit one. You may never need it, but when you do, you'll need it badly. The day cannot be far away when they become required equipment on all seagoing yachts.

Remember to check fire extinguishers and battery-powered equipment at regular intervals. Safety gear is expensive, but it is a false economy not to buy the best.

## Cruising Gear

It is surprising how much more comfortable an island cruise can be with the right equipment on board. Here are some extra items we have found invaluable or essential over the years:

*Dinghies* are essential both for laying second anchors and for landing, as well as visiting other yachts or exploring interesting nooks and crannies. Most people buy inflatable dinghies, most commonly an Avon or Zodiac type, both European dinghies that have a well-deserved reputation for durability. An eight-footer is the minimal family size, and the extra length of a nine-footer is well worth the additional expense (Fig. 3.3). These dinghies, and various well-designed American equivalents like the West design, can be rowed or driven with a small outboard, provided wooden floorboards are fitted. Inflatable dinghies are virtually impervious to angular rocks and beach stones. Leaks are readily fixed with the repair kit provided. They are, however, difficult to tow and can fly at the end of their painters in strong winds, even when trailed astern at anchor. We have even had one fly aboard when a strong westerly got

up behind us on passage from Scorpion to Oxnard! Inflatables are ideal for smaller yachts. They can be stowed on deck easily, even double as a life raft if a $CO_2$ bottle is carried.

There are many cheap plastic and inflatable dinghies on the market, which are really little more than play rafts for swimming pools or sheltered beaches. These

Fig. 3.3 — *The Avon eight or nine-foot inflatable dinghies can be recommended strongly for use in island anchorages.*

dinghies are unstable in even slight surge, are impossible to maneuver in any breeze, in fact, are downright dangerous. Nor do they last long under normal sailing conditions. We cannot, in all conscience, recommend them for use at the islands.

Larger yachts often carry fiberglass or wooden dinghies, either on deck or on stern davits. Some have masts and sails, others outboard motors. Fiberglass dinghies can carry heavy loads and are very versatile. A Sabot or sailing Dyer Dhow can be fun on a lengthy cruise. But they take up valuable storage space, and if towed, slow down your boat considerably. Anyone who has been caught out with a partially swamped dinghy on a tow line in a rising wind off Santa Cruz knows how difficult it is to bring it aboard.

Generally, inflatables are the best bet for island or coastal cruising.

*Boarding ladders* should be part of any 25-35 foot yacht's equipment, certainly any vessel whose topsides are too high for a swimmer to clamber over in a swell. Ideally, you should have a permanent ladder of stainless steel attached to your boat, one that folds up out of the way at sea. Some manufacturers now offer such a stern-mounted option on their larger boats. We strongly recommend fitting one. Such installations should allow you to recover a man overboard at sea. They are certainly more effective than the collapsible types commonly sold in marine chandleries. Most collapsible boarding ladders have the advantage of stowing conveniently but the disadvantage of demonstrating their most irritating collapsible qualities when a swimmer is trying to use them. The amusement wears thin quickly. The best type are those that hook into rigid brackets mounted on the topside. Some people fit steps to the stern, an effective situation for yachts with vertical transoms which do not have vane steering gear.

Electronic navigation instruments have become fashionable options for cruising yachts in recent years. While useful, they can also become defective at the slightest provocation. We are biased to the extent that we recommend fitting the minimum for Channel cruising. This minimal inventory consists of:

*A depth sounder* which records soundings in fathoms and feet either by digital display, a revolving light, or conventional dial. Some models come with a warning buzzer, but a vigilant skipper hardly needs this luxury. Make sure you buy an instrument that can be read in bright sunlight from the cockpit. The delicate circuitry must be well isolated from seawater and damp air, the transducer mounted amidships near the keel. Bulkhead-mounted models are ideal.

Depth sounders are valuable not only for measuring depths in island anchorages, but for locating your position near the coast on foggy days. By spotting the moment you cross the 20, 10, and 5 fathom lines, you can obtain some idea how close to the coast you are from the chart. Kelp beds often lie in 50 feet or so of water. If necessary, too, you can lie offshore in 10 fathoms or more and await a lift in the fog to determine your position. This technique works well provided you have kept an accurate DR plot and are not among pinnacle rocks. We once found Morro Bay entrance on a passage from San Francisco to Santa Barbara. A combination of DR and fathometer readings took us to a position off the entrance where we could wait for a dense fog to lift. When the grey curtain lifted for a few minutes, we were able to slip into the entrance with ease. Depth sounders are invaluable when navigating near the dangerous sand spits at the east ends of San Miguel and Santa Rosa Islands.

*A log* is most desirable for cross-Channel passages on foggy days. Electronic logs are accurate if precisely calibrated and provided you keep their underwater fittings clear of kelp. An electromechanical type with flush hull fitting is more expensive but unlikely to foul. A good log will give you not only boat speed but distance run as well. Perhaps best of all for cruising is a mechanical through-hull device like the Sumlog, which is cheap, accurate, and very reliable. It is, however, essential to keep the cable lubricated. Some perceptive skippers use the Walker log which you trail over the stern. An accurate watch is also useful aboard.

*Apparent wind speed and direction indicators* are essential for racing, but of marginal value for cruising. After a while you learn how to gauge wind direction and strength by using telltales, the feel of the breeze, and the appearance of the sea. Who cares whether the wind is 28 knots or 32 — we hope you are securely reefed down or anchored in this type of breeze.

*A good tool kit* is essential for island cruising. It should include tools to tighten every screw and bolt on the ship, including stern gland fittings and keel bolts, good wire and bolt cutters, and an axe for emergencies. A set of socket and open-ended wrenches for your engine should be added to the manual and tool kit supplied with the motor.

Spare parts should include:

Shackles of all types found on the boat, also cotter pins.
At least one spare snatch block.
Spare sheets, warps, and small stuff for emergency repairs.
Plugs for through-hull fittings.
A spare turnbuckle in case one appears worn or in imminent danger of collapse.
Rigging wire, wire clamps, and electrical tape.
LPS 1-2-3, WD 40, and lubricants for all equipment.
Stainless steel hose clamps to duplicate all such connections aboard . . . several can be hooked together to form a single clasp.
Stove parts (depending on type on board).
Fiberglass repair kit.
Sailmaker's needles, twine, and spare dacron scraps.
Points, oil filters, plugs, belts, and gaskets for the engine (these should depend on the type of fuel used).
Engine manual.
Powerboats — spare battery and Perko switch.
Flashlight batteries and spare globes for all lights.
Fire extinguisher refills.
Starter handle for the engine.
An extra winch handle.
Top-off fuel for engine and spare water in jerry cans.
Spare engine oil.

This list is by no means exhaustive. You should consult any one of the many books on coastal and ocean cruising for recommendations for longer passages.

*Navigation equipment* should include parallel ruler or protractor, dividers, a hand-bearing compass, and a pair of good quality 7 x 50 binoculars. A hand-bearing compass can be invaluable, and is vital for taking bearings on shipping. We particularly recommend the French made Mini Compass. You can hang it around your neck and it is practically unbreakable. A Radio Direction Finder (RDF) is valuable in thick weather.

However, most boats which cruise locally do not seem to carry one. If you plan to sail to Mexico or north of Point Conception, you might consider adding one to your inventory. Don't forget a pencil!

Several luxury items can make life more comfortable. *Cockpit cushions* are wonderful for sunbathing and leisurely passages, but they can tumble all over the place when the boat heels. *Flopper-stoppers* are said to reduce your motion while at anchor in swell-disturbed coves. An inexpensive plastic type has recently come on the market and is reported to work surprisingly well. Most skippers try to anchor their boats in calm spots and to use a second anchor for mooring head to surge to minimize rolling. Rigging flopper-stoppers involves more lines and preparation. To many people, they are a luxury.

If you plan numerous Channel crossings or long passages up and down the coast, we recommend you invest in an *electric autopilot* that operates off your tiller when the boat is under power. Having cruised many hundreds of miles under power with automatic steering, we could never be without an autopilot for a longer passage. Your crew arrives far fresher and keeps a much sharper lookout during passage. Autopilots are not cheap, and it is worth paying a little more for good weatherproofing and reliability. *Wind vanes* are becoming increasingly popular. However, they are hardly essential for local cruising unless you cross the Channel very frequently.

## Domestic Equipment

Most people rarely spend more than a few days at the islands and keep their galley equipment simple. Alcohol stoves and iceboxes are the basis of most yacht galleys, although kerosene or gas stoves and refrigerators are becoming more commonplace.

When planning a galley and provisioning for an island cruise, figure on precooking as many meals as possible, equipping your boat with the necessary utensils for reheating and cooking simple meals, and washing up. If you need more elaborate skillets or other items for a particular trip, you can always bring them aboard especially. Equip your galley with:

Kettle, frying pan and one or two saucepans. Nesting utensils are very convenient.
Salad bowl, colander, spatula, tongs, oven gloves.
Plastic glasses, mugs, plates, cheap stainless steel utensils.
Plastic bags, can openers, corkscrews, salt and pepper shakers, kitchen knives.
Plenty of Tupperware bowls, containers, and storage boxes.
A small cutting board that fits over the sink.
A bucket and washing-up bowl; dish towels and sponges (have deck and table sponges of different colors), aluminum foil and Saran wrap.
A garbage container (lined with plastic bag).

Many people store food and drink in an ice chest they bring on board for each trip. We can fit ours into an enormous icebox, which is a great convenience. A plastic bag-sealing unit at home enables you to precook meals, freeze them and simply heat up on board with minimal mess and washing up. Precooked casseroles are ideal for island cruising, and make a stove with an oven highly desirable.

An elementary point: make sure your water tanks are full before you take off! One is always hearing stories of people brushing their teeth in beer, salt water, or wine! Many newer yachts are fitted with pressure water systems. Most are abominations, for the pumps are unreliable, waste water, and make a horrible noise.

The important thing to remember is there are absolutely no facilities at the islands, so you must be completely self-contained. And don't forget the matches!

**NEVER DUMP GARBAGE OVERBOARD
OR ON THE ISLANDS**
Seal it in a plastic bag and stow in a convenient cockpit locker. There are garbage scows at the entrance to some Catalina harbors, where you can dump your refuse.

## Clothing

The Channel is a relatively mild marine environment by the standards of the Pacific Northwest or the Bay area. Even so, a good supply of warm clothes is necessary, even on summer days. There are relatively few days when one can cross the Channel clad in shorts or a bikini, indeed such days are memorable. The following are essentials in a Channel cruising wardrobe for everyone:

Foul weather gear — this can be the durable, lightweight type, but should have strong, welded seams, high pants that come up to the chest, and adequate zippers and Velcro fasteners. Cheap, dime-store types are a false economy for regular sailors. You'll be surprised how often you use your foul weather gear, even in summer. Everyone should have their own set, but you may want to keep some cheap outfits on board for casual visitors. Some people prefer one-piece suits, or smocks without hoods, in which case a sou'wester is desirable. It is a matter of personal preference.

Many California sailors prefer to invest in a waterproof flotation jacket, which doubles as an emergency vest. Make sure you buy a Coast Guard-approved type. These garments are somewhat more bulky, but are invaluable for cool evenings and when racing. Again, a matter of personal preference.

Adequate footwear — while bare feet may look nautical, they can be downright dangerous on a heeled deck or even in moderate weather. Broken toes are no fun on a yacht. Everyone should have a good pair of rubber-soled shoes. Cheap J.C. Penney or Sears tennis shoes have good deck-grip soles at a fraction of the cost of expensive deck shoes or moccasins that can cost you well over $30 and wear out just as rapidly. You'll replace several pairs of cheap shoes that last a surprisingly long time for the price of a more expensive shoe. Flip-flops are fine for going ashore at a marina, but have no place on the islands or on deck. Leather sandals are useful for walking on sidewalks ashore, but not for deck work.

Rubber boots are invaluable on a rough day and for winter dinghy work. The new, lightweight French type are both colorful and durable. Wear them with thick socks to minimize condensation, slightly oversize so you can shed them easily if you fall overboard.

At least one sweater more than you think you need is a universal and classic rule, which applies in the Channel, too. The thick, oiled sweaters found in many yachting stores are admirable for any season. So plan on taking a lighter sweater with you, or a windbreaker for warmer days.

A sun hat, good sunglasses with a string so you can store them around your neck (and sailing gloves, for those who like them) are essentials. So is a good knife and a small marlinspike.

Jeans, a watch hat, shorts, and changes of underclothing make up most people's wardrobes. A canvas carryall can serve as a pillow as well as a convenient receptable for each crew member's belongings.

## Paperwork

Your registration certificate and a copy of your insurance policy should always be on board, as well as your radio license, if you possess a VHF. Landing on Santa Cruz and Santa Rosa Islands is forbidden without permission or a landing permit. You can obtain these from the following addresses (for San Miguel and other islands, see below):

*East end of Santa Cruz* (from Coche Point to Sandstone Point): Mr. Pier Gherini, 230 La Arcada Building, Santa Barbara, California 93101, or Mr. Francis Gherini, 162 South A Street, Oxnard, Cali-

fornia 93030 (no charge is made, but owner's regulations must be adhered to).

*Remainder of Santa Cruz:* Santa Cruz Island Company, 515 South Flower Street, Los Angeles, California 90017, (213) 485-9208. In 1978, the permit fee was $30/calendar year, or $7.50 for 30 days. The company issues permits in collaboration with the Nature Conservancy.

*Santa Rosa:* Vail and Vickers, 123 West Padre Street, Suite D, Santa Barbara, California 93105 (you may only land at Becher's Bay in daylight).

Do *NOT* land without a permit. You are trespassing and liable to prosecution if caught by a patrol. The Santa Cruz Island Company (Nature Conservancy) permit forbids lighting of fires, importation of animals, collection of flora, fauna, and archaeological remains. Make sure you obey these conditions and carry your permit when ashore. This applies to any crew member from your yacht, so have several copies made. Permits are not issued on the islands.

If you plan to fish or spearfish, you must have the necessary Department of Fish and Game permits. There are added restrictions within National Monument territory. The islands are closely patrolled and even slight infractions of rules regarding season, weight, or size of catch are subject to heavy fine.

## Charts and Pilot Books

Even experts on the Channel take care to carry complete chart coverage of the area they plan to cruise, charts updated from the Coast Guard's *Local Notices to Mariners* that can be consulted at any Harbormaster's office. Charts can be purchased at most marine stores.

The following charts provide basic coverage of our cruising area (Fig. 3.4).

*Passage Charts* (new numbers are given):
18700 Point Conception to Point Sur 1:216,116
(this covers N approaches to the Channel)

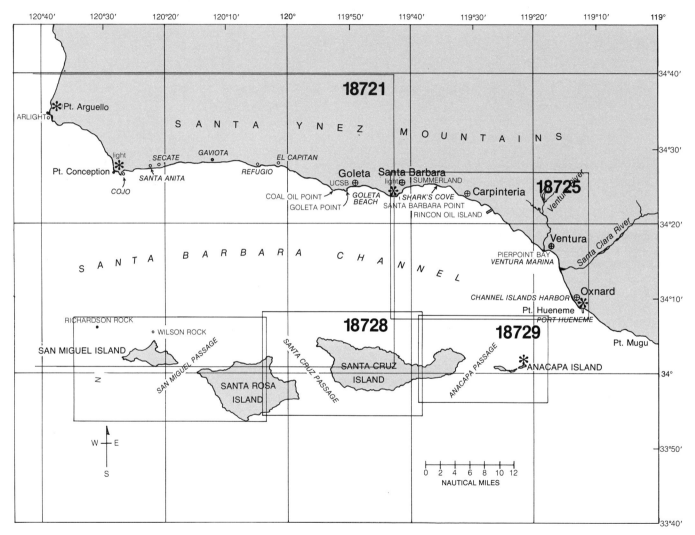

Fig. 3.4 — *U.S. Government chart coverage for the Santa Barbara Channel.*

18720 Point Dume to Purisima Point 1:232,188
18721 Santa Rosa Island to Purisima Point 1:232,188
18740 San Diego to Santa Rosa Island 1:234,270
18725 Port Hueneme to Santa Barbara 1:50,000
(with plans of mainland harbors)

*Large Scale Charts:*
18757 Santa Catalina Island 1:40,000
18759 Santa Catalina Island Harbors 1:10,000
18762 San Clemente Island (18763, 18764 for harbors)
1:40,000
18756 Santa Barbara Island 1:20,000
18755 San Nicolas Island 1:40,000
18729 Anacapa Passage 1:40,000
18728 Santa Cruz Channel 1:40,000
18727 San Miguel Passage 1:40,000

U.S. Coast Pilot Number 7 covers the Santa Barbara Channel and is readily obtainable locally. It is designed for large vessels, however, and deals with islands and harbors in incomplete generalities from the small craft point of view. They do, however, contain all necessary regulations to navigate in commercial harbors and marine traffic lanes.

Most yachts rely on publications designed for cruising vessels. *Pacific Boating Almanac* (Southern California, Arizona and Baja), published by Western Marine Enterprises, Box Q, Ventura, California 93001, appears each year. It is a useful, inexpensive compilation of information about the Pacific Coast by an expert seaman. It should be on every small boat, contains information on facilities, fishing, freshwater lakes, marinas and anchorages. Every year useful articles appear on such topics as first aid offshore. The data on fishing is invaluable, the sailing directions accurate but rather generalized, given the scope of the book. *Sea Guide, Volume I* — Southern California by Leland R. Lewis and Peter E. Ebeling, Sea Publications, 2nd ed., 1973, is a luxury coffee table type of publication that covers the Santa Barbara Channel in a generalized way. Much of its data comes from official publications. The aerial photographs are superb.

*Chart Guide for Southern California 1975, Chart Guide for Catalina, 1977* are compendia of information based on official charts which are widely used by regular visitors. They are published by Edmond Winlund, Chart Guide, P.O. Box 2311, Anaheim, California 92804.

All these publications are admirable for planning a cruise. The *Almanac* is especially useful as a reference book. It contains a mass of information on radio frequencies, addresses, and facilities, as well as tide tables.

TABLE 3.1
*VHF RADIO INFORMATION*
*Channels for Small Craft*

| | |
|---|---|
| 16 | Emergency channel |
| 6 | Ship-to-ship intersafety channel |
| 9 | Ship-to-ship, ship-to-shore non-commercial channel |
| 12 | Harbormaster working channel |
| 13, 14 | Ship-to-ship channels for port and other navigational purposes |
| 15 | Shore station recreational channel |
| 17 | Ship-to-shore recreational channel |
| 68, 69, 70-72, 78 | Recreational boating ship-to-ship and ship-to-shore channels. Used by yacht clubs and marinas. Santa Barbara and Ventura Yachts Clubs are on Channel 68. |
| 24, 26 | Commonly used ship-to-shore telephone channels |
| 24, 26 | San Pedro Marine Operator |
| 25 | Santa Barbara Marine Operator |
| WX-1) | Weather Channels, Santa Barbara, |
| WX-2) | Los Angeles, San Diego |

Note: The Coast Guard now monitors CB radio frequency 27.065 MHz (Channel 9) at Channel Islands Harbor, *for emergency calls only.*

Fig. 4.1 — *Sailing in "Windy Lane" with a single reef in the main and smaller genoa.*

# CHAPTER 4

# *Cruising Hints*

"Local knowledge" is a mysterious commodity that every newcomer to a cruising area keeps hearing about. It conjures images of old salts and pipe-smoking fishermen leaning over a breakwater rail, contemplating the ocean and uttering words of wisdom about weather, winds or windjammers. There is nothing at all mysterious about local knowledge. It is merely experience of a cruising area, experience gained over long years of sailing in the same area. After a while you develop your own favorite anchorages, know where the wind shifts are, and accumulate your own weather signs. The Santa Barbara Channel has its fair share of local knowledge, of phenomena like "Windy Lane," the "Potato Patch," and, of course, many stories about the terrors of Point Conception. This chapter covers such local cruising lore and describes problems you are likely to encounter while cruising in the Channel. It makes no pretense at being comprehensive and is no substitute for practical experience on the water.

Hopefully, however, we can prepare you for some of the surprises our area can spring on you.

## Passage Making in the Channel

The hazards of passage making in the Santa Barbara Channel are easily summarized: strong winds, swells, fog, oil rigs and shipping lanes. Each merits special discussion.

### Winds and Passage Making

The Channel weather is normally moderate, and any trip to and from the islands is likely to involve at least some motoring. Rare are the days when you can sail all the way from the mainland to your anchorage without drifting in a calm for a while. When leaving the mainland, you should depart either early in the morning before the westerlies get up, in which case you may end up motoring all the way, or later in the day, say after 1100, when the likelihood of a good breeze is stronger. In either case, be sure to check weather forecasts in advance and look for telltale signs of strong winds at the islands. These include tumbling white clouds, sharp island profiles and bands of pearly haze. If you have the slightest doubt about the weather offshore, try radioing a yacht that is already at the islands, or don't go.

A passage from Santa Barbara to Santa Cruz Island is straightforward enough and is much simplified if you use the profiles of the mountains as a guide to the location of anchorages (Chapter 7). In foggy weather, you will have to lay off a compass course. We give the key courses for offshore destinations with our descriptions of the major harbors, below. The 25-mile passage offshore from Santa Barbara can take anything between three and six hours depending on wind, swell, and the speed of your boat. If you leave fairly early in the morning, you can expect to pick up a west to SW wind under normal conditions about halfway across. This wind will strengthen and veer to west as you approach Santa Cruz Island and come under the influence of the land.

Some seven miles off the island, you normally encounter a marked strengthening of the wind as you enter what is commonly known as "Windy Alley," "Windy Lane," or simply "The Slot" (Fig. 4.1). The breeze can strengthen quite suddenly from, say, 10 knots to 25, and it behooves you to be prepared for a quick reef or change down to a smaller jib. The U.S. Coast Pilot puts it well: "During NW weather, boats crossing the Channel from the mainland usually encounter heavier seas as the islands are approached. The belt of rough seas . . . lies along the north shores of the islands and is about six miles wide . . . strangers are cautioned that good seamanship sometimes calls for returning to the mainland rather than attempting Windy Lane when rough seas are encountered."

The stronger winds close to the islands gradually build up during the day and die soon after sundown. Be warned, however, that there is no set pattern, and strong winds can blow close to the islands at any time of the day or night, *even when it is calm near the mainland.* Windy Lane is the reason why open boats should not attempt the Channel crossing without escort. Surprisingly, steep seas can rear up in a few minutes. Do everything you can to avoid a passage through Windy Lane in the wake of a winter storm. The WNW winds have been known to reach velocities of over 50 knots with dangerous, breaking seas. Clear skies may tempt you offshore, but are often a sure sign of strong winds.

Many people leave the mainland hard on the wind, laying a course as far west on Santa Cruz Island as possible. They then ease sheets for their chosen anchorage as they approach land and can identify the landmarks. It also enables them to use the Windy Lane breezes to maximum advantage. It should be emphasized there are many days when winds are gentle off the islands and Windy Lane is quiet. The trouble is that weather conditions are unpredictable and highly localized.

When bound from Santa Barbara to Santa Rosa or San Miguel Islands, you are well advised to motor the long miles to windward at night or during early morning hours when the air may be calm — but don't bet on it. Santa Rosa Island is easily laid on the starboard tack if one motors to Goleta and then sails offshore. Many people motor up to Refugio anchorage, spend the night and then take the westerly across to Cuyler Harbor on San Miguel Island the next day. If you elect to sail direct, you can expect to spend many hours getting to your destination, unless, of course, the winds are from SE. Under those circumstances, you should be prepared for the possibility of strong westerlies after a front has passed through.

People cruising from Channel Islands or Ventura to the islands can often take advantage of an early morning offshore breeze that blows out of the NE from the mainland on clear days. If you leave at 0400 or at dawn, you can often rely on several hours of favorable wind which can carry you as far as Scorpion or

Fig. 4.2 — *"The westerlies can funnel through the straits with considerable force." Carrington Point at the NE extremity of Santa Rosa Island, on the west side of Santa Cruz passage.*

Prisoner's. Although the early morning departure can be a hardship, the sunrise and clear beauty of the islands makes the effort well worth the trouble. Yachts from Santa Barbara can enjoy a pleasant weekend cruise in the right conditions by taking the afternoon westerly to Channel Islands, then leaving for the islands early the next day. After breakfast, or a full day at Santa Cruz Island, they can take the westerly home in the afternoon. The same offshore morning breeze once carried us from Channel Islands as far as the Rincon on a beautiful morning on a memorable passage. Beware, however, of riding strong post-frontal northeasterlies up-Channel toward Santa Barbara. They can be very gusty indeed.

The Anacapa passage and the analogous channels between Santa Cruz and Santa Rosa, and Santa Rosa and San Miguel are windier spots, too, for the westerlies can funnel through the straits with considerable force (Fig. 4.2). This is particularly true of the Santa Cruz and San Miguel passages where wind speeds can reach 40 knots or more, even on days when the Channel itself is quiet. Passage winds die down east of Johnson's Lee on the south side of Santa Rosa and by Gull Island near Santa Cruz. A well-equipped vessel will be able to handle the stronger winds of the passages by reefing or changing sails. However, be prepared for sudden changes in wind and sea conditions.

When island hopping from Santa Cruz to Santa Rosa, or on to San Miguel, it is probably best to motor to windward in the calm morning hours if you are pressed for time. You will frequently encounter bumpy swells on your way from Santa Rosa to San Miguel as you pass from the relatively sheltered waters of the Channel to the long swells of the open Pacific.

San Miguel is notorious for its strong winds, which are localized and unpredictable. A crossing from Cojo anchorage or from north of Point Conception can be very bumpy. Special care should be taken when approaching San Miguel from north or NW. There are numerous unlighted dangers and outlying rocks difficult to spot even in very calm weather. A morass of kelp and heavy surge make this an inhospitable area even for local fishermen. Although there are temporary anchorages in the area, we recommend you keep clear.

## Entering the Channel

Entering Santa Barbara Channel from north involves rounding Point Conception, a passage we describe below. Suffice to say here, you will probably encounter either bumpy and foggy conditions or strong winds and clear skies off Point Conception. When south bound, it is probably best to keep three or four miles off the mainland, unless bound for Cojo anchorage to minimize gusts blowing off the land. If bound for San Miguel, keep well offshore but give Richardson Rock and the west end of the island a wide berth (Fig. 5.2), and keep a sharp eye out for unlighted Wilson Rock, NE of Cuyler Harbor. You can expect the strong WNW wind to moderate as you enter the Channel, sometimes with dramatic suddenness. Beware of strong gusts blowing down the canyons between Point Conception and Gaviota or even further eastbound. These gusts can surprise you even on calm days.

Fig. 4.3 — *Conspicuous white sand dune two miles east of Point Mugu, a key landmark for entering the Santa Barbara Channel.*

Entering the Channel from the south is straight-forward except for the complication of the Pacific Missile Range (see below). Bound into the Channel from Catalina Island, your first landfall may be the conspicuous white dune at the foot of the cliffs 2.0 miles east of Point Mugu (Fig. 4.3). Mugu itself is a conspicuous, semi-detached rock lying at the end of the cliffy shoreline that ends in the long, dreary sand spit that extends 10 miles to Point Hueneme. Another landfall closer to Point Hueneme can be made on the conspicuous two-chimney power station that lies 2.0 miles from the point.

The strongest afternoon westerlies blow close inshore. Often you will pick up a 20 knot breeze as you approach Point Mugu, which will give an entertaining beat past the Air Force Base. Sometimes the jets taking off from the runway will pass close overhead, wailing like banshees. The area off the base is patrolled when missile firing is in progress and you may be asked to wait while a shoot takes place. Stronger wind may persist off Point Hueneme and for several miles as you enter the Channel. If you are lucky enough to encounter an offshore breeze, you can enjoy a magnificent run into the Channel, as we once did, bound from Santa Barbara Island to Santa Barbara Harbor. The passage was a rough one, in a fierce Santa Ana that had us leaving the island anchorage in a hurry. Skies were clear over the mainland as we hurried NW under storm jib and triple reefed main. Bioluminescent showers burst aboard as the Santa Ana shrilled in the rigging. In the small hours, the wind moderated from 40 knots to less than 20. Anacapa light guided us into the Channel, the sparkling lights of Port Hueneme glittering to starboard in the warm wind. As the sun rose over the Santa Ynez Mountains, we passed the oil rigs off Santa Barbara and drifted into the harbor as the wind dropped at the warm dawn. Passages like this make cruising the Channel a memorable experience.

When approaching the Channel from SE, look for the hump of the west end of Anacapa Island and the mountains of Santa Cruz Island, which appear before the low-lying mainland. Remember that visibility is usually far from ideal owing to fog, haze, smoke, or — dare we say it — smog, and your landfall may be at short range. An accurate DR plot and a good radar reflector are essential under these conditions. An RDF set, using Anacapa Island radio beacon, can relieve much anxiety. Beware of shipping in the Channel between Anacapa and the mainland, especially on the Anacapa side of the passage. Ships pass through the narrows at great speed and also go outside the islands on their way offshore.

**Hazards: Seas and Swells**

Sea and swell conditions in the Channel can be both

Fig. 4.4 — *Large swells generated by a distant Pacific storm sweeping into the entrance of Cuyler Harbor, San Miguel, on a cloudy, rain-filled day. "Sea and swell conditions are important factors in the planning of longer passages in the Channel."*

rough and complex. Often a considerable swell will be running on flat, calm days, generated by storms thousands of miles offshore. Sometimes Santa Anas will allow you to surf to windward on these swells. Even a 20-knot breeze in Windy Lane can produce sharp, steep seas in only a few hours. Sea and swell conditions are important factors in the planning of longer passages in the Channel (Fig. 4.4).

The term "sea" refers to water disturbances caused by wind velocities both in the local area and further away. *Swells* develop when these disturbances move out downwind from their place of origin, often for hundreds, even thousands, of miles. The heights of seas and swells are measured as the vertical difference between wave crests and troughs in feet. Thus, a six-foot wave measures six feet from trough to crest. The waves may have a period of, for example, 20 seconds, the time it takes successive wave crests to move past the observer. Obviously the height and interval of waves are of vital importance to the small boat sailor. Swells are often a greater danger to a vessel than the winds that generate them, persisting after the gale has passed overhead.

The Southern California coast is battered by swells formed far offshore. As they move eastward toward the coast, the swells gradually subside, expending their final energy on the coast. As the swell approaches the coast, it may be affected by rapid shallowing which tends to heighten the waves. Islands and headlands can bend the direction of swells to conform to the shape of the coastline. Pacific swells are often bent or refracted round the flanks of the offshore islands which shelter the mainland. As you sail along the mainland, indeed, you can pass from a calm area to a bumpy one, depending on how the swells are being filtered through the island passages. You'll normally find rougher swells at the ends of the Channel, and in the island passages. Sometimes tropical cyclones or intense winter storms far offshore bring heavy swells to the Channel. You should be careful when passage making at these times, for the movement of the boat can be vicious if there is no wind to keep you moving. A small auxiliary is almost powerless in such conditions.

Some of the steepest seas in the Channel are encountered in Windy Lane, where rapidly increasing afternoon winds can impose a one or two foot *wind wave* on top of a four foot swell in an hour or so. These, and other, wind waves are often oblique to the prevailing swell, and may give you some uncomfortable surprises over the topsides. Keep hatches closed and be prepared to ease off downwind under such conditions. Cross-swells can occur after winter storms, with a SE sea imposed on a westerly swell. The corkscrew motion from this situation has to be experienced to be believed. Our 30-35 knot NW winds after winter storms can generate three to five foot waves within an hour or two in smooth water. If the wind blows over a swell, you can have very nasty sea conditions indeed. Safety harnesses are essential under these conditions.

Swells over eight feet are fairly rare in the Channel, but the prudent skipper will listen carefully to reports of sea and swell while planning a passage.

A few locations near the islands should be avoided in all but the calmest conditions. These include the so-called Potato Patch one to two miles off the west end of Santa Cruz Island, and the west end of San Miguel.

## Tides and Currents

Currents in the Santa Barbara Channel are unpredictable, generally weak and little understood. According to the U.S. Coast Pilot, they can run at speeds of up to one knot through the passages between the islands, although locally they are known to be stronger. Directions of the currents in the Channel depend greatly on wind conditions, and can vary from summer to winter.

The normal current circulation in the Channel is thought to approximate that in Figure 4.5, although this can vary seasonally. Inshore near the mainland, currents rarely flow more strongly than one-quarter to one-half knot, except off Point Conception where they can be severe. When bound from Santa Barbara to Ventura or the Channel Islands, it pays to stay inshore *if* the current is flowing. You can observe the current moving past the fairway buoy off the harbor and shape your course accordingly. There are rotary current patterns around Anacapa and Santa Cruz Islands, with different currents on both sides of the passages between the islands. A larger rotary pattern is found in the west

part of the Channel, to the extent that it may behoove you to stay inshore when northbound from Santa Barbara to Point Conception and well offshore when southbound, where the current may flow east and where the westerlies blow stronger. It should be stressed that the currents shown in Figure 4.3 are little known, and this is only a provisional diagram. Actual conditions may vary considerably. In general, however, the U.S. Pilot argues that a weak current sets east in the spring and west in the fall and winter. The so-called Davidson current flows north along the California coast in winter, while the California current flows south in the summer. These affect seasonal currents in the Channel.

Tidal streams in the Santa Barbara Channel are generally weak and have little effect on navigation. The mean tidal range at Santa Barbara is 3.6 feet, at Port Hueneme 3.7. Tidal streams are gradually weak, but set along the north shore of the Channel at a speed between 0.5 and 1.0 knot, and reach a velocity of one knot in the

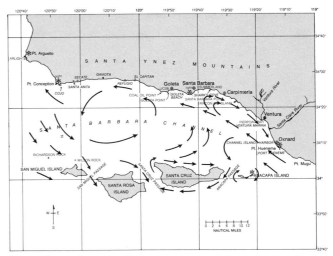

Fig. 4.5 — *A generalized diagram of the currents in the Santa Barbara Channel. This is a highly provisional map, which takes no account of seasonal variations.*

passages between the islands. When bound for Ventura from Santa Cruz Island on a flood tide, be prepared sometimes to allow for a one knot tide close to the mainland, three-quarter knot on the ebb. The Pilot adds, "It has been observed that a strong inshore set prevails on a rising tide in the deep waters of Hueneme Canyon. In general, there are conflicting currents, at times quite strong, around the slopes of the submarine valleys both here and off Point Mugu."

The only time that tides may be of concern to a cruising yacht are when anchoring in a shallow cove, securing alongside a fixed pier, when entering Santa Barbara Harbor when the entrance channel has shoaled, and at times when you want to lift out your mast with a crane that needs some elevation above water level to do the job. Tide tables can be obtained from the National Ocean Survey of the U.S. Department of Commerce, from many marine gas stations and chandleries. You should use these to determine your tides. Tidal constants for the major features in the Channel are given in these tables. You can also obtain complete tidal information from the *Pacific Boating Almanac,* published annually.

## Hazards: Fog

Fog and low clouds are such a common phenomenon in the Channel that one becomes almost blasé about them. On many days, the fog remains several hundred feet above the surface, leaving visibility of 0.5 mile or more. Channel crossings under these circumstances are safe enough, provided a compass course is laid off and a close lookout kept for shipping. Your landfall is likely to be about a mile off, when perceptible darkening of the fog betrays the presence of land, or a white flash surf breaking at the foot of a cliff. Hoist a radar reflector under these conditions and have your foghorn handy. An RDF will enable you to home in on Santa Barbara or Anacapa Island.

Thick fogs are a much different situation and a real hazard. A Channel crossing under these conditions is foolhardy. You will be crossing two busy traffic routes where large freighters will be on passage at full speed. The land will be invisible until you are literally aground. Postpone your trip, or, if caught out, stay out of shipping lanes, hoist a radar reflector, sound the fog signals required by law, and keep a very sharp lookout. Inshore, it is better to anchor in shallow water and wait for the fog to lift than to risk shipwreck. You should sound a bell at intervals not exceeding two minutes if at anchor. Remember, however, that sound signals can be highly deceptive.

The major radio beacons in the Channel are listed in Table 4.1.

**TABLE 4.1**
*RADIO BEACONS*

*MARINE*

| Beacon | Kcs. | Range | Signal |
|---|---|---|---|
| Anacapa | 323 | 10 | . / . (AN) |
| Ventura | 314 | 10 | ...-/-- (VM) |
| Channel Islands | 308 | 10 | -.-./-.. (CI) |
| Santa Barbara | 294 | 10 | .../-... (SB) |
| Point Arguello | 302 | 150 | --- (O)* |

*This beacon operates in a sequence of major radio beacons that repeats continuously. Arguello is No. 3 and 6 in the sequence, each beacon operating for a minute (see official publications).

*AEROBEACONS* (use with caution)

| Los Angeles International | (LAX) | 332 Kcs |
|---|---|---|
| San Nicolas Island | (NSI) | 203 Kcs |
| Point Mugu | (NTD) | 224 Kcs |
| Santa Barbara | (BA) | 338 Kcs |

## Hazards: Shipping

We regard big ships as the greatest hazard to small craft in the Santa Barbara Channel (Fig. 4.6). As a glance at charts shows two purple-bordered bands, representing traffic lanes for north and southbound vessels, slash through the Channel. Most large ships passing through

51

our waters will keep to these lanes unless they are bound for the U.S. Navy Base at Port Hueneme or to the inshore tanker moorings off Ventura, Carpinteria, or Ellwood. But they are under no legal obligation to do so, and you may encounter large ships elsewhere. A particular hazard in the Channel are tugs towing huge barges at the end of very long towlines (Fig. 4.7). On several occasions we have sailed with crew members who have gaily attempted to steer between tug and barge, not realizing they are connected! This is tempting at night, when the tug and barge are at a considerable distance and can be mistaken for two vessels. Be familiar with lights that identify a towing vessel to prevent this mishap occurring. And make sure your crew knows them too.

International law requires small craft to keep out of traffic lanes, and to cross them only when necessary, and then as nearly at right angles as possible. You are also required to keep clear of large, less easily maneuverable vessels in restricted waters — and that includes traffic lanes. While some ships keep a sharp lookout and are courteous to small craft, many appear to ignore them completely. Remember you are in the equivalent of a VW Beetle up against a huge semi-truck: sail defensively.

When crossing the Channel, the following principles should govern your attitude to passing ships:

Fig. 4.6 — *"We regard big ships as the greatest hazard to small craft in the Santa Barbara Channel."*

— Keep out of the traffic lanes except when absolutely necessary. Cross them by the shortest route possible.

— Keep a sharp 360 degree lookout for ships. How many times has a large ship suddenly appeared astern, because you haven't been keeping a watch behind you? A 360 degree lookout is especially important in foggy or rough conditions and should be maintained at least every five minutes.

— Hoist a radar reflector in fog and on passage at night. Make sure you have a functioning masthead light and the correct navigation lights. Carry a high-powered flashlight that can be shone on your sails to show your position.

— Take bearings on ships converging on you. If the bearing is constant, you are on a collision course.

— If you see first a red light (portside) and then a green light (starboard), or both at once, the ship is heading straight for you. Under these circumstances, it is probably safer to alter course *in good time* and to keep out of the other vessel's way, even if legally she should keep out of your way. Avoid last-minute alterations of course.

— If the other vessel alters, maintain your original course. She may signal her intentions by one or two blasts on her whistle. That is a sure sign of a course alteration.

— *If in doubt of the other vessel's intentions, alter course early, and sufficiently conspicuously so that she can see what you are doing.*

— Do NOT carry on regardless and insist on your rights. They may not have seen you. Don't go close to a large ship just for a look or leave decisions to the last minute.

— Brief your crew on the danger of shipping, on the need for a close lookout, and on the need to call the skipper in cases of even the slightest doubt. Never engage an autopilot or vane steering gear and forget to keep a lookout.

The international rules for prevention of collision at sea and the inland regulations control navigation for

Fig. 4.7 — *A tug towing two barges in the Channel. Do not attempt to pass between tug and tow.*

all ships, and you should obey them implicitly, especially with vessels of your own size or slightly larger. Avoid fishing boats and give space to large vessels in narrow harbor channels. It is no excuse to be ignorant of the rules in our congested waters. With large ships, the issue for small vessels is survival and safety, not a blind insistence on your rights. IF IN DOUBT, GET OUT OF THE WAY.

## Hazards: Oil Platforms

The oil controversy rages on in the Santa Barbara Channel, with environmentalists pitted against Big Business in a never-ending struggle over offshore drilling. Whatever your views on the controversy, you have to take account of the many oil platforms that mark our waters (Fig. 4.8). The largest concentration lies off Santa Barbara and Carpinteria, others off Anacapa, Ellwood, Refugio, and others between Gaviota and Point Conception and off Ventura. Oil rigs are clearly marked on the larger scale charts, and you should keep yourself aware of new platforms and also of temporary drilling platforms, such as are sometimes found off Anacapa and Santa Rosa Islands. Oil platforms are brilliantly lit and display white or fl. white lights at each corner, as well as sounding foghorns (2 sec/20 sec). Constant launch traffic links the rigs with the mainland.

Oil platforms can be useful markers on thick days and at night. Each has a name — Hilda, Heidi, and so on — posted on the rig. Treat oil platforms with great respect. Do not approach closer than 200 feet, and never tie up to them. Some of them are surrounded with substantial mooring buoys, which are sometimes unlit. Keep an eye out for isolated oil slicks offshore. Often unreported, these small spills are just as hard to clean off your topsides.

Drilling vessels operate in the Channel, their anchor marked by orange and white buoys with lights Fl. W 4 sec. Do NOT pass between the buoys and the drill ship. Details of drilling operations are listed in *Local Notices.*

## Night Passages

Night passages in the Channel present no great difficulty, provided your ship is correctly lit. It is inadvisable to attempt a landfall on the islands at night, even on a brilliant moonlit night, unless you have vast confidence in your knowledge of the anchorages and their approaches. The mainland can be very confusing, especially in the Ventura-Point Hueneme area where the harbor lights are surrounded by the brilliant lights of the cities around them. Santa Barbara Harbor clusters at the foot of downtown, but the approach is straightforward if you identify the more powerful Santa Barbara Point light (Fl. 10 sec) and then follow the coastline to the breakwater.

There are relatively few major lights in the Channel area. Here are the principal lights, with their characteristics as of January 1, 1978 (check light lists for corrections):

*Major lights:*

Point Arguello (Gp. Fl (2) 30 sec., 26 miles)
Point Conception (Fl. 30 sec., 26 miles)
Anacapa Island (Gp. Fl (3) 60 sec., 26 miles)

*The most important mainland lights:*

Santa Barbara Point (Fl. 10 sec., 25 miles)
Point Hueneme (Fl. 5 sec., 22 miles)

*Island lights:*

San Miguel Island — Richardson Rock (Fl. 4 sec.)
(buoys) — Point Bennett (Fl. R 4 sec.)
Santa Rosa Island — South Point (Fl. 6 sec., 9 miles)
Santa Cruz Island — Gull Island (Fl. 4 sec., 6 miles)
(buoy) — Valley Anchorage (Fl. 2½ sec.)

Harbor lights are discussed in later chapters.

We identify special night navigation problems at intervals in the pages that follow.

Fig. 4.8 — *"Whatever your views on the oil controversy, you have to take account of the many oil platforms that dot our waters."*

## Anchoring and Ground Tackle

Adequate ground tackle is a fundamental requirement for any cruising in the Santa Barbara Channel. By "adequate," we mean:

— A main anchor of adequate weight for your length and displacement.

— Anchor line of more than sufficient diameter and length to hold you in a gale.

— A second anchor and line heavy enough to hold your boat in an emergency or when your main anchor drags.

— Chafing gear for your anchor line.

— An anchor buoy, fender, or bleach bottle for the end of your anchor line in case you have to slip it in an emergency and return later to recover it.

Your boat should have strong cleats for securing anchor lines and some convenient means of storing both anchor and rope. A bow roller, hawse pipe, and chain locker, or a separate compartment, are ideal, but far from standard on California yachts. Larger vessels may need an anchor winch, which can be either electrically or manually powered. Small yachts should be able to pull up their anchors by hand or by using a halyard or sheet winch.

Considerable debate surrounds the best type of anchor for island cruising. Most people swear by the Danforth type, which is excellent in sand and holds well on gravel bottoms. Make sure you purchase the Hi-Tensile type. C.Q.R. plow anchors are popular with larger yachts and are advisable in sand or mud. They also work well in kelp or rocks. A few yachts are using a new form of Wishbone anchor, which seems to be highly effective (except, perhaps, on rocks), and easy to stow. Whatever anchor you choose, the secret is to buy one of adequate size for your boat and to mate it with the correct weight of chain and adequate warp diameter. You'll sleep better at night!

Most local yachts anchor with a 30-foot length of chain secured to the anchor and then a long nylon anchor line. This arrangement is easy to handle on deck and makes less noise on bumpy nights. It holds well provided you use at least six times the depth of water at high tide and the anchor is well dug in. Anchor chain as opposed to line gives you much more weight below the surface, but is rejected by many on account of its weight aboard. You should carry a minimum of 150 feet of anchor line. Chain is, of course, far more resistant to chafe.

The second anchor should be a Danforth, with a length of chain and lighter line than the main anchor. But the rig should be capable of holding your boat in a very strong wind.

Anchoring is an art at the best of times, and a vital art at the islands. What makes island anchoring fascinating is the double challenge of persistent surge and limited space. The small size of the anchorages and the congestion in popular coves means that many people use two anchors to hold them head to surge and clear of their neighbors. As a general principle, we strongly recommend you use only one anchor whenever possible. Should a beam wind spring up, you will then swing head to wind. With two anchors, a strong breeze can place a drastic strain on your beam and cause even well-set anchors to drag without warning. The ideal is probably an anchorage full of vessels anchored on "Bahamian Moors," where anchors laid at 180° to one another are carried to the bow (Fig. 4.9c). This technique minimizes swinging. Unfortunately, however, most people lay anchors bow and stern and you must either move elsewhere or do the same.

If anchoring with two anchors, lay ample scope of chain and line at bow and stern, and make sure the anchors are well dug in. To anchor like Fig. 4.9d is to invite certain trouble if a wind fills in. The main anchor is lying on the bottom and the chain and line lies on top of it. The second anchor is too slack. Only the calm weather is holding the yacht in place.

When anchoring in a small cove, explore the anchorage first, decide where you are going to anchor, and then make your final approach. Figure 4.9 shows three ways you can lay your anchor in comfort. The critical point is to judge where to drop anchor so that

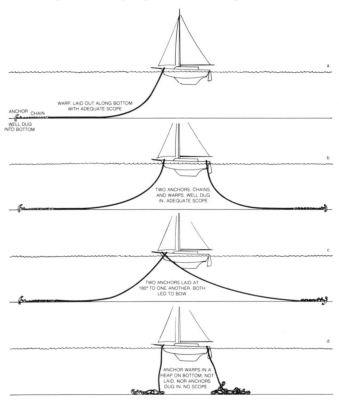

Fig. 4.9 — *The well anchored sailing vessel at the islands*

a. *Lying to a single anchor*

b. *Lying to a stern anchor*

c. *"Bahamian moor," used in shallow water or when swinging room is limited. You lay two anchors 180 degrees in opposite directions and swing in a narrow circle.*

d. *How not to anchor at the islands, or anywhere!*

the boat is in the ideal position you chose in the first place. Only experience can tell you whether you place the anchor in the correct location. Do not hesitate to lay it a second time, even a third, until you are absolutely satisfied and can sleep in peace.

If you anchor with two anchors, you will normally take out your second anchor in the dinghy. Load the anchor, chain, and some line in the stern of your dinghy, then pay out the line from the boat as the oarsman rows in the chosen direction. Once the dinghy is over the spot you have chosen, drop the anchor, allow it time to reach bottom, and haul taut. Some skippers prefer to lay either bow or stern anchor, then pay out double scope before laying the other anchor and centering the two lines. Remember that the weight of the chain and scope of the line will count as much as a heavy anchor. You should be careful to anchor clear of steep cliffs where the swells rebound off the rocks and cause you to rock unnecessarily.

The golden rules of anchoring at the islands are simple enough:

— Lay anchors with ample scope and ensure they are dug into good holding ground.

— The first person anchored has prior rights to space. You cannot usurp his safe anchorage.

— Anchor clear of other people, and make sure your anchors are clear of those of other yachts. Ask fellow owners where their anchors lie.

— Do not lay more than two anchors. More are unnecessary if you have dug in your first pair correctly.

— Insist that yachts that endanger your safety move to a better berth — but do this tactfully!

— Display the correct anchor lights. The Coast Guard patrols the island coves regularly and has been known to ticket offenders.

— Avoid rafting except as a temporary measure. Surge can destroy your topsides against your neighbor.

Anchoring at the islands is simple enough if you take care to anchor securely in the first place. The ideal anchorage depth for a 30 to 40-foot yacht is probably about 25 to 35 feet, and not too close to the beach. If you want, lay a second anchor or line ashore, but make sure it is secure and does not bring you too close to shore.

Weather conditions at the islands can be unpredictable, and at times downright dangerous. Strong down canyon winds, or vicious NE winds can make the most sheltered cove on the northern coast of Santa Cruz Island a serious hazard. Coves like Fry's and Pelican offer good shelter against the prevailing westerlies (see Table 5.1). But much of Santa Cruz can be lethal under strong Santa Ana type conditions. Only one rule applies if you suspect that such conditions are about to arrive or descend upon you — GET OUT — FAST! Often downslope or onshore winds can fill in at speeds of over 30 knots with almost no warning. About the only advance notice on the north coast of Santa Cruz Island is the very dry atmosphere, clear visibility, offshore smog, and an uncomfortable swell from NE in a flat calm. *If these conditions suddenly arrive, get out and return to the mainland or heave to offshore.* The wind may not materialize, in which case you can return to your anchorage. But if it does, you are not trapped on a lee shore in a crowded anchorage under conditions where it is almost impossible to get out. Riding it out can be a survival situation. So — watch your weather, and be prepared to move out fast, even on the calmest summer day. See Table 5.1 for refuge anchorages in different conditions.

## Congestion

Congestion is a way of life at Santa Cruz Island and, to a less extent, elsewhere. On major holiday weekends, you may find as many as 90 boats in Pelican (Fig. 4.10). Popular anchorages like Fry's may shelter 20 boats on an average summer weekend. Only rarely will you have such an anchorage to yourself. The only effective way to

Fig. 4.10 — *Congestion in Pelican Bay on a holiday weekend. "Congestion is a way of life at Santa Cruz Island and to a less extent elsewhere."*

live with congestion is to be prepared for it. Have alternate anchorages in mind. They may be less comfortable, but at least quieter. You can anchor in deeper water away from the most popular spots. Provided you lay ample scope, you should be comfortable enough in calm weather. If you join the crowd, or are an early arrival whose berth becomes crowded by later yachts, you are at their mercy. The problem for late arrivals is to lay anchor properly, to avoid swinging into other people or fouling their lines. This requires fine judgment, careful consideration of other peoples' safety, and the use of your second anchor first so you align your boat parallel to the others.

Here are some pointers:

— Always lay a second anchor *if* everyone in a crowded anchorage is using two anchors. *However*, if at all possible, avoid this method of anchoring, especially in unsettled conditions.

— Lay ample scope and buoy your main anchor, even your second anchor as well.

— Avoid fouling other peoples' lines and do all you can to prevent other yachts anchoring over yours.

— Try to anchor in a congested cove under power. To do so under sail is grossly irresponsible, unless your engine has failed.

— Have adequate insurance and carefully log all collisions with details of damage received to either vessel.

— Lastly, if you have any doubts whether there is room, go elsewhere. The room for error is so small that an insecure berth simply isn't worth it.

Fouled anchors are commonplace in crowded anchorages. If you are unlucky enough to foul your anchor, either lift your anchor with your buoy rope servicing as a trip line or lie to your other anchor while you recover your fouled one by taking the line out in a dinghy. A scuba diver may be in the anchorage. Do not hesitate to ask for help, as he can easily spot, and even solve your problem. Most divers are delighted to assist, and will often check to see if your anchor is securely dug in, or not fouled.

Horror stories about congested anchorages abound, of noisy parties and badly anchored yachts drifting upon their neighbors at night. Boat owners shout at each other and run generators at all hours of the night. Congestion is now such a fact of cruising life in the Santa Barbara Channel that we have to approach it as a practical problem, just as important as safe anchoring or heavy weather strategy. All we can beg people to do is to be tolerant of others, unselfish in their partying and considerate in their use of generators, and responsible and cooperative as far as safe navigation and anchoring are concerned. After all, the Channel and its many anchorages are for all of us to enjoy. Let's help make them enjoyable for everyone afloat! We hope the sailing directions which follow contribute to this enjoyment, and enable you to explore the many charming anchorages that are quiet all year-round.

---

## WARNING

Keep a close look out for commercial fishing traps, marked by rubber floats, plastic bleach bottles, and other devices lying in or just outside the mainland kelp beds and off the islands. These inconspicuous markers are hard to sight on sunny and foggy days. Their lines can foul your propellers.

---

## Additional Reading for Part One

The writing of Part I involved reading many dozens of books and obscure articles. Few of our sources are worth putting on your cabin bookshelf. But here are some favorite books we find invaluable companions.

*There was a grandeur in everything around, which gave almost a solemnity to the scene; a silence and solitariness which affected everything. Not a human being but ourselves for miles; and no sound heard but the pulsations of the Great Pacific.*

Every cruising boat in California should carry a copy of Richard Henry Dana's *Two Years Before the Mast*, Macmillan, New York, 1841. This immortal book can be bought at any bookstore, yet the author sold it for $250! Dana's descriptions of early California, of Santa Barbara and "Buenaventura" are classics. They add a unique perspective to the Channel.

Peter and Jane Howorth, *Foraging Along the California Coast*, Capra Press, Santa Barbara, 1977, is a must, an invaluable compendium of data about the shorelines of the West Coast.

Hillary Hauser and Bob Evans' *The Living World of the Reef*, Walker, New York, 1978, is a useful guide to underwater life at the islands.

Those interested in local flora should carry Clifton E. Smith, *A Flora of the Santa Barbara Region*, Santa Barbara Museum of Natural History, 1976, which is a mine of information.

Bird watchers should carry Howard L. Cogswell's *Water Birds of California*, University of California Press, Berkeley and Los Angeles, 1977. This valuable guide contains a mass of information on birds and bird watching, as well as accounts of individual species. The

University of California Press also publishes invaluable guides to the mammals, native trees and shrubs, and seashore life and plants of Southern California that are available in most bookstores. The UC Press guides are invariably authoritative and well written.

Unfortunately, no one has yet written a definitive history of the Santa Barbara Channel area or of the Chumash Indians. Our accounts were compiled from a variety of sources, and by consulting expert researchers. Leif C.W. Landberg, *The Chumash Indians of Southern California*, Southwest Museum, 1965, is very useful. You can obtain some historical background by buying anecdotal histories in local bookstores. But beware — many of the stories they tell are unverified by rigorous historical inquiry! A fascinating account of California life in the mid-nineteenth century emerges from Alfred Robinson's *Life in California*, first published in 1846 and reprinted by Peregrine Press, Santa Barbara, 1970.

Edith Buckland Webb, *Indian Life at the Old Missions*, Lewis, Los Angeles, 1952, is a rare classic.

For Catalina, try Alma Overholt (updated by Jack Sargent), *The Catalina Story*, Catalina Island Museum Society, P.O. Box 366, Avalon, CA 90704.

Chapter Two was largely compiled from Emil S. Kurtz' invaluable National Weather Service pamphlet *Southern California Weather for Small Boaters*, Salt Lake City, 1971.

There are innumerable books on safety afloat, navigation, and passage making, and we assume you will choose those which best reflect your interest. Much of these chapters was written from our collective experience of the Channel, and that of the experts who checked our manuscript.

Incidentally, don't forget to take lots of paperbacks with you, to read and trade with other boats, also decks of cards, dice, Scrabble, and other such games. In 1977, everyone seemed to be trying to swap copies of *Trinity!*

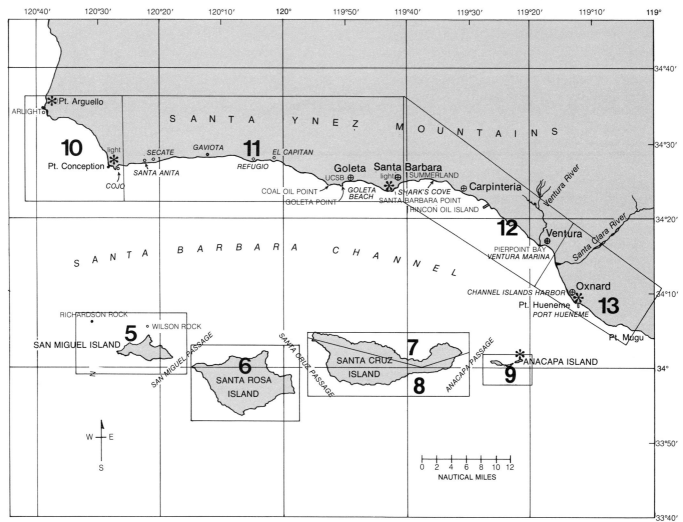

120°40'  120°30'  120°20'  120°10'  **120°**  119°50'  119°40'  119°30'  119°20'  119°10'  **119°**

34°40'

Pt. Arguello
ARLIGHT

S A N T A   Y N E Z   M O U N T A I N S

34°30'

**10**
Pt. Conception

light

SECATE  GAVIOTA  **11**  EL CAPITAN
SANTA ANITA  REFUGIO

COJO

Goleta  Santa Barbara
UCSB  light  SUMMERLAND
COAL OIL POINT  GOLETA  SHARK'S COVE  Carpinteria
GOLETA POINT  BEACH  SANTA BARBARA POINT
RINCON OIL ISLAND

Ventura River

34°20'

**12**
Ventura

Santa Clara River

PIERPOINT BAY
VENTURA MARINA

S A N T A   B A R B A R A   C H A N N E L

CHANNEL ISLANDS HARBOR  Oxnard
Pt. Hueneme  **13**
PORT HUENEME

34°10'

RICHARDSON ROCK

WILSON ROCK

**5**

SAN MIGUEL ISLAND

SAN MIGUEL PASSAGE

SANTA CRUZ PASSAGE

SANTA CRUZ
ISLAND  **7**

ANACAPA PASSAGE

**9**  ANACAPA ISLAND

Pt. Mugu

N

**6**
SANTA ROSA
ISLAND

**8**

ANACAPA PASSAGE

34°

W — E

S

33°50'

0  2  4  6  8  10  12
NAUTICAL MILES

33°40'

*Chapter Numbers*

# Part II:

# Sailing Directions - Western Offshore Islands

Chapters 5 - 9 cover the offshore islands in the Santa Barbara Channel; chapters 10 - 13 cover the mainland. Sailing directions conclude with Santa Barbara Island and a brief note on the eastern islands — Santa Catalina, San Nicolas and San Clemente.

---

**TABLE 5.1**
*REFUGE ANCHORAGES*

This book contains frequent warnings to clear out of anchorages when certain conditions appear imminent. The big question is — where do you go? This table, developed by Peter Howorth on our behalf, summarizes which anchorages are safest in different conditions. It includes anchorages at the islands and west of Santa Barbara, not the few anchorages in the east mainland coast of the Channel. *Be certain to look up detailed descriptions of each anchorage in text before making your approach.*

---

*WARNING*
The information in this Table is based on many years of experience in all weathers. However, in the final analysis, the judgments about anchorages are yours, based on conditions in them at the time of your arrival. *If in doubt, head to port if possible, or stay offshore and ride out the bad weather, clear of all dangers.*

---

*NW CONDITION* (Strongest and most prevalent from mid-March to mid-May)

Monitor wind speed and direction by listening to weather reports from Point Arguello and San Nicolas Island.

If wind averages out at over 12 knots north or NW at Point Arguello and San Nicolas Island, use this table to determine which anchorages are safe for refuge.

Natural weather indicators, detailed in *Table 2.2,* may also be used to determine wind velocities which can be applied to this table.

Anchorages are listed in order of preference for each area.

### NW CONDITION
### WIND SPEED AND DIRECTION

| | 12-19 north to NW | 20-29 north to NW |
|---|---|---|
| **San Miguel Island** | Cuyler Harbor<br>Tyler Bight<br>Crook Point | Cuyler Harbor<br>Tyler Bight |
| **Santa Rosa Island** | Johnson's Lee or<br>Becher's Bay<br>Eagle Rock | Johnson's Lee or<br>Becher's Bay north of pier<br>Eagle Rock |
| **Santa Cruz Island** | On north side: protected anchorages from Fry's Harbor east<br>On south side: Malva Real or protected anchorages from Coches Priestos east<br>Willows<br>Forney's | On north side: protected anchorages from Fry's Harbor east<br>On south side: Albert's<br>Hungryman's or<br>Yellowbanks<br>Smuggler's<br>Malva Real (windy but safe) |
| **Anacapa Island** | East Fish Camp<br>Frenchy's | East Fish Camp |
| **Pt. Arguello to Gaviota** | Secate<br>Cojo<br>Gaviota | Secate<br>Cojo<br>Gaviota |
| **Refugio to Goleta** | Refugio,<br>Goleta or<br>El Capitan | El Capitan<br>Goleta<br>Refugio |

### NW CONDITION
### WIND SPEED AND DIRECTION

| | 30-30 north to NW | Over 40 north or NW |
|---|---|---|
| **San Miguel Island** | Cuyler Harbor<br>Tyler Bight | Cuyler Harbor |
| **Santa Rosa Island** | Johnson's Lee or<br>Becher's Bay,<br>north of pier | Johnson's Lee or<br>Becher's Bay,<br>north of pier |

| **Santa Cruz Island** | On north side: Fry's Harbor or Pelican; protected anchorages east of Scorpion<br>On south side: Albert's Yellowbanks Smuggler's | On north side: Pelican<br>On south side: Yellowbanks or Albert's |
|---|---|---|
| **Anacapa Island** | None | None |
| **Pt. Arguello to Gaviota** | Secate<br>Cojo or Gaviota<br>(if unable to return to port) | Secate |
| **Refugio to Goleta** | None | None |

*NE CONDITION* (Strongest and most prevalent from September to November.)

Monitor wind speed and direction by listening to weather reports from Point Mugu.

If wind ranges from 15-20 knots and more NE, use this table to determine which anchorages are safe for refuge. Natural weather indicators, detailed in *Table 2.2,* may also be used to determine wind velocities which can be applied to this table.

Anchorages are listed in order of preference for each area.

### NE CONDITION
### WIND SPEED AND DIRECTION

| | 15-19 NE | 20-29 NE | 30-45 NE |
|---|---|---|---|
| **San Miguel Island** | Cuyler Harbor<br>Tyler Bight<br>Crook Point | Cuyler Harbor<br>Tyler Bight<br>Crook Point | Cuyler Harbor<br>Tyler Bight<br>Crook Point |
| **Santa Rosa Island** | Johnson's Lee<br>Becher's Bay<br>Eagle Rock | Johnson's Lee<br>Southeast Anchorage | Johnson's Lee<br>Inside Talcott Shoal (shallow draft power-craft only) |

| | | | |
|---|---|---|---|
| **Santa Cruz Island** | On north side: Protected anchorages from Pelican to Lady's On south side: Coches Prietos Willows or Malva Real Forney's | North part of Christy's Forney's Fraser Cove (north of Forney's) | Between Christy's and Forney's (if you can't reach Johnson's Lee |
| **Anacapa Island** | East of Cat Rock | None | None |
| **Pt. Arguello to Gaviota** | Secate Cojo Gaviota | Secate Cojo Gaviota | Secate Cojo Gaviota |
| **Refugio to Goleta** | Refugio El Capitan Goleta | Refugio El Capitan Goleta | Refugio El Capitan |

## NE CONDITION
## WIND SPEED AND DIRECTION

| | 45-60 NE | Over 60 NE |
|---|---|---|
| **San Miguel Island** | Cuyler Harbor Tyler Bight | Cuyler Harbor Tyler Bight |
| **Santa Rosa Island** | Inside Talcott Shoal (shallow draft power-craft only) In lee of west end (watch for sub-merged rocks) | Inside Talcott Shoal (shallow draft power-craft only) In lee of west end (watch for sub-merged rocks) |
| **Santa Cruz Island** | Between Christy's and Forney's if you can't move | None |
| **Anacapa Island** | None | None |
| **Pt. Arguello to Gaviota** | Secate Cojo | Cojo Secate |
| **Refugio to Goleta** | Refugio | None |

**SE CONDITION** (Common from October to April)

Monitor wind speed and direction by listening *for several hours* to *all* coastal weather stations from Point Piedras Blancas to San Diego. If increasing SE winds are coming your way, use this table to determine which anchorages are safe for refuge. Natural weather indicators, detailed in *Table 2.2*, may also be used to determine wind velocities which can be applied to this table. *Remember that strong NW winds often follow SE storms. Anchorages safe in SE conditions can quickly become dangerous lee shores if the wind shifts to NW.* Anchorages are listed in order of preference for each area.

## SE CONDITION
## WIND SPEED AND DIRECTION

| | 12-19 SE | 20-29 SE | 30-50 SE |
|---|---|---|---|
| **San Miguel Island** | Cuyler Harbor | Cuyler Harbor | West side of Harris Pt., well clear of breakers and wash rocks (watch for shift to NW as storm passes, then head into Cuyler Harbor) |
| **Santa Rosa Island** | SE anchorage Inside Talcott (shallow draft powercraft only; watch for shift to NW as storm passes, then head to Santa Barbara or Becher's Bay) | Inside Talcott Shoal (same caution as for 12-19 SE) | Inside Talcott Shoal (same caution as for 12-19 SE) |
| **Santa Cruz Island** | Potato Harbor (*best* natural anchorage in SE storm, but watch for shift to NW as storm passes) Fraser Cove North of Christy's Chinese Harbor, east side | Potato Harbor Fraser Cove North of Christy's | Potato Harbor |

63

| | | | |
|---|---|---|---|
| **Anacapa Island** | None | None | None |
| **Pt. Arguello to Gaviota** | Secate | Head for nearest harbor away from advancing front (Morro Bay or Santa Barbara*) | Head for nearest harbor |
| **Refugio to Goleta** | Head for Santa Barbara* | Head for Santa Barbara* | Head for Santa Barbara* |

*Santa Barbara is a lee shore in SE storm; get there before wind increases.

*SW CONDITIONS* (Prevalent from May through August)

Since this wind is normally relatively moderate, most protected anchorages will suffice.

*FOGGY CONDITIONS* (Especially from late May to July)

Most protected anchorages will provide adequate shelter, as wind is usually moderate in fog. Fogs are most prevalent from dusk to mid-morning. By monitoring weather reports from nearby stations, you can sometimes predict movement of fog toward you. Certain areas are nearly always fog free, owing to warm offshore winds and nearby land configurations. Use this table as a guide to sunny anchorages.

| | Moderate to heavy fog | Peasoup |
|---|---|---|
| **San Miguel Island** | Crook Point | Crook Point |
| **Santa Rosa Island** | Johnson's Lee or Becher's Bay | East Point to Becher's Bay |
| **Santa Cruz Island** | Gull Island to San Pedro Point | Smugglers (if anywhere) |
| **Anacapa Island** | None | None |
| **Pt. Arguello to Gaviota** | Arlight to Jalama Cojo to Gaviota | Cojo to Gaviota |
| **Refugio to Goleta** | Usually none | None |

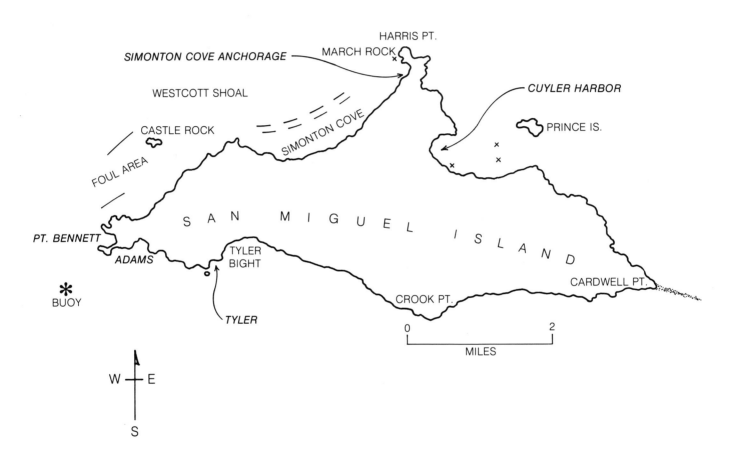

HARRIS PT.

MARCH ROCK

SIMONTON COVE ANCHORAGE

CUYLER HARBOR

WESTCOTT SHOAL

PRINCE IS.

CASTLE ROCK

SIMONTON COVE

FOUL AREA

S A N   M I G U E L   I S L A N D

PT. BENNETT

TYLER
BIGHT

ADAMS

CARDWELL PT.

BUOY

CROOK PT.

TYLER

0                          2

MILES

W — E

S

*(Based on U.S. Government Chart 18727)*

Fig. 5.1 — *San Miguel Island, with major features and anchorages mentioned in the text.*

# CHAPTER 5

# *San Miguel*

San Miguel Island is managed by the National Park Service. At present the island is open to the public on a limited access basis, both to protect the large seal and sea lion rookeries and to avoid accidents with the unexploded bombs and ammunition that occasionally turn up underfoot. San Miguel has a resident manager and is patrolled constantly. A permit to visit must be obtained from the Channel Islands National Monument office in Ventura (805) 644-8157. You cannot obtain it at the island.

## Sailing Directions

San Miguel is the most remote of the Santa Barbara Channel Islands, a desolate and windy place that has a charm all its own (Fig. 5.1). The island is 7.6 nautical miles long and up to four miles wide. You can see the two hills on San Miguel as far as 20 miles off on clear days, for the 800-foot humps stand out on the horizon even if the lower slopes of the island are invisible. San Miguel is notorious for its strong NW winds, which often spring up at night. Even in moderate NW weather offshore, the local winds can reach 50 knots. Once covered with dense brush, the island was denuded by drought and decades of sheep ranching. The sheep and the winds destroyed the brush cover. The western part is now sand dunes, while stunted grass and scrub covers the remainder.

Do not visit San Miguel until you have had considerable experience cruising in the Channel and of heavy weather sailing. San Miguel weather is unpredictable and dangerous. Even in calm conditions, heavy Pacific swells can roll into seemingly sheltered anchorages and seriously impede progress under power. The golden rules of cruising San Miguel are simple enough:

Fig. 5.2 — *WARNING: Do not attempt to approach the west end of San Miguel from offshore in thick or rough weather.*

— Pick your weather and monitor weather forecasts constantly.

— Avoid the west end of San Miguel. There are many off lying dangers and often heavy swells.

Passage to San Miguel can be made from Cojo, Secate, Refugio, or Goleta, an easy, if sometimes bumpy, reach across the mouth of the Channel. You can make your miles to windward from Santa Barbara in the calmer water inshore. As usual in the Channel, the calmest conditions for a crossing are in the early morning or at night. Many Santa Barbara vessels leave harbor after sundown and motor directly to San Miguel, arriving there by early morning. If the sea is calm, this is a straightforward passage except for the shipping lanes. An autopilot makes everything more comfortable for all hands, provided a good lookout is maintained. The return home is a different matter. Once we set our spinnaker just outside Cuyler Harbor and ran all the way down to Santa Barbara on the afternoon westerly with an ideal breeze. As the sun set we lowered the spinnaker off Santa Barbara Point, broad reached to the harbor entrance. The west wind dropped at Stearn's Wharf, a gentle SE air then took us to our slip without using the engine! Talk about ideal passage making!

When bound for San Miguel from Santa Cruz or Santa Rosa Islands, plan to motor to windward in the early morning, leaving at first light. Most days, you should reach San Miguel before the westerly fills in. While South Point on Santa Rosa is lit, San Miguel is not, so night passages are not recommended unless you have reliable radar. If you want to sail to San Miguel, prepare yourself for a long, and often wet, beat to windward. Only truly hardy types should try this particular passage under sail. Above all, beware of sailing off San Miguel on a dark night. There are many outlying rocks, and unlit dangers. Even with a full moon and perfect conditions, navigation can be hazardous.

Approaching San Miguel from north of Point Conception needs some care. Plan to keep well off the mainland, clear of strong winds that funnel round Point Conception. As you approach San Miguel, keep a sharp lookout for the following outlying dangers:

— Richardson Rock, 5.5 miles NW of Point Bennett. This isolated rock is 53 feet high and white topped. A lighted whistle buoy lies 0.5 miles NW of the rock. Do not pass between this lighted rock and San Miguel at night, to avoid the foul areas closer inshore.

— Wilson Rock, 2.2 miles NW of Harris Point, only 19 feet high. A reef extends about one mile WNW from the black rock. This shoal is covered with breaking water even in a slight swell. Further foul ground lies south and SW of Wilson Rock.

— Castle Rock, a three-headed outcrop 1.6 miles NNE of Point Bennett. This 180-foot landmark is normally surrounded with dense kelp, and the nearby shoals break in moderate swells.

Although San Miguel itself is unlit, the following lighted buoys mark off lying hazards:

— Richardson's Rock whistle buoy (Fl 4 sec.)
— Whistle buoy off Point Bennett (Fl. R. 4 sec.).

Note that Wilson Rock is unlit, so a NW approach at night could be foolhardy. Neither of the San Miguel lighted buoys is visible from any great distance.

---

*WARNING*
Do not attempt to approach the west end of San Miguel in thick weather (Fig. 5.2). Soundings give no warning of the hazards described above.

---

For a first visit to San Miguel, you are best advised to approach the island from Johnson's Lee on Santa Rosa, picking perfect conditions to venture westward.

For planning purposes, assume weather patterns west of South Point on Santa Rosa will be similar to those of San Miguel — frequently boisterous.

The extreme west end of San Miguel is readily identified by the long, jagged bluff of Point Bennett.

The 74-foot high bluff rises to 337 feet further east. A lighted whistle buoy lies 0.8 miles SW of the point (Fl. R. 4 sec.). The west end of San Miguel is mantled with extensive sand dunes that extend across the island. The NW coast is backed by low cliffs and trends NE to a low lying spit that extends NW. A patch of rocks and shoals heavily infested with kelp extends NW of the spit for nearly a mile. This area is known as Westcott Shoal, much of it covered with a minimum depth of 28 feet. 0.6 miles further north lies a natural oil spring with a minimum depth of 15 feet. The entire coastline between Westcott Shoal and Point Bennett is foul with rocks and kelp. Castle Rock and its off lying boulders is conspicuous. Kelp beds and breaking water often extend a mile or more offshore of Castle Rock.

---

*WARNING*
Give the stretch of coast described above a wide berth in all conditions.

---

**Simonton Cove**
East of Westcott Shoal, the coast forms a gradual bight 2.4 miles long and 0.6 miles wide. This bay, known as Simonton Cove, is blanketed with kelp. Some covered rocks lie up to 0.3 mile offshore just west of the center of the bay. Approach the beach with great care and only in calm sea conditions, keeping a lookout for sub-surface rocks and kelp.

**Anchorage**
Simonton Cove is fully exposed to NW and west winds, and a lively surge commonly enters the bay. Shelter from SE winds can be found by anchoring under Harris Point (Fig. 5.3). To anchor in Simonton Cove, identify Harris Point and March Rock immediately on the west side of this conspicuous landmark. Then steer toward shore, keeping a close lookout for kelp and breaking water. Anchor (rock and sand) according to

draft, tucked in under the cliffs for maximum shelter according to prevailing conditions. Fifteen feet will be found at a considerable distance from the beach. Simonton is preferable to Cuyler in SE conditions. If anchored in SE conditions, be prepared to move to Cuyler if the wind shifts to NW.

## Cuyler Harbor (Fig. 5.3)

Harris Point is the most prominent landmark on the San Miguel coast, a bold and precipitous promontory that is connected by a saddle to a 485-foot link 1.0 mile south of the headland. Harris can be identified from far offshore, a dark and menacing symphony of rock and stunted grass. You can safely approach Harris Point to within 0.5 mile. Cuyler Harbor lies immediately SE of Harris Point, one of the most famous anchorages in the Santa Barbara Channel.

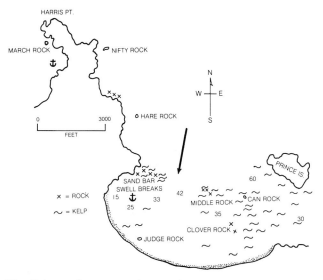

Fig. 5.3 — *Plan of Cuyler Harbor, showing anchorage under Harris Point in Simonton Cove.*

*(After U.S. Goverment Chart 18727)*

### General Description

Juan Cabrillo may have died in Cuyler in 1543. The harbor, named after its original government surveyor, has been a favorite anchorage for explorers, sealers, fishermen, and cruising people ever since. The anchorage is sheltered from NW to SW winds, but exposed to strong NE or SE winds. A fine, sandy beach lies round the anchorage, formed by a bight of volcanic cliffs that are a shoulder of the 485-foot hill behind Harris Point. The cliffs are mantled by sand dunes on the south side of the anchorage. Prince Island guards the eastern approach to Cuyler, is often alive with hundreds of sea birds. Cuyler Harbor is a comfortable and uncongested anchorage with good holding ground. But a nasty surge can roll in and strong winds sweeping over the cliffs have to be experienced to be believed.

### Approach (Figs. 5.3-5)

(Have Chart 18727 in front of you.)

When approaching from any direction, identify Harris Point, which is unmistakable with its conspicuous hill, shoulder and steep cliffs. Steer for the point until the other landmarks are spotted. When approaching Cuyler from the NW, give wide berth to Wilson Rock, which is often difficult to spot.

Approaching from any direction between east and NW, you should identify the following landmarks:

— Prince Island, at the east side of Cuyler, 288 feet high. The seaward face of this huge rock is precipitous and black, lies 0.4 miles offshore.

— Nifty Rock, 39 feet, 250 yards offshore, 1000 yards SE of Harris Point.

— Hare Rock, a 56-foot pinnacle 300 yards offshore, 1110 yards SSE of Nifty Rock.

— The conspicuous sand dunes behind Prince Island.

— Judge Rock, a small, black rock near the west end of the sandy beach. A smaller outcrop, Gull Rock

Fig. 5.4 — *"View of Cuyler's Harbor from north."* *Original surveyor's profile of this important anchorage which can still be used in conjunction with Fig. 5.3. Survey by Lieutenant James Alden, 1852.*

*(Published in the* Annual Report of the Superintendent of the Coast Survey, 1853.)

lies on the beach 0.3 mile ESE of Judge Rock. Do not confuse the two.

— Middle Rock, 0.5 mile WSW of Prince Island, dries at low tide — a shoal area.

Entrance to the anchorage lies one-third of the distance between Prince Island and Harris Point cliffs. Shape your course to stay about 300 yards east of Harris Point cliffs. If arriving from the east, keep offshore of a line between Prince Island and a point midway between Bat and Hare Rocks until you are close to the cliffs. Such a course will keep you clear of the kelp and foul ground that lies inshore of Prince Island. Once Bat Rock has been identified, shape your course to stay at least 0.4 mile offshore. A reef extends over 300 yards east of the NW extremity of the anchorage. Use your depth sounder to avoid this danger. Breaking water will be found on this shoal even in moderate weather. Give it a wide berth. Once clear of the shoal, alter course west toward the beach.

In thick weather, or when uncertain of the minor landmarks, follow the following directions, from the U.S. Coast Pilot:

*Bring Harris Point to bear 261 degrees true (246 degrees M), distant 1.7 miles, and the west point of Prince Island to bear 181 degrees true (167 degrees M), distant 1.3 miles; thence steer 209 degrees true, heading midway between Middle Rock and the west point of the entrance, and when the south point of Prince Island bears 084 degrees true (069 degrees M), anchor in five to seven fathoms.*

You can also approach Cuyler through a channel south of Prince Island, passing between the island and San Miguel itself. However, the area is heavily overgrown with kelp and is difficult to negotiate. Minimum depth is said to be 18 feet. Clover Rock (awash at LW) and Can Rock (four feet high) lie SW of Prince Island (see plan). They should be given a wide berth, and a course shaped to pass midway between Can Rock and Prince Island and offshore of Middle Rock will bring you to the main entrance channel. Do not try to pass between Can and Clover Rocks without local knowledge and perfect visibility.

### Anchorage

Inside the anchorage, the bottom shoals gradually toward the beach. Anchor according to draft, tucked in

Fig. 5.5 — a. *Cuyler Harbor from NE. Use in conjunction with Fig. 5.3.*
   b. *Approach to Cuyler Harbor from NE.*

under the cliffs to gain maximum protection from the wind. Fifteen to 20 feet of water will be found up to 200 yards offshore (soft sand). Watch out for the foundations of an old pier at the south corner of the anchorage. Choose your anchorage with care, paying particular attention to:

— The necessity of leaving in a hurry if wind or surge become dangerous.

— Swells rolling into the beach at low tide.

— Surge entering the anchorage round Bat Rock.

You can sometimes anchor at Cuyler in the calmest conditions and then find yourself rolling wildly in a dangerous surge. Make sure you give yourself enough space to swing and to leave if necessary.

Heavy swells can break in the entrance in rough weather. Entering or leaving Cuyler under these conditions is suicidal.

### Landing and Facilities

Landing by permission only, and then on the beach. Watch for breaking swells. No facilities, except for a small freshwater spring on the beach.

## Cuyler to Tyler Bight

---

### WARNING
A government-designated Danger Area extends over the east half of San Miguel Island. You should check the regulations in Chapter 2 of the U.S. Coast Pilot.

---

East of Cuyler, the coast trends SE past Bay Point to Cardwell Point. The black/grey bluffs at the east end of Cuyler gradually fall away to sea level, the scrub-covered coastline sloping into the water. A sandy beach masks low lying Cardwell Point, fronted by a conspicu-

ous, low sandspit that extends ESE for about 0.5 mile. This area is constantly shoaling, and underwater dangers extend almost a mile offshore. The sandspit is fortunately fairly obvious, as its white-yellow sand can be seen from some distance (Fig. 5.6). Even in calm weather, Pacific swells break with great force on the spit, throwing cascades of spray into the air. Further breaking water is caused by clashing currents in San Miguel Passage that meet the prevailing swells. Cardwell Point is treacherous in heavy weather. Use your depth sounder to warn yourself of rapidly shallowing water in thick weather. A Navy target buoy sometimes lies south of the spit.

---

### WARNING
Give Cardwell Point a berth of at least 1.5 miles. When bound through San Miguel Passage, keep closer to the Santa Rosa shore.

---

Two outlying rocks are located 400 yards south of Cardwell Point. Extensive kelp beds are found on both sides of the point. From Cardwell Point, San Miguel slopes gradually to the shore. A yellow-white sandy beach bounds the surf, wrapping round inconspicuous Crook Point, the south promontory of the island. Keep well offshore to avoid the kelp growth along this stretch of coast.

The low lying coastline, bounded by high bluffs, trends WNW beyond Crook Point. There is little to interest cruising yachts in this area, although you can land a dinghy in a small cove just west of Crook Point. Fishermen anchor east of Crook Point along the inner edge of the kelp and 0.5 to 1.0 mile east of the point. This area provides good shelter in moderate NW and NE winds, but beware of the breaking reef a mile east of Crook Point.

Give the coast a wide berth to avoid Wyckoff Ledge, 1.4 miles west of Crook Point. This ledge and its

Fig. 5.6 — *Sand spit off Cardwell Point, San Miguel, in a heavy swell. Give the spit a wide berth in all conditions.*

associated kelp beds lies 0.5 mile offshore with a least depth of nine feet. The kelp beds provide an excellent boundary beyond which it is dangerous to navigate inshore, for a number of submerged rocks lie between Wyckoff Ledge and Tyler Bight, which opens up on your starboard bow. The entrance to the bight is normally mantled with dense kelp beds that mask submerged rocks, some lying as close as three feet from the surface.

## Tyler Bight Anchorage

### General Description (Fig. 5.7)

A useful and little-known anchorage with good protection from west and NW winds. Even when winds are blowing over 40 knots offshore, Tyler is relatively calm, partly because of the off lying kelp beds that filter the swell.

### Approach

Tyler Bight is bounded by a high bluff at the NW end of the anchorage, which protects the bay from west to NW winds. The bluff is streaked with yellow dune sand and has a sandy beach at its foot. Once you have identified this conspicuous bluff, look for white-topped Judith Rock, which lies at the west entrance of the bight, close inshore. Then shape your course to bring the rock north of your vessel, distant 0.5 mile, or further offshore if the kelp beds are dense inshore. Then alter course shoreward, aiming to pass between the kelp patches and leaving Judith Rock 200 yards to port.

### Anchorage

Although the Pilot recommends anchoring in seven fathoms, with Judith Rock bearing 250 degrees *M*, 500 yards distant, you can also move as close inshore as seems prudent in prevailing wind and swell conditions (but see WARNING below). Sound your way to a berth in 18-25 feet (sand), tucked under the cliff and as much in the lee of Judith Rock as possible. Look out for kelp and be prepared to leave in a hurry if weather conditions deteriorate.

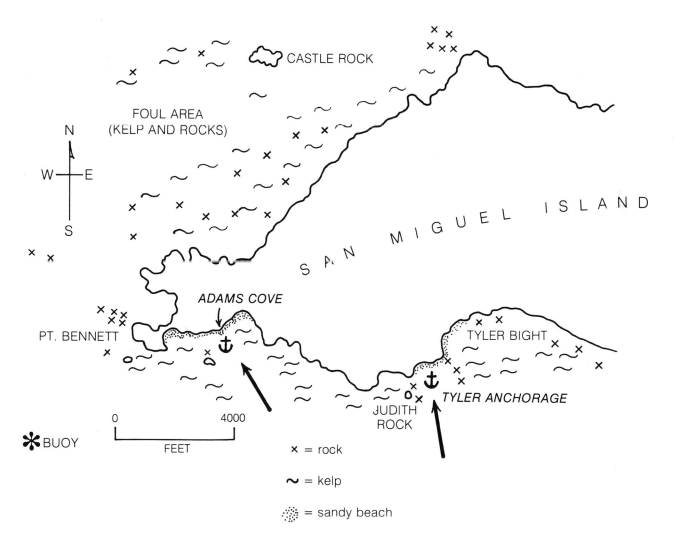

CASTLE ROCK

FOUL AREA
(KELP AND ROCKS)

N
W — E
S

S A N   M I G U E L   I S L A N D

*ADAMS COVE*

PT. BENNETT

*TYLER BIGHT*

*TYLER ANCHORAGE*

JUDITH
ROCK

0        4000

FEET

**✱**BUOY

✕ = rock

∼ = kelp

⦂ = sandy beach

Fig. 5.7 —
a.  *Plan of Adams Cove and Tyler Bight.*

*b. Approach to Tyler Bight from west.*

*c. Tyler Bight anchorage from east with Judith Rock.*

Do not approach the Tyler Bight anchorage from ESE for there are dense kelp beds and sub-surface rocks.

State Park Service regulations forbid anchorage closer than 300 yards to the shore between Judith Rock and Castle Rock on the NW coast. Your anchor spot should be chosen accordingly.

Landing is forbidden in this area because of rookeries.

### Tyler Bight to Point Bennett

From Tyler Bight, the coastline remains low lying and is covered with extensive patches of sand dunes. This can be a windy corner and should not be approached except on a calm day. Low, rocky outcrops bound the shore, as it forms a last small cove before joining a sandy beach and low spit that joins Point Bennett to the island. Two rocky islets lie close inshore south of the point.

## Adams Cove (Fig. 5.7)

### General Description

This small indentation lies immediately east of Point Bennett, and gives some shelter from west to NE winds. However, a nasty surge can roll into the anchorage even in calm weather. Adams is at best a temporary berth in fine weather, or an emergency.

### Approach and Anchorage

Identify Point Bennett and its sandspit. Adams Cove lies at the east end of the sandy beach that extends east from the point, a sloping bluff of rocks and sand forming the indented cove.

Once the indentation has been identified, feel your way in with depth sounder and an alert lookout on the foredeck. Anchor in 30 feet off the beach (rock and sand), but be prepared to leave at a moment's notice if winds come up (see WARNING above). Sea elephants and many seals are to be seen on the spit to the east.

Our directions for San Miguel may sound like pronouncements from a Prophet of Doom. A doomsday note is justified. San Miguel can be very dangerous and you are advised to navigate conservatively in its vicinity. Local fishermen have many small anchorages they use for days on end. They have acquired an intimate knowledge of San Miguel over years of fishing. No casual visitor can acquire similar knowledge haphazardly in a few short trips. Everyone should treat San Miguel with the respect it deserves.

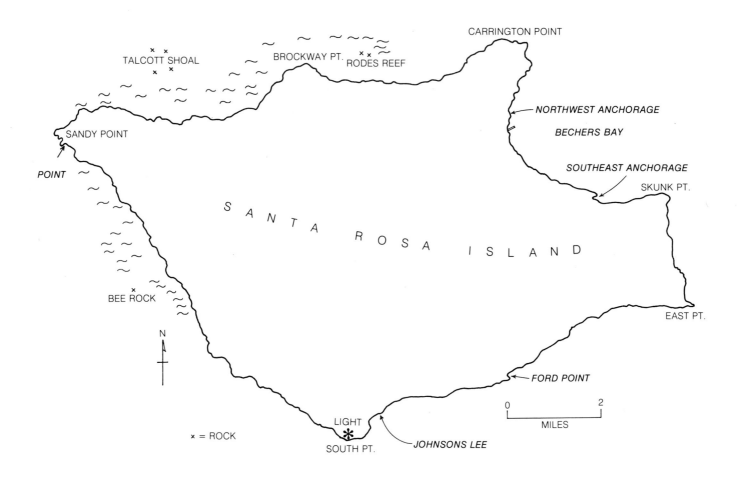

CARRINGTON POINT

NORTHWEST ANCHORAGE

BECHERS BAY

SOUTHEAST ANCHORAGE

SKUNK PT.

EAST PT.

TALCOTT SHOAL

BROCKWAY PT.

RODES REEF

SANDY POINT

POINT

SANTA ROSA ISLAND

BEE ROCK

N

FORD POINT

0 2
MILES

x = ROCK

LIGHT

SOUTH PT.

JOHNSONS LEE

Fig. 6.1 — *Santa Rosa Island, with major features and anchorages mentioned in the text.*

CHAPTER **6**

# *Santa Rosa*

Santa Rosa Island has had a colorful history, as a hunting ground for sea otters and as a cattle ranch (Fig. 6.1). The second largest of the offshore islands, Santa Rosa is about 15 nautical miles long from east to west and nine miles across at its widest point. Unlike Santa Cruz, Santa Rosa lacks natural harbors, has generally steep-to coasts and extensive offshore kelp beds. The highest point of the island is 1589 feet above sea level.

Santa Rosa can normally be seen from the mainland on a clear day, although its profile is less spectacular than that of its larger, easterly neighbor. Like San Miguel, Santa Rosa is not an island to be trifled with, for sudden gale-force, downslope winds and strong westerlies can easily catch the small boat sailor unawares. Once, while beating from Gull Island off the south coast of Santa Cruz to Johnson's Lee on Santa Rosa, we were caught by a sudden NW blow that funneled through the Santa Cruz Passage. Hastily, we reefed down our 32-footer to a storm jib and triple-reefed main and beat along the south shore of Santa Rosa. Fortunately, the sea was flat and we enjoyed an exhilarating sail with spray blowing horizontally. We came to anchor at Johnson's Lee with considerable difficulty against the strong wind. The wind screamed through the rigging until 0200, when it dropped as suddenly as it had risen. The unpredictability of Santa Rosa weather makes it unwise to take chances with faulty gear or inadequate preparation.

Fig. 6.2 — *Bechers Bay, NW anchorage from east. The ranch buildings and pier (arrow), are useful landmarks for this spot. "Some vessels anchor under the cliffs 0.5 mile north of the pier, where sometimes smoother water and more shelter may be found."*

## Sandy Point to Becher's Bay

Sandy Point is a conspicuous, rocky point that forms the west extremity of Santa Rosa Island. White sand dunes over 400 feet high extend inland from Sandy Point and are conspicuous from seaward. A small rock, four feet high, lies off the point. Two peaks, 465 and 485 feet high, respectively, rise inland off Sandy Point. The 10-fathom line extends north from the west end of Santa Rosa 1.5 to 2.0 miles offshore. Irregular swells and breaking water may extend a considerable distance offshore, even in moderate weather. Talcott Shoal, a mile NE of Sandy Point, has a minimum depth of 10 feet (rock). This entire area, indeed the whole north coast of Santa Rosa, should be given a berth of at least two miles to avoid both shallow water, confused seas in rougher weather, and kelp beds that can extend up to three miles offshore.

The north coast trends east to Brockway Point, a low spit with high bluffs behind it 300-500 yards inland. A peak 534 feet high rises 2.2 miles SE of the point. Beaches on this stretch of coast have nothing to offer small boat sailors and are obstructed by kelp.

Rode's Reef, a patch of three submerged, kelp-covered rocks with a minimum depth of 7.5 feet lies 1.2 miles ENE of Brockway Point, 0.8 mile offshore. The swell breaks on this reef. If you keep 3.0 miles offshore, you will be well clear of Rode's Reef and other offlying dangers. The north coast continues in a shallow bay of steep cliffs that trend NE to Carrington Point, the NE extremity of Santa Rosa. This shoreline should also be given a wide berth.

Carrington Point rises to a peak 452 feet high, 0.75 mile inland. The seaward face of the point is bold and rocky, and 0.8 mile long. Beacon Reef lies 0.4 mile north off Carrington Point, minimum depth 14 feet. To avoid concealed rocks, stay at least 1.0 mile off the land.

The east shore of Santa Rosa Island is dominated by Becher's Bay, a large, open bight, 4.5 miles across. Becher's Bay is backed by low cliffs that are highest near Carrington Point. The bluffs are 100-feet high at Coati and Corral Points just south of Carrington, but the 100-foot contour recedes behind the low cliffs. A ridge of higher ground extends east from the high spine of the island down to sea level at the south end of Becher's Bay. The cliffs taper away and end in the sandy spit known as Skunk Point. Becher's Bay is generally steep-to, with kelp beds lying up to 0.5 mile offshore. Shallower water extends further from land off Skunk Point, which should be passed at least a mile offshore.

# Becher's Bay Anchorages

### NW Anchorage (Fig. 6.2)

**General Description**

An open roadstead with a pier that serves as the supply anchorage for the cattle ranch. NW anchorage provides fairly good shelter from the prevailing NW winds, but it can blow hard at night. Strong winter swells can swing around Carrington Point and break in the anchorage, sometimes with little warning.

**Approach**

Approaching from north or NW, identify Carrington, Coati and Corral Points with their bold cliffs. The land will appear somewhat featureless until you are within a mile or so of the anchorage, for the pier tends to merge with the cliffs when viewed at a distance, especially when approaching just before sunset. Once, however, the trestles of the pier are identified against the brown cliff, steer for the pier and select your anchoring spot. When approaching from the south, steer inshore from Carrington Point about one mile, where the cliffs become lower, until you identify the pier.

At night, you can sometimes use the lights of the ranch house which lies inshore of the pier as a leading mark for the anchorage.

**Anchorage**

Some vessels anchor under the cliffs about 0.5 mile north of the pier, where sometimes smoother water and fair shelter may be found, in an opening between the kelp beds. If anchoring off the pier, in 30 feet or more, position yourself well clear of the mooring buoy, in a berth where you gain maximum shelter from the cliffs consistent with a kelp-free anchorage. Do not anchor near shore, especially in winter, because of the extensive undisturbed breaker zone. There is 16 feet at the end of the pier.

Gusty winds can blow through NW Anchorage, especially at night. Rough weather brings heavy surge, but Becher's is a wild and interesting spot for an overnight stay. The holding ground is good, but you should clear out if the wind fills in from NE or SE.

**Landing and Facilities**

At the pier, by permit only. No facilities.

### SE Anchorage (Fig. 6.3)

**General Description**

SE Anchorage lies 1.5 miles west of Skunk Point but is little more than a shallow bay offering limited shelter from SE winds. The anchorage is normally bumpy and not recommended for an overnight stay except in perfect conditions.

**Approach**

From the north or NW, identify Skunk Point with its sandy spit, and shape your course to close with the land one mile west of the point. Southeast Anchorage lies in an indentation of the land where sandstone cliffs join the sandy beach. Once the indentation is identified, steer to enter the anchorage 200 yards east of the deepest indentation of the cove. From SE, pass well offshore of Skunk Point and close with the land at the indentation.

**Anchorage**

Off the beach in 25-35 feet (sand). Although holding ground is good, there is always a surge. Beware of recent shoaling in this anchorage. Anchor in a good least depth at low tide to avoid bumpy breaker swells, or even the danger of bouncing on the sand. Southeast is a good temporary anchorage. An overnight stay is not recommended.

Fig. 6.3 — *SE Anchorage, Bechers Bay, from NE, distant 1.5 miles.*

## Skunk Point to Ford Point

The coastline between Skunk Point and East Point, the SE corner of Santa Rosa Island, is low lying with a sandy beach. Higher ground behind the low sandy spit trends SE to end in East Point, a fairly bold, rocky headland. East Point should be given a wide berth, for there are off lying dangers, including a rock in the kelp, minimum depth 16 feet, 0.7 mile north of the point. A shoal with minimum depth of 22 feet lies just SE of Skunk Point. Keep at least 1.5 miles offshore of the SE corner of Santa Rosa unless anchoring close inshore. It is possible to anchor off the beach between Skunk Point and East Point, sheltered by the coastline and kelp beds in 12-25 feet (sand). This is better than Becher's in heavy winter swell conditions. A first visit with someone having local knowledge is recommended. The shore between Skunk Point and East Point is sometimes difficult to identify at night. Breaking water occurs off Skunk Point even in moderate conditions, where strong currents can sometimes set you NW or inshore. Give this dangerous point a wide berth.

The south coast of Santa Rosa slopes steeply into the Pacific, with a series of dry canyons flowing into the ocean. Low cliffs and sandy beaches occur most of the distance between East Point and Ford Point, but rocks will be found close inshore, and you should keep at least 0.5 mile off in 30 feet or more.

Two anchorages are frequented by fishermen — Eagle Rock and Ford Point.

## Eagle Rock Anchorage

### General Description
A useful anchorage under the cliffs with good shelter in moderate NW and NE conditions.

### Approach
Eagle Rock lies 1.9 miles west of East Point, off a conspicuous white-yellow bluff, which is readily identified from east or west. Another rock lies close inshore just west of the bluff. Once Eagle Rock and the bluff are identified, alter course to close with the shore east of the rock. Do not attempt to pass between Eagle Rock and the shore without exploring the area in a dinghy first.

### Anchorage
In the lee of the bluff and cliffs in 15-30 feet (sand), clear of kelp and other obstructions.

## Ford Point Anchorage (Fig. 6.4)

### General Description
A temporary anchorage in the lee of a small point that offers little shelter for a prolonged stay. A pleasant, sandy beach lies nearby.

Fig. 6.4 — *Ford Point anchorage.*
*Beware of kelp in the entrance.*

### Approach
Ford Point is a low, rocky promontory that lies 4.2 miles west of East Point. Once the point is identified, steer to pass just inshore of the headland. Give the rocks off the point a wide berth (at least 200 yards) and sound your way into the anchorage.

## Anchorage

Off the beach in 15 feet or less (sand) where maximum shelter can be obtained. Do not set yourself too close to the breaker line, and be prepared to clear out if the surge gets up.

---

### WARNING
The swell can come up quickly in these anchorages, especially when tropical storms are off the Mexican coast.

---

## Ford Point to Johnson's Lee

The coastline between Ford Point and Johnson's Lee is somewhat featureless, with low cliffs and steep slopes and canyons behind them. The bottom is rocky, some kelp found close inshore which thickens as you approach South Point which is conspicuous. Johnson's Lee lies immediately NE of South Point.

## Johnson's Lee (Fig. 6.5)

### General Description

Many people claim Johnson's is the best anchorage on Santa Rosa, but it can be uncomfortable in winter and spring. The open roadstead faces SE and offers considerable shelter from west to north winds. An abandoned military base overlooks the anchorage, complete with empty barracks and a substantial Navy pier which becomes more dangerous through disuse every year. A thick kelp bed provides some shelter from the swells that roll toward the beach. The anchorage is fairly comfortable in moderate weather.

### Approach

Johnson's Lee is easy to find, for the anchorage lies immediately NE of South Point, the southernmost extremity of Santa Rosa. Approaching from San Miguel, simply identify South Point and its light, then pass 0.5 mile off and alter course into Johnson's Lee to the east (Fig. 6.5). The abandoned buildings of the military base on the slopes above the anchorage are visible from a long distance. Steer for the pier immediately below them. These same buildings and South Point are your landmarks for approaching Johnson's Lee from Santa Cruz (Fig. 6.5). Keep outside the kelp beds as you approach the anchorage, then thread your way through the seaweed toward the pier. Do not attempt this anchorage at night without local knowledge.

### Anchorage

Anchor just inside the kelp bed in 25-35 feet (sand). Avoid anchoring close to the north shore of Johnson's Lee. The bottom is rocky and holding poor. Do not

Fig. 6.5 — *Johnson's Lee*
*From SSW, distant 1.0 mile, taken from east point where you can head inshore. The incinerator chimney on the ridge to west of the base buildings can be seen from a long distance in clear weather. Do not head inshore until the pier is abeam.*

Fig. 6.6 — S.S. Chickasaw *impaled on the rocks of South Point makes a good navigational landmark.*

attempt, either, to secure alongside the pier which is sadly decayed and extremely hazardous in the surge.

Strong downslope winds can blow in Johnson's Lee, and you should clear out at the slightest sign of a southeaster.

Fair anchorage can be obtained off the beach 0.5 mile east of Johnson's Lee in settled conditions, if the main anchorage is congested.

## South Point to Sandy Point  (Fig. 6.6)

South Point can be identified from a long distance, a conspicuous rocky promontory 100 feet high, which rises steeply to a height of 460 feet. A peak of 603 feet lies behind the point. Brown, steep cliffs several hundred feet high and about 0.5 mile long extend SW from the point. An automated light (Fl. 6 sec. 9 miles) is situated 540 feet above sea level on the point. You cannot see it from Johnson's Lee. Extensive kelp beds can form off the point.

From west, South Point is unmistakable, for the wreck of the *S.S. Chickasaw* is impaled on the rocks west of the point (Fig. 6.6). The rusty hull and superstructure seem in good shape until you approach the wreck and see swells breaking against the dilapidated vessel and inside the hull. Although people do visit the wreck on quiet days, do not take a small vessel close to shore as submerged rocks and ledges extend some distance offshore.

*WARNING*
Do not visit the *S.S. Chickasaw*. She is in imminent danger of breaking up. Her rusty plates are extremely hazardous.

The high ground slopes down to the shoreline as you approach Cluster Point, 3.5 miles NW of South Point. Rocks and ledges make Cluster Point dangerous to approach closer than 0.75 mile . Shape your course for San Miguel or Sandy Point to pass offshore of Bee Rock, 2.5 miles NW of Cluster Point. Bee Rock is only five feet high and normally surrounded by dense kelp beds that extend offshore between Cluster Point and the end of Santa Rosa. Another 10-foot high outcrop lies close SE to Bee Rock. The entire area is rock studded and smothered with breaking water in even moderate weather. Do not attempt to pass inside Bee Rock. The passage is often thick with kelp and rocks lie close offshore.

The coastline, with its low, vertical cliffs, gradually slopes to NW, ending in the dunes of Sandy Point. Keep well offshore as San Miguel Passage opens in front of you and only head inshore if you plan to visit Sandy Point Anchorage.

## Sandy Point Anchorage (Fig. 6.7)

### General Description

A small, little-known anchorage at the extreme west end of Santa Rosa, offering shelter from north and NW winds. Few people visit this exposed landing which is both remote and desolate, and, at best, a fair weather day anchorage.

### Approach

Identify Sandy Point, then a small bight formed by a dark brown-grey headland, extending about 400 yards seaward from the general NW-SE trend of the coast. Always approach this anchorage from SE. Sound your way carefully toward the bight, steering to pass into the middle of the bay. Keep a sharp lookout for submerged rocks and have someone con the ship from the bow.

### Anchorage

Once inshore, anchor in the bight in 12-18 feet (sand),

avoiding kelp and rocks. The protected swinging area is very limited. Be prepared to leave in a hurry if swell or wind come up.

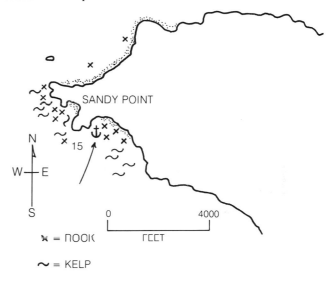

Fig. 6.7 — *Plan of Sandy Point anchorage. "Always approach this anchorage from SE."*

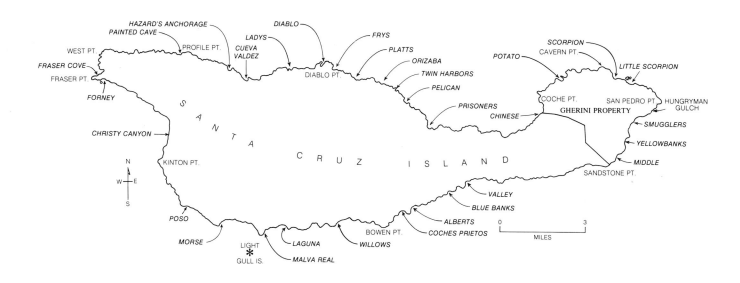

Fig. 7.1 — *Santa Cruz Island, with major features and anchorages mentioned in the text.*

# CHAPTER 7

# *Santa Cruz-North Coast*

## Important Note

*Landing on Santa Cruz Island is forbidden without a landing permit, which must be obtained on the mainland. Landing permits are NOT issued on the island.* You can apply for landing permits as follows:

For those portions of the island controlled by the Nature Conservancy, once owned by the Santa Cruz Island Company. Coche Point to Sandstone Point west (Fig. 7.1):

Santa Cruz Island Company
515 South Flower Street
Los Angeles, California 90071
(213) 485-4208

An application form can be obtained either from this address or from harbormasters' offices, yacht clubs, or chandleries. A $30.00 fee is charged (1978).

For the eastern part of Santa Cruz (Fig. 7.1):

Mr. Francis Gherini
162 South 'A' Street
Oxnard, California 93030
(805) 483-8022
or
Mr. Pier Gherini
1114 State Street
230 La Arcada Building
Santa Barbara, California 93101
(805) 966-4155

No charge is made, but owners' regulations must be obeyed.

*Landing permits have stringent conditions attached to them, to which you and your crew must adhere.* The anchorages are patrolled by Santa Barbara County Sheriffs and the Department of Fish and Game. Allow at least a week to 10 days for processing of your application.

DO NOT LAND WITHOUT A PERMIT.

## Approaching Santa Cruz Island from Santa Barbara

The distinctive skyline of Santa Cruz Island makes landfalls easy on clear days, for several of the best anchorages lie below conspicuous hills or mountain profiles that can be identified from the mainland.

Santa Cruz Island lies slightly over 20 miles off Santa Barbara. On a clear, sunny day, you can see the low slope of San Pedro Point at the east end as it climbs gradually to the high ground that rises above Scorpion Harbor. This high ground undulates for some miles, then falls away behind a deep fold in the hills, lowest point on the north coast. Prisoner's Harbor lies at the nick of this fold. The skyline climbs again east of Prisoner's where Pelican lies below a distinctive conical hill, the second in a series of six humps that run from east to west along the summit of the island. Once past these humps, the mountain ridge rises to the highest point of Santa Cruz Island. Fortunately, this lies above Diablo Point, an excellent leading mark for Fry's, Lady's, and other close-by anchorages. Another distinctive conical hill west of this high point marks Cueva Valdez. The backbone of the island slopes away gradually until steep cliffs of the West End are reached. An ancient beach line, millions of years old, can be seen as a distinctive platform extending about three miles east of West Point. It forms the precipitous cliffs that mark the west end of the island.

Steer for these landmarks — we mention and illustrate most of them in connection with the anchorages described below, and you should have no trouble finding your destination on a clear day. In thick weather, lay off a compass course for Diablo Point, West Point, Prisoner's Harbor, or some other conspicuous landmark easy to identify at close range.

Steer only toward conspicuous landmarks in foggy weather unless you have an intimate knowledge of Santa Cruz Island. You may not see anything as you close the land, often until you are less than a mile offshore. Although there are no outlying dangers, an accurate DR plot is essential in fog.

A night approach to Santa Cruz Island is not recommended without local knowledge. The island is lit by Gull Island light on the south coast (Fl. 4 sec.). The only other night landmark is a conspicuous patch of lights marking a radar station high above Valley Anchorage, visible from both sides of the island on clear nights.

## General Sailing Directions (Fig. 7.1)

The west end of Santa Cruz Island is steep-to, the abrupt end of a three-mile terrace of cliffs that fall precipitously into the Pacific. You can approach close inshore between West and Profile Points, for a look at some fascinating rock formations and soaring sea birds. The cliffs are particularly impressive on a foggy day when the mist comes and goes in delicate wraiths along their dark faces. You should keep well clear of this coastline in rough weather. Although some small boats have spent the night tucked into tiny nooks in the cliffs, we do not recommend it. Strong winds can funnel down over the cliffs, dumping grit and sand on your decks and blowing you against the cliffs.

Fig. 7.2 — *Approach to Painted Cave from north, distant 0.5 mile.*

Spectacular cliffs lead east to Profile Point, so called because of its distinctive shape when viewed from east or west. Painted Cove, just west of Profile Point, is a favorite excursion for small craft visiting the north coast of Santa Cruz Island. You can also enter three caves that lie 1.10 miles west of Painted Cave, where the cliffs are steep-to and it is possible to anchor temporarily under the shelter of the land off the middle cave in a patch of sand among the rocks and kelp that litter the bottom. These caves have large entrances and fascinating rock formations. Lights are unnecessary. The water is calm except when the Channel swells are up.

## Painted Cave

Painted Cave is not an anchorage, merely a fascinating spot to lie off and visit by dinghy. It is easily reached on a calm day from Cueva Valdez. The area should be avoided if a heavy surge or strong westerly is blowing. Best visit Painted Cave in the morning, when conditions are calm.

The cave lies in the second indentation west of Profile Point, the entrance being relatively inconspicuous (Fig. 7.2). Many people confuse it with a larger-mouthed sea cave just east. Although some people take large powerboats into the mouth of the cave and secure them to the rocks inside, we prefer to lie off the cave and go in by dinghy in relays. And, of course, a sailing yacht can do nothing else.

The walls of the cave are about 80 feet high at the entrance, flanked by boulders. The ceiling rises to over 125 feet inside and slopes down to about 20 feet at the rear. Magnificent greens, yellows and reds can be seen on the walls as you row your dinghy into the cave. Row to the end of the first section, over 600 feet into the cave. Then alter course hard to starboard into the side chamber, which extends 150 feet in total darkness. You will find rock shelves and a beach where seals and sea lions lie ashore. As your flashlights light up the chamber, the sea lions will scramble into the water and leave you in possession of their home.

*On no account try to enter Painted Cave in a heavy surge.*

The coastline trends slightly SE beyond Profile Point, but continues precipitously with few outlying dangers. Some trees appear on the hillsides as you reach the classic anchorages of the north coast.

## Hazard's Anchorage

A sandy beach and slightly indented cove 0.75 mile west of Cueva Valdez anchorage, offering limited shelter in prevailing westerlies. The cove is easily identified as it is the only conspicuous sandy beach between Cueva Valdez and Profile Point. There are no off lying dangers. Anchor in 25-30 feet (sand) off the beach and lay plenty of scope. For some reason, this pleasant, calm weather anchorage has been neglected in recent years, although well-known in the 1950s. But it becomes sloppy in even moderate west wind or surge.

Steep cliffs of the west portion of the island are now less precipitous as we near Cueva Valdez with its reddish cliffs and fine caves.

## Cueva Valdez Anchorage (Fig. 7.3)
(NOAA chart spelling is Cueva Valdaze.)

### General Description
Cueva Valdez is a popular anchorage for family cruises. Many boats congregate here on fine summer days. For those with landing permits, the magnificent sandy beach is a paradise for children, while the caverns are well worth exploring. Unfortunately, however, a nasty surge can roll into the anchorage without warning, making Cueva Valdez uncomfortable.

Fig. 7.3 — *Cueva Valdez anchorage*
*a.  Approach from five miles offshore. Arrow indicates anchorage*

*b.  Approach from east Arch Rock to port in foreground. Left arrow indicates Arch Rock, right arrow the anchorage.*

*c. Entrance to the anchorage, caves on right.*

**Approach**

Cueva Valdez is easy to identify from some miles offshore, for it lies immediately below a sharp, pointed, conical hill on the skyline of the island (Fig. 7.3a). Once this hill is identified, keep the ship's bow on the summit until the details of the coastline are picked out two or three miles offshore. The sandy beach of the anchorage will now be spotted immediately below the pointed hill, bounded on the west by a steep hillside. Caves are in the base of this hillside and can be picked out about 1.5 miles offshore. Steer for the midpoint between the two sides of the cove and head for the beach, sounding carefully, for it shelves rapidly.

When approaching from west or from Painted Cave, skirt the coast about a half mile offshore, clear of all dangers as the coast recedes slightly SE. Cueva Valdez will open up, and the caves become visible west of the beach, once abeam. When the caves are in sight, steer for the middle of the anchorage, staying at least 100 yards off the west shore of the cove.

From east, start looking for the anchorage once a rock with a hole in it west of Lady's is abeam (Fig. 7.3b). Cueva Valdez is the first sandy beach beyond the rock, and lies 1.75 miles west of this landmark. The north cave will be identified in a fold in the cliff when you are about a mile out of the anchorage. Course may be safely set for them, leaving the east promontory of the anchorage at least 0.25 mile to port. Once this point is abeam, head for the center of the anchorage (Fig. 7.3c).

**Anchorage**

The most sheltered anchorage in prevailing west conditions is off the cave entrances in 20-25 feet (sand) under shelter of the cliff (Fig. 7.3d). Everyone normally lies in a parallel line off the beach, each new arrival anchoring east of her neighbor and leading a second anchor inshore. We advise you to lay considerable scope, for the bottom shelves rapidly. There is 60 feet of water only a hundred yards from the beach. Holding ground is generally good, but look out for patches of

*d. Caves in anchorage.*

*"An uncomfortable surge can set into the anchorage. Get out when the swell comes in."*

kelp and sea grass. Anchorage on the east side of Cueva Valdez should be avoided if possible in westerly conditions. There is often bad surge, as well as patches of slippery kelp and rock on the bottom. A second anchor is recommended to reduce motion at anchor. This is an anchorage where a Bahamian moor is useful.

**Landing**

By permit only. Land by dinghy in the south cave entrance and on the beach.

---

### *WARNING*

Cueva Valdez is open to the NW, and an uncomfortable surge can set into the anchorage (Fig. 7.3e). Get out when the swell comes in, or when a strong NW or NE wind is forecast. The swells often develop in mid-afternoon and become most uncomfortable at sunset, after which they commonly decrease.

---

The landscape east of Cueva Valdez is considerably less precipitous than the west end of the island. The east promontory of the anchorage slopes gradually into the ocean, and the north slopes of the high spine of the island fall away more gradually to cliffs that are about 75 feet high. The stretch of coast between Cueva Valdez and Arch Rock can be approached to within 0.25 mile with impunity, but there is little to attract a small vessel except some fine scenery.

The next landmark is Arch Rock, a conspicuous outcrop that lies immediately offshore of another flat-topped rock (Fig. 7.3b). The two rocks form a conspicuous point of land that should be given a berth of about 400 yards. Lady's Cove lies 0.5 mile east of Arch Rock, immediately east of the steep cliffs that face the two outlying rocks.

## Lady's Harbor    (Fig. 7.4)

**General Description**

Lady's Harbor consists of two parts, the main

Fig. 7.4 — a. *Lady's Harbor entrance from west. The arrow indicates the entrance.*

b. *Lady's Harbor entrance from east, showing Arch Rock. Arrow shows entrance.*

c. *Lady's and Little Lady's anchorages from NNW. Altitude 2000 feet.*

d. *Little Lady's anchorage.*

anchorage and a smaller cove to the east, often called Baby's. The main anchorage is a magnificent spot for one or two yachts in calm conditions. Lady's tends to be congested in the summer and can experience bad surge when the swell offshore is still relatively moderate. The main anchorage is reported to be surprisingly calm in strong NE winds. Little Lady's (Baby's) is only a fair weather anchorage, which is potentially suicidal in rough west conditions, for the prevailing wind and swell head right into the entrance.

### Approach

Lady's can be hard to find from offshore. You are best advised to steer for the pointed hill above Cueva Valdez and to identify both that anchorage and Arch Rock when two or three miles offshore. The entrance to the cove lies 0.5 mile east of Arch Rock.

From the west, leave Arch Rock 0.25 mile to starboard. Diablo Point can be seen to the east in the far distance, with the sloping profile of the eastern promontory of Lady's in the middle distance (Fig. 7.4a). This promontory can be identified by a conspicuous patch of grey soil that caps the ridge as it slopes into the water. The west side of the anchorage is less prominent, lying 200 yards south. Set your course midway between these two points. Hold this course until the land is close ahead and the main Lady's anchorage opens up to starboard. Little Lady's lies 100 yards south of the easternmost promontory. The course midway between the two points will take you to the entrance passage for the latter.

From the east, leave Diablo Point 0.25 mile to port and pick up Arch Rock (Fig. 7.4b). Aim to approach the land 0.5 mile east of the rock, and identify the east side of Lady's by its grey capping when 0.5 mile west. Leave the promontory 200 yards to port and alter course inshore when the main anchorage opens up to port.

### Anchorage

*Main Anchorage.* Once the main cove is open to the south, steer for the beach midway between the two cliffs (Fig. 7.4c). Kelp extends off the east side of the entrance and sometimes extends across the cove. There is between 45 and 50 feet of water in the narrowest part of the entrance. Sound your way in, keeping midway between the cliffs, until the depth sounder reads 25-30 feet. Then choose your anchorage spot. It is probably best to lie in the middle of the cove, or nearer the west cliff in 15-20 feet, but beware of getting too close to the rocks where backwash can be uncomfortable. The bottom is generally sandy, but good scope should be laid. A second anchor is essential, even if no other boats are present. There is barely enough room to swing safely.

Fig. 7.5 — a. *Approach to Diablo Anchorage from Diablo Point (arrow shows entrance).*

*Little Lady's (Baby's)* has a more hazardous approach, for the narrow passage into the anchorage is often bumpy, with some breaking water and formidable surge (Fig. 7.4d). Also, there is little room to turn once inside. Boats over 35 feet should bear this in mind, especially if other vessels are already anchored in the cove. The entrance is midway through the rock-girt passage, where a least depth of 30-35 feet will be found, also some isolated rocks. The bottom is rocky and care must be taken to avoid a 20-foot patch immediately north of the passage, where thick kelp is sometimes found. When going through the passage, maintain sufficient speed to give you steerage way in the steep swells that can run into the entrance. Once through the passage, slow down in 25 feet and prepare to anchor off the beach in 15-20 feet (sand). The most sheltered place is on the SW side, under the cliff, but watch for swell and rocky patches. This small anchorage can only accommodate a few boats.

### Landing (both anchorages)

Those with permits can land on the sandy beaches in both coves. A small stream with refreshing bathing pools runs down to Little Lady's.

## WARNINGS

The two Lady's anchorages are small, and subject to surge even in quite moderate conditions. Do not try to anchor in Lady's if more than a few yachts are present. There is not enough room to avoid endangering others if conditions blow up, and you drag. The surge can roll in and cause considerable discomfort. In these circumstances, it is best to anchor elsewhere. Strong canyon winds can blow at night. Your second anchor should be laid carefully to guard against swinging.

## SPECIAL WARNING — LITTLE LADY'S (BABY'S)

Little Lady's is fully exposed to west winds and swell. It should be regarded as a calm weather anchorage only. You should clear out at once if it shows any sign of becoming a difficult lee shore. Do not sail in with a leading wind, as there is little room to turn. The entrance can be rough for dinghies, even if conditions both inside and outside are quiet.

*b. Entrance to Diablo anchorage on a windy day with some surge running into the cove. Best anchorage is under west wall of the bay.*

The coastline east from Lady's to Diablo Point is steep to with sheer cliffs. Most people head straight for Diablo Point, the most conspicuous headland on the north coast of Santa Cruz Island. Diablo Point slopes steeply into deep water, and lies immediately north of the highest point of the island. Give the point a berth of at least 0.25 mile, for irregular swells often form off Diablo from the effects of waves breaking against the steep cliffs, and offshore current.

Diablo anchorage lies immediately west of the point, Fry's Harbor 0.5 mile east. Two large islets lie off the west shore of Diablo anchorage, and are conspicuous when approaching from west.

## Diablo Anchorage (Fig. 7.5)

### General Description
A relatively large anchorage, a viable alternative to Fry's Harbor in quiet conditions. Although Diablo suffers from uncomfortable surge in moderate west to NW conditions, it is rarely congested.

### Approach
Approaching from Santa Barbara, set course for Diablo Point. When a mile offshore, the anchorage will open up immediately west of the point. The two off lying islets already mentioned will be seen west of the beach. Steer midway between them and the cliffs of Diablo Point.

The west approach from Lady's is straightforward. Steer for Diablo Point with the two rocky islets that form the west side of the anchorage close on the starboard bow. Once they are abeam, distant about 300 yards, the anchorage will open to starboard. Shape your course midway between the islets and Diablo cliffs and proceed to anchorage.

### Anchorage
Seventy feet of water will be found in the entrance to Diablo, 50 feet as the inshore islet is abeam. Proceed toward the beach and anchor in 20-25 feet (sand) nearer the west cliff. A good spot is close to a cave in the west cliff in 22 feet (sand) with sufficient room to avoid backwash from the rocks. Use a second anchor to minimize effects of surge. The beach shelves rapidly inshore of a cave in the west wall of the cove halfway between the beach and the west tip of the land. A loose gravel bottom will be found inshore of the cave.

Fig. 7.6 — *Fry's Harbor* — *a. Approach to Fry's from east showing Diablo Point (arrow shows entrance).*

*b. Fry's Harbor, from north, altitude 2000 feet.*

*c. Anchorage at Fry's. The best spots are well inshore in the central and western parts of the cove, near the small sailing vessel in the picture.*

## Fry's Harbor

### General Description

Fry's Harbor quarry provided the rock for Santa Barbara Harbor Breakwater in the 1920s. One of the most famous anchorages in the Santa Barbara Channel, Fry's is rarely empty. The cove provides adequate shelter in all but extreme conditions, but is subject to strong canyon winds. Surge is rarely a problem here. The anchorage is dangerous in strong NE winds.

### Approach (Fig. 7.6a, b)

The anchorage is easily found when approaching from east or west. Approaching from Diablo Point, the scar from the quarry operations of the 1920s can be seen on the east cliff of the anchorage, above the beach, once one is well east of Diablo. A platform of boulders extends seaward from the beach below this steep cliff, the remains of the landing area for the quarried stone. Until recently, a simple wooden derrick stood at the north end of the platform, but this has now collapsed and forms an underwater obstruction. The beach is tucked behind a shoulder of land, and will not appear until you are close to the entrance. When approaching from east aim to steer about 300 yards inshore of Diablo Point. When Fry's opens up — it lies at the east root of the point — alter course to port and steer for the beach.

Diablo Point lies under the highest point of land in the west half of Santa Cruz. When approaching from the mainland, lay off a course for Diablo, then identify the anchorage when a mile or so offshore and alter course accordingly. Like other popular anchorages, Fry's can often be identified offshore by the white hulls of yachts anchored in its shelter.

### Anchorage

When approaching the anchorage, look out for kelp lying off the cliffs of Diablo Point. Sudden, shifting gusts can blow off these cliffs, so use care when lowering sail in the entrance.

Enter Fry's by steering for a point midway between the two sides of the cove, sounding carefully. Once you have a depth of 50 feet, choose your anchoring spot off the beach according to draft. The best spots are tucked in under the west cliff (kelp and sand), as close to the beach as your boat can safely allow (Fig. 7.6c). A second anchor is usually laid, and should be well dug in. Strong canyon winds can spring up in the anchorage without warning. Fry's is a popular spot and several boats will be found here on most weekends. We have counted at least 20 yachts here on one occasion. Under these circumstances, go elsewhere. If you anchor in a more exposed position or deeper water than usual, be prepared to leave at once if conditions deteriorate.

A small cove lies immediately east of Fry's. Although we have seen yachts anchored here, it cannot be recommended as safe. Dinghy expeditions to this beach are fun, also to the cave 600 feet west of Fry's.

A second cove east of Fry's, although fairly deep, is a good, seldom-used alternative anchorage, known as The Grotto. Beware of fouling your anchor on rocks, however.

### Landing

By permit only, on the sandy beach, safe under normal conditions.

## Fry's Harbor to Prisoner's Harbor

The four miles between Fry's and Prisoner's Harbor is the best known portion of Santa Cruz Island. We describe the coast first, then the anchorages as a group. East of Fry's, you will pass some spectacular cliffs. Deep water anchorages under these cliffs are used by commercial diving and fishing boats. A mile east of Fry's, the coastline slopes more gradually, giving way to low lying cliffs capped by undulating ridges that can be spotted from a long distance by patches of grey soil which mantle the hillsides. This low lying coast is indented with tiny coves, most of which are unsuitable for overnight anchoring, except for Platt's, which lies a mile east of Fry's, and tiny Orizaba anchorage immediately east of a low island 0.6 mile further east. Do not approach the coast much nearer than 0.25 mile, for dense kelp beds flourish in depths of 30-50 feet close inshore.

The point at Twin Harbors is conspicuous from both east and west, and can be identified by the small arch in its outermost end. A low promontory extends seaward a few hundred yards west. The coves on either side of this point form Twin Harbor anchorage.

From Twin Harbors to Pelican Bay, the coast is somewhat steeper, for a ridge of hills runs down to the coastline. The shoreline is deeply indented in places, but there are no suitable overnight anchorages for small craft. Pelican Harbor opens up behind a low bluff with several conspicuous clumps of trees on its west side, while the far side of this popular anchorage is marked by a low promontory with a small, sandy beach on its east side. The high, rocky cliff at the back of Pelican Bay is conspicuous from some distance to seaward.

From Pelican Bay to Prisoner's, the coastline trends SE for just over a mile. Sloping cliffs fall steeply into the ocean. You can skirt the coast about 200 yards offshore. Prisoner's Harbor, with its conspicuous pier and small buildings, will open up on the starboard bow. In all probability, you will identify the deep fold in the hills that leads to the interior of the island long before the pier appears.

Fig. 7.7 — *Orizaba anchorage from NNW, altitude 2000 feet. The yacht is anchored in the best position. Give the island a wide berth.*

Fig. 7.8 — *Twin Harbors approach from east. Arrow indicates arch rock and entrance to east cove.*

## Anchorages Between Fry's and Pelican Bay

### Platt's Anchorage
(Dick's on older charts.)

#### General Description
A large, open roadstead with a small beach, otherwise steep cliffs and deep water. Much frequented by divers and commercial fishing boats. Exposed to prevailing wind and swell.

#### Approach
Platt's lies 1.0 mile east of Fry's. The anchorage is easily identified, for the land falls away sharply on the east side of the bay and the sandy beach is conspicuous. No more precise directions need be given, for the approach is completely safe under normal conditions.

#### Anchorage
The best anchorage is off the small beach in the SW portion of the roadstead (sand). Anchor according to draft and clear out if the wind comes up. Surge can be uncomfortable.

The SE corner of Platt's is heavily infested with rocks and kelp, and should be given a wide berth.

### Orizaba Cove (Fig. 7.7)

#### General Description
Orizaba Cove is a charming spot, but should be visited with care in anything but very calm conditions. It is sometimes used by diving and fishing boats. Excellent shelter from south and west in quiet weather.

#### Approach
When approaching Orizaba Cove from offshore, make a landfall on Diablo or Twin Harbors. If you intend to spend the night in Orizaba, you then have a chance to check on prevailing weather conditions before making the anchorage. In anything but settled conditions, anchor elsewhere.

Orizaba Cove lies immediately east of a conspicuous, low lying rock whose highest point lies inshore. The rock is stained with white bird droppings. Considerable kelp growth will be found around this outcrop. When approaching Orizaba Cove from east or west, steer to pass 200 yards offshore of the rock. Once opposite the east end of this landmark, you will be able to stop and spot the anchorage. The entrance lies between a low bluff covered with conspicuous grey soil to the east (there is a notice board on the point — NO TRES-PASSING), and a rocky cliff, the right hand side of which is capped with similar grey deposit. A small canyon overgrown with trees empties into the rocky cliff at the back of the anchorage. Once you have spotted these landmarks, steer slowly into the mouth of the cove, some 150 yards east of the offshore rock, sounding carefully.

#### Anchorage
The two sides of the tiny cove will close in on you as you steer inshore. Dense kelp lies off the east side of the anchorage, and can fill much of the cove as well. Enter the middle of the cove in 30 feet and anchor in deep water. A second anchor is essential, for the amount of sandy bottom is limited and swinging severely restricted. The best spot is slightly to the west of the center of the cove, but your anchorage should be governed by surge and kelp conditions. You will almost certainly have harbor seals as interested spectators. This is a spectacular spot in quiet weather.

The sandy beach inshore of the entrance rock to the west of Orizaba Cove offers no shelter from surge and west-NW winds, and is not recommended.

#### Landing
By permit only. Land on rocks and pull your dinghy clear of water's edge. An inflatable is recommended.

### Twin Harbors

#### General Description
Twin Harbors is a small anchorage which can be

idyllic in quiet conditions, except when an uncomfortable surge rolls in. There are two anchorages, the west one offering little shelter.

### Approach (Fig. 7.8)

This anchorage is best approached from east or west unless you are familiar enough with Santa Cruz Island to set course for its central rock spur from offshore. The east cove lies immediately on the east side of a small arch rock that can be spotted from more than a mile away from west.

Once this conspicuous landmark is in sight, aim to pass 100 yards offshore until the sandy beach of the east anchorage opens up to port or starboard. Then alter course inshore, giving a wide berth to a rocky ledge on the east shore of the arch rock. A small rock lies just offshore of the arch, which should also be avoided.

### East Anchorage

Enter the cove and steer for the middle of the beach. Sixty feet of water will be found in the entrance off the arch rock. Sound your way toward the beach and anchor in 20-25 feet (sand and some rocks) some 150 feet off the beach near the west cliff. A second anchor is essential, especially if you are in the company of other boats. The west side is most sheltered.

### West Anchorage

Twin Harbors west anchorage is somewhat larger and has limited shelter from swell or wind. The sandy beach will be seen west of the arch rock. Sound your way into the beach and anchor according to draft. We would not recommend this anchorage as anything more than a lunch stop. Island ironwood trees abound in the nearby canyon.

## Pelican Bay (Fig. 7.9-10)

### General Description

Pelican Bay is the most famous and popular of all Santa Cruz Island anchorages. Although the scenery is magnificent, Pelican Bay can be bumpy, the holding ground is patchy, and landing is tricky. Pelican has the advantage of generous size and is a favorite destination for Yacht Club or Power Squadron cruises from the mainland. Yacht races from Santa Barbara occasionally end in Pelican, or round a temporary mark off the entrance. Fifty years ago, Ira Eaton ran a hotel at Pelican Bay, the remains of which overlook the bay. He used to ferry his passengers across the Channel in his boat called *Sea Wolf*, until she blew ashore at Santa Barbara in a southeasterly in December 1927.

### Approach

One can locate Pelican far offshore by setting course for a conspicuous pointed hill with a step to the east, and a steep, conical profile to the west (Fig. 7.9). This landmark lies west of the lowermost point of Santa Cruz Island behind Prisoner's. Identify the hill and steer for it until you can identify the Pelican landmarks a mile or two offshore. White hulls of yachts are often more conspicuous than the anchorage landmarks, and you may spot your future neighbors first. The low bluff with two summits, and a patch of trees that form the west side of Pelican will be the first landmark identified from offshore. Steer to pass 100 yards east of this landmark, which will take you into the anchorage. A sandy cove close east of the anchorage can sometimes be spotted offshore.

This same bluff is the best landmark from east or west, when approaching along the island coast. The patch of trees referred to above will aid in identification of the bluff from west, as will a distinctive notch in its base. Conspicuous yellow rocks on the west cliff of Pelican are visible when arriving from the east. Approaching from either direction, steer for the bluff until both sides of the anchorage can be identified, or it opens up on port or starboard bow. There are no off lying dangers and you can safely alter course inshore at this point.

The east shore of Pelican ends in a low point marked by the tall spines of century plants on its summit. These

Fig. 7.9 — *Santa Cruz Island from north, an aerial shot showing the coastline from Potato to Pelican. Arrows indicate major anchorages, from east: Potato, Chinese, Prisoner, Pelican.*

Fig. 7.10 — *Pelican Bay, approach to anchorage from north, altitude 2000 feet.*

once formed part of the landscaping of the resort hotel that flourished at Pelican 50 years ago. A NO TRES-PASSING sign also marks this promontory.

### Anchorage

More than 50 feet of water fill the entrance. Most vessels drop anchor in 25-35 feet of water farther inshore. The favorite anchorage is in the shelter of the west cliff, sufficiently distant to avoid back-surge from the rocks (Fig. 7.10). Later arrivals often anchor in the middle of the bay close inshore. The bottom is littered with patches of kelp, which can cause a badly set anchor to drag if the wind comes up. It is said the best holding ground is in the center of the anchorage, but opinions differ. Make sure your anchors are well dug in, in case they slip on a patch of kelp. An irritating east chop can fill in during the night, the result of gentle mainland land breezes. A single anchor enables you to swing to the chop.

### Landing

By permit only. Landing can be effected at a set of ruined steps that once led to the hotel on the cliff at the SE corner of the anchorage. Beware of surge and slippery rocks. Lift your dinghy out of reach of waves and rising tides, leaving enough room for others to do the same. In calm weather, you can also land on the sandy beach in the cove (Tinker's Harbor) immediately east of Pelican itself. The canyon behind the anchorage flows into this bay which is not, however, a suitable overnight anchorage as it is unsheltered. Even on quiet days, a steep chop can break on this steeply shelving beach, and you may receive a wetting. There are fascinating walks through nearby canyons and the coast is worth exploring by dinghy.

---

---

## Prisoner's Harbor (Fig. 7.9, 7.11)

### General Description

This is one of our favorites, because of its attractive surroundings and also because it is rarely congested. Prisoner's is the main landing for the Santa Cruz Island Company. A Navy boat brings supplies to Prisoner's each week. The buildings, pier and tall eucalyptus trees give this spot a unique feeling, for the rocky coves elsewhere on Santa Cruz Island seem to be in a different world. Prisoner's is, however, less sheltered than some other anchorages, especially from the east.

### Approach

From the mainland, Prisoner's lies below the lowest point of land on Santa Cruz' north coast, where a fold of land gives access, through a large canyon, to the central valley (Fig. 7.9). When approaching from the NE or NW, simply steer for this low point until pier and buildings can be identified. From that point, head for the pier.

From east or west, the approach is just as straightforward. Once around Cavern Point, west of Scorpion Anchorage, skirt the coast to Coche Point. By this time you should be able to see the pier. The pier and buildings behind Prisoner's bear 240 degrees M from Coche Point. When skirting the coastline from the west, keep 200 yards offshore from Pelican until the coast recedes SE more sharply, and the cliffs fall sharply into the ocean. The pier will then open up on the starboard bow as you follow the coastline SE. Head for the pier, leaving the cliffs at least 200 yards to starboard. The barns inshore of the pier are conspicuous from a considerable distance. A small lookout building will be seen on the hillside behind the landing.

### Anchorage

Steer for the pierhead until you are in 50 feet, then shape your course for your chosen anchoring spot (Fig. 7.11). There is 12 feet along an imaginary line extending west of the pierhead (sand). Depths between 15 and 35 feet will be found north of this line, in sand, mud and silt. Do not anchor inshore of the pierhead, for the bottom shelves rapidly. Choose your position according to surge and wind conditions, and make sure you lay plenty of scope, as the holding ground can be a little weak. Your anchor may slip on the hard sand or eel grass. The most sheltered berths are close under the west cliffs. Securing alongside the pier is forbidden. Anchoring east of the pier is possible, but more exposed.

### Landing

By permit only, and then only in areas which are not posted as "closed to permit holders." Land on beach, and be prepared to get your feet wet.

---

---

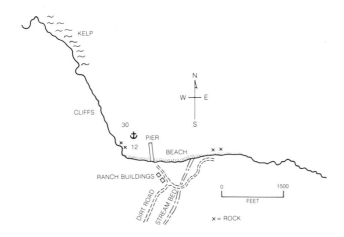

Fig. 7.11 — *Prisoner's Harbor* — *a. Plan of Prisoner's adapted from NOAA Chart 18729.*

*b. Prisoner's Harbor from north, altitude 2000 feet. Best anchorage is west of pier.*

## Prisoner's Harbor to San Pedro Point (Figs. 7.9, 7.12)

The west side of Prisoner's consists of a steeply sloping hillside, with red-brown rocky cliffs, shelving steeply into the anchorage. East of the canyon that gives access to the interior at Prisoner's, the coast again rises steeply. The shoreline is indented, but sloping cliffs prevent easy access onshore. It is possible to anchor off the isolated beaches between Prisoner's and Chinese Harbor in moderate westerly weather. Do not anchor too close to the gradually shelving beach because of swells. At Chinese, the steep coast turns NE and trends east toward Cavern Point. High, rocky cliffs fall sheer into the water, and it is possible for divers and fishermen to work close inshore. The only landing between Chinese and Scorpion is at Potato anchorage, described below. Seen from a distance, and from the west, the cliffs dip steeply two miles SW of Cavern Point, and just north of Potato, giving way to the lower topography of the east part of Santa Cruz. But the coastline itself remains steep and inhospitable for landing. Cavern Point is steep-to, and leads to a high, sheer, red-brown cliff that marks the western extremity of Scorpion anchorage. A fold of hills behind Scorpion gives way to the steep cliffs and rocky outcrops that back Little Scorpion, while a conspicuous beach extends along the back of Scorpion anchorage. After Little Scorpion, the coastline is markedly lower and cliffs bound gently sloping, grassy slopes that lead inland to higher ground. San Pedro Point forms the easternmost extremity of Santa Cruz Island.

The stretch of coast from Little Scorpion to San Pedro Point is steep-to, but should not be approached closer than 200 yards. Patches of kelp can occur off the point and close inshore, while interesting blow-holes and fine spring flowers are features of this stretch of coast. Seals are still commonplace off the many rocks near the water's edge. When approaching San Pedro Point, beware of sudden wind increases as you round the point and enter the windy Anacapa Passage that

**103**

Fig. 7.12 — *Santa Cruz Island from NE, showing coastline from Middle Anchorage to Cavern Point. Arrows indicate major anchorages. From left to right: Smugglers, Little Scorpion, Scorpion.*

separates Santa Cruz Island from Anacapa Island. In the 1858 Sailing Directions, we learn that "a site for a lighthouse at the eastern end of the island has been reported upon and recommended by the Superintendent of the Coast Survey to the Lighthouse Board." It was never built.

## Chinese Harbor (Fig. 7.9)

### General Description

Chinese Harbor is little more than a large, open roadstead, used by passing ships in the nineteenth century. Oil boats sometimes use it today. Few yachts or fishing boats spend the night off this open and exposed beach in an anchorage which is bumpy in almost any conditions. A fumarole, the only one on the offshore islands, can be seen smoking in the NE cliff of the anchorage several hundred feet above the beach. Chinese Harbor offers moderate shelter in NE winds.

### Approach

The approach is straightforward. From west, identify Prisoner's Harbor pier, and follow the coastline to the white-brown cliffs that slope to Chinese Harbor three miles SW of Cavern Point, which can be identified from a long distance even on misty days. The best anchorage lies in the NE corner of Chinese. You should steer for the NE end of the beach to reach this spot. Approaching from Potato or Scorpion, keep 200 yards offshore until the shoreline indents at Coche Point toward the beach that forms Chinese anchorage. The fumarole will normally be identified when 0.5 mile from the anchorage. Aim to have the fumarole on the starboard bow as you approach the beach.

### Anchorage

Anchor according to draft, sounding your way to the beach, and avoiding patches of kelp. The best anchorage appears to be in a position where the fumarole cliff bears about SE, in 25-30 feet (sand), but you should use your judgment in choosing the best spot. A second anchor is unnecessary except to control boat motion.

### Landing

On the beach, with permit. Take careful note of swell conditions before attempting a landing.

Fig. 7.13 — *Potato Harbor from west altitude 2000 feet. Enter midway between the rocky point and the island. Arrow shows entrance.*

---

*WARNING*
Chinese Harbor is a lee shore in the prevailing west winds, and offers no shelter under such conditions. It is also said to be windy and uncomfortable in SE weather.

---

## Potato Harbor (Figs. 7.9, 7.13)
(Potato Harbor was once known as Tyler's.)

**General Description**
A picturesque anchorage in a narrow bay in the steep cliffs east of Prisoner's Harbor which is, however, exposed to the prevailing westerlies. Potato offers shelter from NE and SE winds, which can, however, blow down from the cliffs in strong gusts, and complete protection from swells out of these directions. Be prepared to move out quickly if the wind shifts to NW, however.

**Approach**
From west, locate a patch of white cliffs west of Cavern Point. Potato lies just east of these white slopes. The narrow entrance can be identified as you close with the land, a prominent rock lying off the south side of the indentation.

Approaching from east, around Cavern Point and pick up the north side of Potato entrance, the second prominent headland beyond Cavern. A patch of white cliff will be seen halfway up the slope immediately behind this low, sloping headland. Pass 0.5 mile offshore until the entrance opens up to port.

Enter Potato by steering midway between the entrance headland and steering for the beach, sounding carefully.

**Anchorage**
Sound your way toward the beach, keeping slightly to north of the center of the bay. Anchor off the beach in 25-90 feet (sand), avoiding rocks and kelp in the NE corner of the anchorage and the shallower water on the south side. The anchorage is sometimes covered with tar and oil.

---

*WARNING*
Potato is a lee shore in prevailing westerly winds and swells. You should clear out at the first sign of stronger winds. The anchorage cannot be recommended for an overnight stay except in settled weather.

---

## Scorpion and Little Scorpion Anchorages (Fig. 7.14)
(Known as East End Anchorage on 1882 chart.)

**General Description**
Two well-known anchorages, known as Scorpion

Fig. 7.14 — *a. Scorpion and Little Scorpion from NE, distant 1.5 miles. The arrows identify the anchorages, Little Scorpion on left.*

*b. Little Scorpion from west, with rock at east end of Scorpion on the starboard bow.*

*c. Little Scorpion from the entrance, showing kelp beds and best anchoring spot SE of detached rocks.*

and Little Scorpion, lie east of Cavern Point and are especially popular with vessels from Ventura or Channel Islands. Little Scorpion is the more popular of the two, for it offers more shelter than its west neighbor. Also, the holding ground in Scorpion is sometimes unsatisfactory. Scorpion is the main landing for the Gherini Ranch on the island. A pier extends seaward at the NW side of the anchorage.

## Approach

Approaching from Santa Barbara, both anchorages are readily identified at a distance by finding low lying San Pedro Point and the distinctive hump of the hill behind Cavern Point (Fig. 7.14a). You should then be able to identify a saddle of land between the easternmost peak of high ground and the summit of the foothill ridge to the east. Scorpion lies in front of a conspicuous cleft in the cliff below the saddle. Steer for this cleft until pier and rocks west of Little Scorpion can be identified.

Approaching from east, identify Cavern Point, and two detached rocks lying inshore and to the east that shelter Little Scorpion (Fig. 7.14b). Steer to pass 200 yards offshore of these rocks, a course that will bring you into Scorpion. From the west, simply follow the coast east from Cavern Point until the rocks of Little Scorpion are identified ahead and the anchorage opens up ahead.

## Scorpion Anchorage

Enter the anchorage by steering for the pier, giving offshore rocks at the east end of the bight a wide berth (Fig. 7.14b). Avoiding the kelp to the west and off the bay, sound your way to anchorage south or east of the pier in 35-40 feet (mud, sand and kelp). Anchor between the pier and a pyramid-shaped rock to the east, for the best kelp-free berth. Anchorage can be obtained west of the pier, but beware of extensive kelp beds under the steep cliffs. Lay plenty of scope and a second anchor. Clear out if the wind fills in strongly from NW or NE, or if the smell of bird droppings becomes unbearable.

---

### WARNING
Anchorage in Scorpion can be insecure owing to kelp on the bottom. Make sure your anchor is well dug in.

---

## Landing

By permit only, on the beach or at the pier. The whole coast, especially the cliffs and caves, are worth exploring by dinghy in the calm early morning.

## Little Scorpion Anchorage (Figs. 7.14b, c)

Give the two white-stained rocks west of Little Scorpion a berth of at least 100 yards to avoid kelp beds, and enter the anchorage midway between steep cliffs to the east and these outcrops. There is 60 feet in the entrance. A sandy bottom gives excellent shelter in 22-45 feet in the lee of the two rocks. Anchor as close to the rocks as you can, consistent with your draft. A second anchor is essential, both to minimize surge and to prevent you swinging into the kelp south of the clear water and immediately west of the rocks. Little Scorpion is often congested, and is suicidal in strong NE winds. Afternoon winds can gust strongly in summer.

## Landing

Landing is not recommended, but you can explore the cliffs, caves, rocks, and kelp beds from a dinghy.

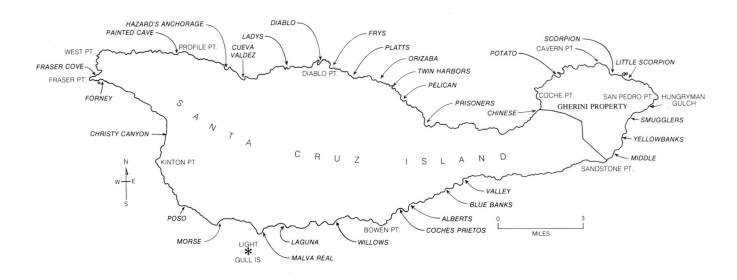

Fig. 7.1 — *Santa Cruz Island, with major features and anchorages mentioned in the text.*

# CHAPTER **8**

# *Santa Cruz-South Coast,*

Many people visiting Santa Cruz Island for the first time cross from Channel Islands, stopping at Anacapa Island on the way. This route provides convenient access to the attractive anchorages on the south coast of Santa Cruz Island, easier access than is possible by approaching them through the bumpy Santa Cruz channel. Here, we describe the coasts of Santa Cruz Island from San Pedro Point along the east, south and west shores, as far as West Point (Fig. 7.1).

Approaching from Channel Islands or Anacapa, Santa Cruz Island appears as a steep mountain chain, tailing off to the low lying NE corner. When crossing to Santa Cruz Island from these directions, expect a strengthening of the afternoon breeze in the Anacapa Passage. Much stronger NW winds funnel through this passage on many days, so much so that you may have to reduce sail. Beware of the effects of current against wind in the passage, which can result in short, steep seas. Smaller craft, especially outboard fishing boats, are best advised to make this crossing in the calmer hours of morning, although it can blow in Anacapa Passage at any time.

---

### *WARNING*
All south coast anchorages are subject to heavy surge from tropical storms off the Mexican Coast which can come in without warning, especially in summer.

---

San Pedro Point is low, but steep-to, with some outlying kelp and rocks (Figs. 7.12, 8.1). Give the east end of Santa Cruz Island a berth of 0.5 mile. East of San Pedro Point, the steep, red-brown cliffs are indented with small, rocky caves, the most prominent of which lies 0.5 mile SW of the point. Hungryman Gulch terminates in this cove, which can provide some shelter in 15 feet (sand and rock). But beware of rocks and kelp lying off the beach in the middle of the bay. Late nineteenth century charts describe this as a "small boat landing," but few vessels use it today. The shore trends SW into Smuggler's Cove, the major anchorage at the east end of the island, 1.25 miles SW of San Pedro Point.

Fig. 8.1 — *Smuggler's Cove from SE on a calm day. The best anchorage lies NE of the olive groves seen on the hillside behind the anchorage.*

## Smuggler's Cove

### General Description

A large, open roadstead which provides shelter for large numbers of small craft in calm weather, Smuggler's has the advantage of being easy to find, but suffers from frequent heavy surge and strong offshore (NW) winds at times. We have spent the night in Smuggler's riding to a 35 pound Hitensile Danforth, 90 feet of chain, and 90 feet of heavy-duty dacron hawser in an offshore wind of at least 45 knots, gusting even higher (far stronger gear than most people normally carry). Without adequate ground tackle, this anchorage can be uncomfortable and hazardous. But Smuggler's is an attractive place with groves of olives and fine eucalyptus trees overlooking the cove.

### Approach (Fig. 8.1)

Approaching from Anacapa or Channel Islands, the yellow-brown cliffs of the SE shore of Santa Cruz Island can be seen from a long distance on a clear day. Identify the northernmost of these light-colored bluffs which lie immediately SW of Smuggler's, also low lying San Pedro Point. Steer for the point on the coast where yellow cliffs merge with the lower shoreline. Smuggler's will open up on your starboard bow as you approach the land.

When looking for the anchorage on passage along the island, from the south coast follow the yellow cliffs into the open bay, keeping sufficient distance offshore to avoid the extensive kelp beds off the coastline. As the roadstead opens up to port, you'll see the serried rows of olive trees on the NW slope of the bay. Once Smuggler's is identified, shape your course for the middle of the cove until near the head of the anchorage. Smuggler's can be found from the north by following the coastline from San Pedro around into the bay.

### Anchorage

Anchorage can be obtained almost anywhere in Smuggler's on a sandy bottom in 25-40 feet. The best shelter lies under the cliffs on the NW side of the cove. Make sure you anchor sufficiently far enough offshore to minimize effects of ground swell. Beware of shallowing at the head of the anchorage. Insure, too, that you anchor clear of other people, in case they drag when a downslope wind blows. Lay plenty of scope.

---

### WARNING
At the first sign of a swell from NE on calm, dry, clear days, or of smog offshore warning of an impending Santa Ana, clear out of this anchorage AT ONCE. Also leave if a SE swell and dark clouds indicate an approaching southeaster.

---

## Yellowbanks Anchorage (Fig. 7.12)

### General Description

Another open roadstead that provides an attractive

alternative to Smuggler's in both calm and heavy NW weather. Yellowbanks is usually less congested than its neighbor, but provides much greater protection from NW winds, although slightly more exposed to prevailing swells, which wrap around the island from north or NW, or from Mexican tropical storms to the south.

### Approach

As for Smuggler's, but the anchorage lies under the yellow-brown cliffs to the SW of the former. As you approach the NE extremity of the yellow bluffs (see above), identify the steep, high cliff that marks the SW side of the Yellowbanks and the steep, V-shaped canyon that runs into the head of the anchorage. Yellowbanks is separated from Smuggler's by a low lying cliff and point. A shallow reef and some kelp lies off this spot, which should be given 0.5 mile clearance. Watch for kelp in the entrance as you steer for the canyon mouth. Beware of an isolated rock in 18 feet that uncovers at low tide off the south side of the bay.

### Anchorage

Off the beach in 20-35 feet (sand, rocks and pebbles). Do not anchor too close in, to avoid disturbance from ground swell. A second anchor is advisable. You should clear out at the first sign of a NE or SE wind. Watch for rapid shallowing near the beach. The amount of sheltered water for anchorage is relatively small.

SW of Yellowbanks, the island turns west at a conspicuous yellow-brown cliff, formed by a ridge that runs down to the shore from the center of the island. Sandstone Point is visible from a long distance offshore. Extensive kelp beds extend out to sea from Sandstone Point for at least a mile. You are best advised to keep outside them, unless you plan to anchor off the beach at Middle Anchorage or west of the point.

## Middle Anchorage (Fig. 7.12)

### General Description

Little more than a slight indentation in the cliffs, Middle Anchorage is only a calm weather, temporary landing. Even in quiet conditions, a slight swell runs into the beach.

### Approach

Identify Sandstone Point and steer through the kelp, leaving the point 0.75 mile to port. The anchorage lies inside the kelp off the beach. Watch for isolated rocks near the shore on either side of the anchorage.

### Anchorage

Off the beach in 15-35 feet (sand), according to draft. *Do not overnight in this exposed anchorage.*

Fig. 8.2 — *Sandstone Point and SE coast of Santa Cruz Island. Arrows, left: Albert's, right, Valley.*

## Sandstone Point Anchorage

You can also anchor 0.5 mile west of Sandstone Point inside the kelp in 30 feet (rock and sand), in an open bay that offers shelter from NW winds. Again, we don't recommend this as an overnight stop.

The easternmost stretches of the south coast of the island consist of attractive yellow-brown cliffs that fall steeply into the ocean (Fig. 8.2). Fine sandy beaches lie at the foot of the cliffs, but dense kelp can mantle the coastline. Steep canyons run down through the cliffs from the central spur of the island. A conspicuous radar tracking station lies high above the coast and can be seen from a long distance, being brightly lit at night. It is not marked on the chart. Keep outside the kelp until you approach a conspicuous yellow bluff, 800 feet high, which lies 1.5 miles east of Valley Anchorage. A rock (10 feet) lies offshore below the bluff, the most conspicuous feature of the foul rock and kelp area off the coast in this location. This foul ground extends west of the bluff. Do not approach the coast too closely until you are within 0.75 mile of Valley Anchorage.

Fig. 8.3 — *Valley anchorage from south, distant 1.25 miles. Arrows indicate mooring buoy and research station buildings.*

## Valley Anchorage (Fig. 8.3)

### General Description

An open bay now used by General Motors which maintains a field station above the anchorage. Valley is, however, an exposed, calm weather berth, uncomfortable in a surge or strong winds. Low-flying aircraft sometimes come in overhead, for the island air strip lies upslope of the anchorage.

### Approach

Valley Anchorage is easy to identify, as the only buildings on the entire south coast of the island are situated on cliffs overlooking the bight. Trailers and white houses which can be seen from some distance when approaching from the east, are partially obscured by a ridge from the west. A large mooring buoy, with flashing white light (2½ sec.) and radar reflector lies off the houses. A white mooring buoy is located 150 yards SE. Cliffs immediately east of the houses are white colored and conspicuous. Once the landmarks are identified, steer for the buoy. If approaching the anchorage parallel to the coastline, do not steer between the buoy and the west side of the anchorage without local knowledge. A reef and dense kelp beds extend SE from the shore toward the buoy. Once near the buoy, sound your way inshore toward the anchorage.

### Anchorage

Anchor in 35-40 feet (sand) off the beach or secure to the mooring buoy with anchor laid astern to prevent banging against the metal. The buoy can be used if the research vessel is elsewhere — but be prepared to move if she arrives. Avoid anchoring too close inshore; keep clear of the NE area of the anchorage which is kelp and rock infested. A flopper stopper is useful to reduce movement from the constant surge into the anchorage.

### Landing

By permit only, on the beach.

The deep indentation which runs inshore from Valley Anchorage forms the central valley of Santa Cruz Island. Cliffs west of Valley are precipitous and fall sheer into the Pacific. Blue Banks Anchorage is the next indentation in this steep coast, 0.5 mile west of Valley Anchorage. The shoreline is very steep all around the anchorage, with bands of brown, yellow, red-brown that can be identified at some distance.

## Blue Banks Anchorage

### General Description

A shallow indentation in the coast that provides some shelter from west and NW winds. Blue Banks has a constant surge problem, and is at its best in calm summer weather.

### Approach

No conspicuous landmarks mark the Blue Banks

approach. You can find it by looking for the indentation in the land 1.5 miles east of Albert's Anchorage (see below) and 0.5 mile west of Valley. The banded brown-yellow coloring of the cliffs sometimes stands out near the shore, appears blue sometimes, whence the name "Blue Banks." Once the anchorage is identified, plan to enter the cove midway between the two extremities of the indentation.

### Anchorage

Anchor in 25-30 feet, 35 yards or more off the beach, in the center of the cove, or just SW of a conspicuous green rock outcrop. Blue Banks is uncomfortable in any surge and should be avoided in strong winds, even if it provides some shelter from west and NW winds.

Precipitous cliffs continue to trend SW toward the prominent sloping promontory that forms the western side of Albert's Anchorage. This conspicuous and unnamed headland has a characteristic sloping profile readily identifiable from a considerable distance. As you approach, the tilted geological strata stand out on the cliffs. A small, and recent, rock fall can be seen on the east side of the cliff by Albert's. High cliffs between Blue Banks and Albert's end at the beach behind the anchorage, where the headland, a steep slope from the spur of the island, and the cliffs meet.

Fig. 8.4 — *Coches Prietos and Albert's anchorages from south, distant 1-5 miles. Albert's is in shadow as this shot was taken in the late afternoon. Left arrow is Coches Prietos.*

## Albert's Anchorage (Figs. 8.4, 8.5)

### General Description

History does not reveal who Albert was. But his anchorage is a comfortable berth in settled weather with good shelter from west through north. The steep cliff to the west puts the cove in shadow in the late afternoon. A small beach lies at the head of the anchorage. Albert's can be bumpy with surge and is completely exposed to SE. You have a fine view of the SE coast of the island and distant Anacapa from this cove, but Albert's is dark in late afternoon and you may feel closed in.

### Approach

From east, identify the conspicuous, sloping headland, and shape your course to pass 200 yards inshore of the tip of the promontory. The anchorage with its small beach will open up to starboard, immediately inshore of the headland. Once identified, steer into the cove and choose an anchorage spot.

### Anchorage (Fig. 8.5)

Smaller vessels normally anchor 35-40 yards off the beach in 25-35 feet (sand). Good shelter can be found under the steep cliffs in 40 feet off a recently collapsed slab of rock. Look out, however, for underwater rocks and kelp. When the anchorage is congested, anchor in deeper water with plenty of scope. A second anchor can be used to minimize surge effects.

### Landing

On the beach, by permit. Limited access inshore.

When bound west past the headland, give the end a berth of at least 300 yards to avoid isolated rocks and kelp. Once around the headland, Coches Prietos anchorage will open up on your starboard bow.

## Coches Prietos (Figs. 8.4,)

### General Description

A charming cove (Coches Prietos means "Black Pigs"), probably the best anchorage on the south side of

Fig. 8.5 — *Albert's anchorage, showing conspicuous canyon behind the beach. The best anchorage lies between the powerboat and the cliff.*

Santa Cruz Island. Coches Prietos has a fine sandy beach, good shelter from west to north winds, and offers some protection in NE blows. Albert's is best in strong NW winds, however. This beautiful spot is normally crowded with visitors, especially in the summer.

### Approach

The cove is formed by a beautiful, semi-circular, sandy beach at the foot of a valley extending inland. Anchor in 10-25 feet (sand) off the beach. Tuck in behind the kelp and the west cliff as much as possible. Do not anchor too near the beach; a second anchor is normal. Coches Prietos is normally relatively smooth and a comfortable berth if you lay adequate scope. If the anchorage is congested, you may need to anchor near the east cliffs or off the entrance in deeper water. Strong winds can blow down the canyons (see Willow's Warning, below).

### Landing

By permit, on the beach.

Very steep, grey cliffs seem to descend from the heavens into the ocean between Coches Prietos and Willow's Anchorage 2.75 miles west. A mile west of Coches, Bowen Point drops steeply into the Pacific. A small, white rock lies off the end of the point. Dense

kelp beds may be found off Bowen. This brown-grey point has sloping geological strata. The shoreline between Coches Prietos and Bowen is much fouled by rocks and kelp and should be given a berth of 0.5 mile. At night, the flashing light on Gull Island should be spotted as you round Bowen Point.

Steep, grey cliffs continue 1.75 miles west to Willow's Anchorage, which lies just east of a 669-foot peak near the shore.

## Willow's Anchorage
(Alamos Anchorage on 1882 chart.)

### General Description

A popular anchorage, protected from west to north, Willow's is a pretty spot. Surge conditions can be dangerous if even moderate wind comes in from SW. You should avoid anchoring here when high swell is running offshore.

### Approach (Fig. 8.6a)

From east, identify the 669-foot peak with its precipitous cliffs and look for two conspicuous, detached rocks, each 87 feet high that lie about 100 and 200 yards from the shore. The offshore rock is stained white, the inshore pinnacle colored brown-black. These landmarks will guide you to the anchorage, which should not be approached until the outer pinnacle rock is on the starboard quarter. Give this off lying danger a berth of at least 0.3 mile. Dense kelp and hidden rocks lie offshore. Then steer for the beach midway between the cliff and the two rocks.

From west, follow the coastline from Gull Island east until you spot the two pinnacle rocks and Bowen Point 1.75 miles east. A course shaped to approach the land 1.0 miles west of Bowen will open up the landmarks on a safe bearing.

### Anchorage (Fig. 8.6b)

The most popular anchorage lies in the middle of the cove off the beach in 20-35 feet (sand). Larger vessels anchor under the west cliff in 35-50 feet. Lay plenty of scope and a second anchor to minimize surge movement and to leave space for others. The surge in Willow's can build up rapidly, so be prepared to move on if the anchorage becomes intolerable.

You can also anchor in calm weather east of the pinnacle rocks in 35 feet (sand) clear of the kelp, or closer to shore. Look out, however, for the off lying and awash rocks close inshore SE of the beach. This berth is sometimes quieter than Willow's itself, but neither the cove nor this spot can be recommended in bad weather.

Fig. 8.6 — *Willows Anchorage from SW, distant 1.75 miles. Arrow indicates entrance and detached rocks.*

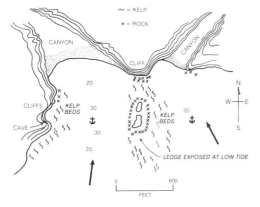

*Plan of Willows Anchorage. Adapted from U.S. Government chart 18728.*

**Landing**
By permit only, on the beach.

Between Willow's and Laguna Harbor two miles west, the steep cliffs are relieved by two conspicuous, sandy beaches with 30 feet close inshore. Neither are realistic overnight anchorages, however. Kelp beds lie inshore along this stretch of coast. Laguna Harbor is immediately west of an unmistakable precipitous, sloping point 571 feet high.

## Laguna Harbor

Chart 18728 calls this a harbor, although it is hard to understand why. Laguna consists of a long, sandy beach below a conspicuous canyon. A steep yellow-brown cliff and a high rock lie just west of the beach, and can be identified at a considerable distance. Anchor off the beach in 35-40 feet (sand) and be prepared for a bumpy stay. Not recommended as an overnight berth.

Fig. 8.7 — *Gull Island from ESE, distant 0.75 mile, showing light tower. A good impression of the coastal landscape of the SW shores of the island.*

As you pass Bowen Point, Gull Island and its light will appear about a mile offshore of low lying Punta Arena (Fig. 8.7). You now have the choice of passing offshore or inshore of the island. On a first visit, we recommend that you pass offshore, giving the lighted rock a berth of 0.5 mile.

Gull Island is 65 feet high and 0.2 mile across, a popular sunning place for sea lions, and many sea birds whose droppings have stained the rocks white. A light (Fl. W. 4 sec. 73 feet, 6 miles) is exhibited from a white pyramidical structure on the summit of the island. Dense kelp beds and both exposed and subsurface rocks surround Gull Island. When bound past the island offshore, you can safely pass 0.5 mile outside the kelp.

Inshore passage requires caution, a good depth sounder, and calm weather, for it is much overgrown with kelp and foul ground (Fig. 8.8). When bound between Gull Island and Santa Cruz Island, identify:

— low lying Punta Arena, which looks like a low ridge extending seaward with a conspicuous, pointed peak sloping steeply upward inshore of the headland,

— Gull Island and its kelp beds,

— as you approach the narrowest point of the passage, watch for the distribution of kelp lying SE of Punta Arena, and north from Gull Island. Keep a close eye for breaking water and rocks awash near Punta Arena.

Once these features are clear, steer carefully between Gull Island and the main island, sounding often. The clear passage lies about one-third of the way between Gull and Santa Cruz Islands, closer to Gull in about 35 feet or slightly less. You should steer for Gull Island itself until kelp beds and smooth water are seen, then shape your course through the passage. *Do not attempt this passage at night, in fog, or in rough weather.* A guide with local knowledge is advisable first time.

There is no good reason to pass inshore of Gull Island unless you are fishing or skin diving. The kelp-protected coast of Santa Cruz Island between Laguna Harbor and Punta Arena is steep and barren with little of interest for small craft. Malva Real anchorage lies in the lee of Punta Arena, however, tucked behind the kelp and rocks off the headland.

## Malva Real Anchorage (Fig. 8.8)

### General Description

A temporary anchorage often uncomfortable with surge in the lee of a desolate and rocky promontory which offers shelter from west to NW winds, especially if you take advantage of the flattening effects of kelp on swell.

### Approach

Once Punta Arena is identified, from east pass inside of the kelp beds, sounding carefully, steering to bring your vessel inshore 250 yards north of the point. From west, you will have to pass inshore of Gull Island, giving the rocks and kelp off Punta Arena a wide berth before heading through the kelp to the anchorage.

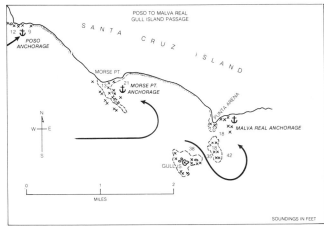

Fig. 8.8 — *Poso anchorage to Malva Real, including Gull Island passage. (Adapted from U.S. Government chart 18307.)*

### Anchorage

Off the pebble beach in 30-35 feet (rock and sand). Anchor inside the kelp if possible, and be prepared to leave quickly if swell or wind conditions deteriorate. This is a fair weather anchorage, but often used by fishing boats.

West of Punta Arena, the immediate shoreline is lower-lying than further east, terminating in low, brown, sandy cliffs, creased by innumerable water gullies. Punta Arena itself is capped with yellow dunes and grey soil. Unless you want to anchor in the lee of Morse Point, keep at least 1.0 mile offshore until this headland is well astern to avoid a zone of kelp and rocks extending SE of the point for 0.75 mile. The bight to the east is called Johnson's Lee, not to be confused with the anchorage of that name on Santa Rosa Island. These off lying dangers break heavily in any swell and are suicidal in a gale. Morse Point has a conspicuous yellow cliff on its east side.

## Morse Point Anchorage (Fig. 8.8)

You can anchor in the lee of Morse Point, a steep-ended promontory with a high rocky ridge inshore of the coast. Anchor in 25 feet (sand), well off the beach between the inner and outer kelp beds to avoid rocks in shallow water. Approach the anchorage from east, skirting the off lying ledge SE of the point. Only recommended as a temporary anchorage in fine weather.

Morse Point runs down to the coast to end in 150 foot yellow-brown cliffs. Viewed from west, the headland has a distinct, stepped profile which is easily identified at some distance. The coast now trends NW into the Santa Cruz Passage, the grey-brown hills of the SW corners of the island sloping down to the shore and ending in low, steep cliffs that front the ocean. A dense kelp bed lies off this coast which should be given a berth of at least 0.75 mile. The shallow bight between Morse and Poso Point and anchorage 1.4 miles NW is exposed to the full onslaught of the SW swell. Larger breakers make the beach unapproachable in any surge.

## Poso Anchorage (Fig. 8.8)

(NOAA Chart spelling is Posa.)

A temporary anchorage in the lee of a steep promontory with a rock at its extremity, conspicuous from NW.

Anchor off the beach in 30-35 feet (sand), giving the end of the point a wide berth, also the kelp. This anchorage is dangerous in any swell, as waves break for a considerable distance off the point.

Kinton Point is the next landmark, a precipitous and conspicuous headland with rocks at its foot. The promontory offers no protection from the prevailing winds, and forms one side of the large bay that marks the west end of Santa Cruz Island. This huge bight curves around to end in Forney's Cove and Fraser Point. The central valley of the island ends in the Christy Valley, the low lying head of the bay. The coastline is steep around Kinton Point and slopes downward to the floor of the canyons that empty into the shore. Low cliffs trend around the bay toward Fraser Point. As you sail NW through Santa Cruz Passage, you will see a mountain chain that forms the north spur of the island on the starboard bow, an impressive background to Forney's Cove at the NW corner of Santa Cruz Island. Black Point is the only conspicuous headland in the bight, about midway between Kinton and Fraser Points.

Most people sail directly across toward Forney's or West Point, for there is little to attract the visitor in this large bight.

## Christy Valley Anchorage

You can anchor off the mouth of the valley in 18-35 feet (hard sand). The best anchorage lies a little north of the valley mouth, close inshore south of the wash rocks, where there is more protection. The anchorage can be identified from a long distance as some white ranch buildings lie behind the beach. A course for these buildings will bring you to the anchorage. Keep at least 0.5 mile off either shore of the bay to avoid kelp and outlying rocks. Christy Valley is a bumpy anchorage and cannot be recommended for a long stay except as a refuge from strong NE winds when the land north of the canyon offers some protection.

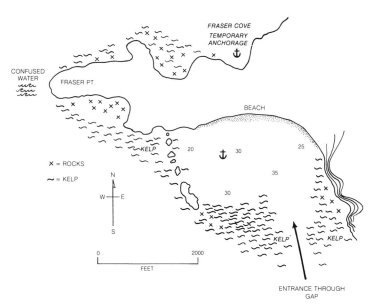

Fig. 8.9 — *Plan of Forney's Cove. (Adapted from U.S. Government chart 18307.)*

## Forney's Cove (Fig. 8.9)

### General Description

Forney's is one of the more popular anchorages on Santa Cruz Island, offering a desolate and fascinating berth amidst spectacular scenery. Skin diving and fishing are excellent nearby. Forney's gives some protection from west and NW, but cannot be recommended if a heavy swell is running. *If a strong offshore wind blows up after sundown, and you are lying at the west end of Forney's, leave the anchorage at once. You are on a lee shore.* We once got caught here in a 45-knot downslope wind and nearly lost our ship, snapping a one-inch anchor line in the small hours of the night because we failed to get out.

### Approach

From north or south, identify Fraser Point, a long,

low lying peninsula that protrudes like a detached islet from the main island. Fraser Point can be approached within 0.5 mile. Once within a mile of Fraser (from south) or with the headland abaft the beam (from north), identify a series of off lying rock islets that lie 0.5 mile east and inshore of the end of the headland. These islets are surrounded by isolated subsurface dangers and extensive kelp beds that extend SE for 0.5 mile. Forney's Cove lies behind these rocks, which provide much of the shelter in the anchorage. When approaching Forney's from west or north, give the south side of the headland and these rocks 0.75 mile berth, keeping clear of the kelp, as you steer SE into the bight beyond Fraser Point. Once the rocks and kelp are well astern, alter course to north to pass through the gap in the kelp between the rocks, which is only about 100 feet wide, and the steep cliffs of the shore. Bound for Forney's from south, leave the rocks and kelp broad on the port bow and steer for a point just over halfway between the cliffs and the rocks, just outside the kelp beds. This course (probably just west of north) will bring you into the cove safely. We should note in passing that Fraser Point is easily identified from offshore in the Santa Cruz Channel, lying 1.5 miles south of West Point (see Warning about the Potato Patch, below).

### Anchorage

Forney's Cove is formed by a semi-circular, sandy beach that ends in steep cliffs to the NE, and in Fraser Point to the west. The off lying rocks and reefs just mentioned provide some protection from prevailing swells. Entering the cove, steer for the beach until rocks and kelp to port are abaft the beam. Then sound your way into an anchor berth between the beach and rocks tucked as far west into the anchorage as conditions and your draft permits. The smoothest water will be found at the head of the cove. Anchor in 15-40 feet (sand, kelp and rocks). Lay plenty of scope and a second anchor to minimize effects of surge. Although people do anchor off pebbly Fraser Beach immediately NE of Fraser Point, we cannot recommend this berth for an overnight stay, and during the day only in the calmest west conditions. It does offer shelter in NE conditions, however.

### Landing

By permit only, on the beach. Look out for the breakers.

---

### *WARNING*

The west end of Forney's is suicidal in the strong NE winds that sometimes occur in fall or winter. *Get out at once if a wind fills in from this direction*, and be especially careful on very dry, clear days.

---

North of Fraser Point, steep cliffs of the rugged NW corner of Santa Cruz Island fall directly into the ocean. Although you can approach West Point within 0.3 mile (look out for the rocks awash at the point), the water off the coast in this vicinity can be very dangerous.

---

### *WARNING — POTATO PATCH*

The so-called "Potato Patch" extends two miles west of West Point, a zone of turbulent water caused by opposing currents in Santa Cruz Channel and the main Channel. In heavy weather, westerly swells are confused by these opposing currents, creating an extensive area of dangerous and turbulent seas. Even on calm days, overfalls caused by the currents can cause the sea to seeth and ripple. In any wind or swell at all, the Potato Patch comes alive with steep-sided, chaotic seas, moving in all directions. The wind spills from your sails; waves can break aboard at any time. *In anything other than calm conditions, round West Point at least two miles off.* Beware, also, of a spot of breaking water one-quarter mile SW of Fraser Point, where swells can build suddenly even in quiet weather.

---

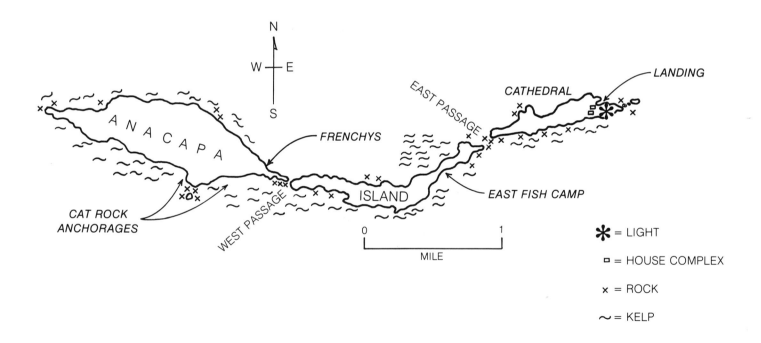

N
W — E
S

LANDING

CATHEDRAL

EAST PASSAGE

A N A C A P A

FRENCHYS

ISLAND

EAST FISH CAMP

CAT ROCK
ANCHORAGES

WEST PASSAGE

0                    1

MILE

\* = LIGHT

□ = HOUSE COMPLEX

x = ROCK

~ = KELP

Fig. 9.1 — *Anacapa Island, with major features and anchorages mentioned in the text.*

# CHAPTER *9*

# *Anacapa*

## Important Note

Anacapa Island, a national monument, is part of the National Park System. You may land on the island, but the west part of the island is off limits because of its important brown pelican rookeries. Stringent regulations protect the island. You may not:

1. Mutilate or interfere with submerged features or wrecks.
2. Take abalone or lobsters for commercial purposes on the north side of the island, use fishing nets inside the kelp beds. Fishing licenses are required.
3. Interfere with the wildlife or archaeological remains on the island.

(For further details, see *Federal Register,* March 17, 1972.)

Overnight camping on the island is by permit only, and limited to 50 persons or less:

For further information, contact:
  National Park Service
  Channel Islands National Monument
  1699 Anchors Way Drive
  Ventura, California 93003
  (805) 644-8157

All accidents at the National Monument must be reported to the Park Service within 24 hours.

Anacapa Island has a remarkable profile, visible for miles on a clear day. The 4.5 nautical miles of Anacapa are nowhere much more than 0.5 mile wide, consisting of three islands, separated by two very narrow passages blocked with rocks and sand. Nine hundred thirty foot Vela Peak forms the west extremity of the island, visible from a long distance, so much so that Portola's supply ship captain Juan Perez named it *"Falsa Vela"* (false sail). Vancouver subsequently renamed the island Anacapa after a Chumash word for mirage — *'anyapah*. The Chumash never lived on Anacapa for any length of time, for the island is waterless. Instead, they visited it in search of shellfish, seals and seal lions. Anacapa has remained uninhabited in modern times except for government personnel and one remarkable individual — Frenchman Raymond Ledreau. He lived at Frenchy's Cove from 1928 to 1956, surviving off the bounty of visitors and fishing.

Vela Peak falls rapidly to the east, giving way to a narrow spine of land that extends 1.5 miles and is 0.2 mile wide, although 325-feet high. Anacapa ends in a mile-long, 250-foot high, level land mass that terminates in an 80-foot high Arch Rock at the east end. The sides of the island are steep and precipitous, so landing can be difficult. Thick beds of kelp hug the shore.

The most significant man-made structure on Anacapa is the cylindrical, white tower of the lighthouse on the east end. Now automated, the light (Gp. Fl. (3) 60 sec.) is one of the most powerful on the California coast, visible 23 miles away in clear weather. The light is 277 feet above sea level and sounds a fog horn every 15 seconds in thick weather. A radio beacon near the lighthouse transmits on 323 KHz (.--. [AW]) with a full range of 10 miles. This light is a vital signpost for navigating this general area at night.

From a distance, Anacapa appears as a single hump, the lower lying east segments of the island not appearing until you are 10-15 miles away. Mirage effects can play strange tricks with Anacapa. On warm days, the island can appear to be swimming on a bed of haze, its peak magnified to strange and distorted shapes. The west end is imposing to approach, a precipitous, desolate peak that tumbles into deep water. We once approached Anacapa from NW on a King Harbor race on a magnificent, calm, August evening. Over 120 yachts were running down to Anacapa, passing close inshore on its south side. Their multi-colored spinnakers, glowing in the soft, yellow evening light, were reflected in the mirror-like water. We sailed close to the cliffs, hoping to pick up some advantage close inshore. The steep sides of Anacapa fell into 60 feet of water or more, the Pacific barely breaking on the island shores. We had never seen the area so calm.

Fig. 9.2 — *The lighthouse landing on Anacapa Island. "Although you can bring a sizeable vessel alongside, this is inadvisable owing to surge."*

## Sailing Directions (Fig. 9.1)

When crossing to Anacapa from the mainland, and unfamiliar with local conditions, you are probably best advised to cross in the early morning when conditions are often calmer. Afternoon west winds can blow strongly near Anacapa and at times near the mainland as they funnel through the east end of the Santa Barbara Channel. If a NE wind is blowing at the mainland, extreme care in crossing to Anacapa is required, as such winds can blow with great force near the island, especially on clear, dry nights.

Anacapa should be approached with caution. Although most of the island is steep-to, thick beds of kelp impede navigation close to the shore. Be particularly careful when approaching Anacapa in thick weather or on a dark night. Deep water extends close

Fig. 9.3 — *Arch Rock and the east end of Anacapa Island from SE, distant 0.5 mile. The lighthouse can be seen 277 feet above sea level.*

inshore and you could literally collide with the land in zero visibility conditions. Many small craft visit Anacapa, but relatively few spend the night in its anchorages, as they are somewhat exposed. Landing on Anacapa can be difficult, especially if a swell is running.

The north coast of Anacapa looks like a bastion of cliffs with a steep peak at the west end from some distance offshore. Indeed, the *Southern California Sea Guide* refers to the profile as "several segments of an outsize freight train." This analogy is apt. Notches in the land that mark the two passages can be identified some distance off and are helpful in locating the two possible anchorages on the north coast of the island.

Extensive kelp beds surround both shorelines of the high west end of Anacapa. An isolated rock lies immediately off the extreme west point, and you should plan to keep at least 0.5 mile offshore at this point. Keep outside the kelp. The west end of the north shore is steep-to, and of no particular interest except for its precipitous cliffs. Extensive kelp beds can grow off this

part of the island. The area around the east passage and the cliffs of Middle Island are heavily infested with kelp. Anchorage may be obtained in Frenchy's Cove, a partially sheltered inlet with a rocky beach at the east end of West Island (Fig. 9.4). Fascinating caves lie in the cliff NW of Frenchy's Cove, but their entrances are opposite often dense kelp beds.

East of the passage, steep cliffs form Cathedral Cove, where anchoring is possible. It lies 0.5 mile west of the Coast Guard landing. Sailing east toward Arch Rock, your best landmark is a cluster of white houses that formerly housed lighthouse personnel. Four white houses with red tile roofs, a communications center, and other structures are situated on the summit of the cliff. They are connected to the lighthouse by a short road. A white-painted concrete wall marks a small indentation in the cliff used as a landing place, where a platform is reached by means of two vertical iron ladders (Fig. 9.6). Although you can bring a sizable vessel alongside, this is inadvisable owing to surge. If you want to leave a dinghy at this platform, you should

**123**

Fig. 9.4 — *Approach to Frenchy's Anchorage and west end of Anacapa from NE, distant 1.25 miles. Arrow indicates anchorage off the beach.*

hoist it up 11 feet onto the platform, as the surge and a blow hole are certain to bang the dinghy against the pier. National Park Service personnel now live in the Coast Guard houses, and there is a small museum. Their provisions and supplies for the lighthouse are hauled up the cliffs with a crane, easily spotted close inshore. Two mooring buoys lie off the landing. This unsheltered spot cannot be recommended as an overnight stop.

Anacapa ends in a sloping promontory and the celebrated Arch Rock, 80 feet high, with a 50-foot natural archway in the middle (Fig. 9.3). Arch Rock is separated from Anacapa itself by a large, flat-topped rock. Give this end of Anacapa a berth of at least 0.5 mile because of kelp and outlying rocks. The white tower of Anacapa Light is conspicuous above Arch Rock, 277 feet above sea level.

Kelp beds can extend along the easternmost part of Anacapa, providing a protective barrier against coastal rocks for small boats. All along this coast, you may see fishing boats and pleasure craft enjoying the rich kelp fisheries. Seals play off the rocks and bask in the sun. The cliffs of the flatter, east island overlook the ocean and fall steeply into the Pacific.

Steep cliffs of Middle Island rise to a 320-foot peak just west of East Fish Camp anchorage (see below). The anchorage is a conspicuous light in the land about 0.5 mile west of the east passage. The east passage, filled with rocks, is somewhat wider than its west relative. Kelp beds lie off this passage, and can congest the approach to East Fish Camp anchorage.

Kelp beds extend up to 0.5 mile offshore along the middle of the south side of the island. The west passage that separates the highest part of Anacapa from its central portion is little more than a sandspit, although an 1856 chart records it as a "Boat Passage" with three feet. Isolated subsurface rocks, some exposed at low tide, lie to the west of this passage, which should be given a wide berth on this side of the island. Even moderate swells can break on the beach with considerable force. We once had a dinghy swamped here.

Cat Rock, a 71-foot isolated outcrop, is the only out-

Fig. 9.5 — *Cathedral Cove from NE, distant 0.40 mile. This is a marginal anchorage even in calm conditions.*

lying danger on the SW side of Anacapa. A temporary anchorage sheltered from NE winds exists east and west of this rock (see below).

The 1856 chart records "boat landings" at the extreme NW corner of Anacapa, also 0.3 mile east of the west passage on the north coast, but they are no longer commonly used.

## Frenchy's Cove (Fig. 9.4)

### General Description
Frenchy's is probably the most sheltered anchorage on Anacapa, but is far from ideal in anything but the calmest conditions. Like Cathedral, Frenchy's is completely open from NW to NE. The anchorage is famous for its tidepools and for caves in the cliffs NW of the cove.

### Approach
When headed for Frenchy's from the mainland, steer for the east end of West Island, where the higher ground ends in the confused rocks of west passage. Shape your course for the narrow passage which will bring you into the wide bight of the anchorage. Frenchy's lies immediately west of the passage, off a rock and sand beach. Approach the anchorage with care, avoiding the kelp beds that can grow offshore.

### Anchorage
Sound your way toward the beach and anchor according to draft in the most sheltered spot possible under the cliffs in 20-30 feet (sand and small rocks). To minimize surge movement, plan on laying a second anchor. The Park Service maintains a mooring buoy in Frenchy's, to which you can tie temporarily, using the rope bridle attached.

### Landing
On the beach. No facilities. Landing can be tricky in a surge.

---

*WARNING*
None of the Anacapa anchorages are completely safe in heavy weather. Plan on clearing out of the north coast anchorage *AT ONCE* if a NE breeze from the mainland fills in.

---

## Cathedral Cove (Fig. 9.5)

### General Description
A marginal fair weather anchorage in one of the most beautiful parts of the island, with partial shelter from north to NW. This anchorage is a possible place to leave your vessel when visiting the lighthouse, whose landing lies 0.5 mile east (Fig. 9.7). Anchoring will probably be limited when the Park Service develops planned underwater nature trails in this cove.

Fig. 9.6 — *Approach to lighthouse landing from NE, distant 0.6 mile.*

Fig. 9.7 — *Approach to East Fish camp anchorage from E distant 1.3 miles. Many seals can be seen along this stretch of coastline.*

### Approach

From the mainland, steer for the conspicuous buildings of the lighthouse complex. As you close the land, identify the landing place and crane, then look for a spire-like rock that in fact is a north/south wall of rock, extending at right angles to the beach. This forms a barrier that gives some shelter from prevailing wind and surge in settled conditions. Eighteen feet will be found between this rock and the beach, but the passage is heavily congested with kelp. Once the spire-like rock is identified, sound your way into the anchorage east of the rock.

### Anchorage

Aim to anchor on a line that places your boat east of the highest point of the spire-like rock, parallel to the rocky wall. This is the most sheltered berth, in about 25 feet (sand and rock). A second anchor is essential, but beware of placing it too close to shore. The bottom shelves steeply and and becomes rocky with poor holding ground. Kelp growth will probably keep you at least 35 feet from the wall of the spire-like rock. Beware also, of sunken wire cable on the bottom NE of the spire rock. You can foul your anchor on this obstruction. On calm days, you can normally spot the cable on the bottom, however.

Anchorage may also be obtained west of the spire-like rock, with some limited shelter from a protruding headland, in 20-25 feet (sand). The surge in this spot is, however, a nuisance. This cannot be regarded as anything more than a temporary anchorage. Cathedral Cove is untenable in a NE wind.

### Landing and Facilities

Land on the sand and rock beach. No facilities. The Park Service rangers patrol this area and may call on you.

## East Fish Camp (Fig. 9.7)

### General Description

An anchorage much used by fishing boats, with a mooring buoy. East Fish Camp provides shelter from west to north winds, although surge sometimes rolls into the anchorage. An adequate overnight anchorage in quiet conditions, and a refuge spot in unexpected, strong westerlies.

### Approach

Identify Cat Rock and East Passage. East Fish Camp lies 0.6 mile west of the passage. A conspicuous bluff, visible from either end of the south side of the island, and a minor indentation in the land form the bight of the anchorage. Once the bight is identified, shape your course for the middle of the bay, finding the clearest route through the kelp.

### Anchorage

In 30-35 feet (sand and rock) as close to the shore as you deem safe, and clear of rocks to minimize effect of surge and maximize shelter. A second anchor should not be necessary in this anchorage unless it is congested. There is only 18 feet of water or less off the beach. East Fish Camp is often heavily overgrown with kelp.

Fig. 9.8 — a. *Approach to Cat Rock anchorages from east. Cat Rock is 0.75 mile distant. Anchorage may be obtained under the cliffs NE of the rock, but the main anchorage lies west of Cat Rock. Arrow shows Cat Rock.*

*b. Cat Rock from west at the spot where you enter the anchorage.*

128

## Cat Rock Anchorages (Fig. 9.8)

**General Description**

The anchorages lie on the south side of Anacapa West Island, about 0.75 mile west of the West Passage, and provides shelter from NW to NE winds. Allegedly, the rock was named after Frenchy's cats who were stranded there by incoming tides.

**Approach (Fig. 9.8a)**

Identify Cat Rock, an outlying rock surrounded by other, smaller rocks. For the west anchorage, alter course to pass inshore 200 yards west of the rock itself. A mooring buoy lies 200 yards offshore at the anchorage. Aim to anchor as close to the shore as possible, to gain maximum shelter of the land, yet far enough out to avoid backwash. Provided you keep 200 yards west of Cat Rock, there are no outlying dangers except for kelp.

**Anchorage (Fig. 9.8b)**

Anchor according to draft as close to the beach as you can, in 30-40 feet (sand).

## East Anchorage

You can also anchor under the lee of the land east of Cat Rock. There is deep water close inshore. Thread your way through the kelp and choose a sheltered spot.

# Part III:

# Sailing Directions–
# Mainland Coasts

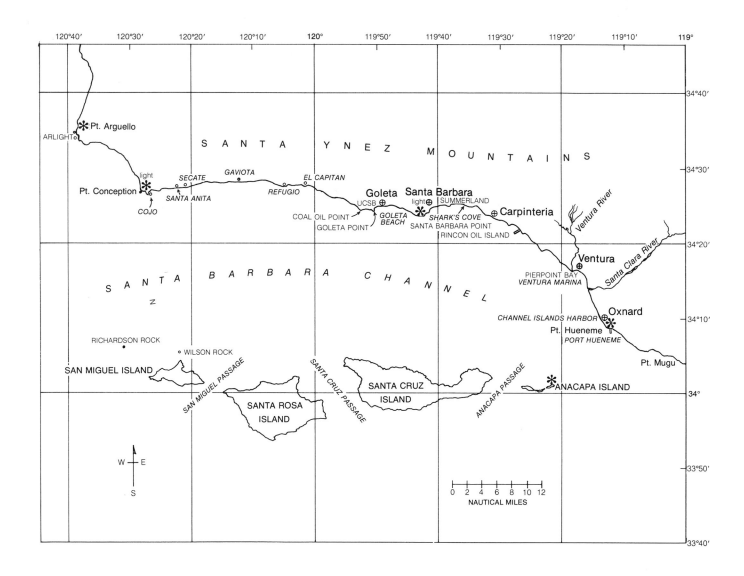

Fig. 10.1 — *Mainland coast from Point Arguello to Point Mugu, with major features and anchorages mentioned in the text.*

# CHAPTER *10*

# *Point Arguello, Point Conception, and Cojo Anchorage.*

## Important Warning

Coastal waters off Point Arguello and Point Conception constitute a Danger Area for Vandenberg missile range. The coastline is divided into 11 zones, some of which are in use most days.

For details of activity, call (805) 865-3405 or 3406 between 0800 and 1600, Monday through Friday, or listen to VHF Channels 6 or 16 at 0900 or 1200 Monday through Friday. You can also call "Frontier Control" on Channel 16. The zones are normally not in use on weekends or holidays. Call before you leave on passage to avoid delays. Also, consult *Local Notices*.

This chapter describes the western approach to the Santa Barbara Channel, the notorious and windy conditions that give the Point Conception area a mystique all its own (Fig. 10.1). As long ago as 1858,

George Davidson, the celebrated surveyor of the California coast, described how he had seen "vessels coming from the eastward with all sail set, and light airs from the north in a very time reduced to short canvas upon approaching the cape." Even in his day, Conception was known as the "Cape Horn of the Pacific." Davidson called it "A peculiar and remarkable headland. Once seen," he added, "it will never be forgotten." Many small boat sailors spend their whole cruising lives south of Conception and never venture further north. They are missing something, for this stormy and desolate corner of California has a great fascination. But a word of warning! This area of the Channel is not for the inexperienced. Keep clear until you know your boat intimately!

# Point Arguello and Point Conception

## Meteorology

The west end of the Santa Barbara Channel is notorious for its gusty winds and confused seas. The coast turns east at Points Arguello and Conception. A new weather pattern develops east of these two points which enjoy local weather of their own. Point Conception is celebrated for its squalls and strong winds. Nevertheless, many small yachts manage to round Conception safely on their journey to and from Southern California. But a successful rounding of the Arguello-Conception land mass requires careful observation of prevailing weather and some understanding of what causes the unusual wind and sea conditions off the cape.[1]

---

Footnote 1

The account of meteorological conditions which follows is drawn from Charles E. Wood, "Understanding Capes and Their Weather," *Pacific Skipper*, October, 1977, which should be consulted for further information.

---

Point Conception is not the only prominent cape on the Pacific Coast with a notorious reputation. Cabo San Lucas in Baja is another windy spot. But both pale into insignificance alongside Cape Horn. Each of these points is the bold edging of a land mass, a promontory backed by mountains which act as a barrier to prevailing winds. Each projects into an area of relatively constant onshore winds, in the case of Conception, the north to NW breeze that blows down the California coast most of the year. Point Conception is an abrupt interruption of the steady onshore winds that have suffered minimal friction loss over the ocean and of the long, regular swells that have traveled over open water for thousands of miles.

When the onshore winds are cool and relatively stable, the effect of Point Conception is to cause the air mass to lift some seven to nine times the height of the cape to windward, leaving a fluky area immediately windward of the promontory. Both sea and wind quiet down and conditions off Point Conception are peaceful. This stable condition usually occurs only at night during periods of cooler, settled weather, when fog is present.

Point Conception rarely enjoys such stable conditions, for there are many factors that act together to make air flows more complex. Frontal systems or pressure changes far offshore can make conditions alter without warning. As a general rule, winds around Point Conception tend to increase during the afternoons. But these stronger winds can last for longer periods of time if onshore wind conditions are inconsistent or stronger than usual.

An unstable onshore wind will result in no lifting. The air mass hits the cape in full flow. It compresses and squeezes past the point in a "venturi" effect that funnels it through a small area at the land and causes wind velocity to rise sharply. As the sun begins to heat up the land, warm air begins to rise in a thermal effect, a sea breeze effect is caused. The sea breeze circulation causes lower pressure at the cape, and the onshore wind further accelerates to fill the low pressure area. Offshore, the downflow of the sea breeze brings gustier upper level air down to the surface. This mixture of sea breeze and upper level, higher speed air is then drawn into the airflow, funneling around Point Conception. The winds at the cape can be 50% to 130% higher than the strong breeze well offshore. In other words, an 18-knot breeze offshore may have a local velocity of 27-42 knots close to the Point. The onshore wind will increase all day as the sea breeze effect gains strength and land heating persists. A wind shadow extends to leeward beyond the cape, and it can extend a distance of 20 to 30 times the height of the point away from the land, or about 1.0 mile off Point Conception.

Swell conditions off Point Conception are rougher than offshore. Swells are refracted around the headlands and are heightened by the increased wind speed. Although turbulent eddies and currents may further

Fig. 10.2 — *Point Arguello from east, distant 1.0 mile.* *(Photograph by Peter Howorth.)*

confuse swells off Arguello and Conception, the roughest conditions will normally be found where the winds are strongest or immediately to leeward of the windiest area.

## Point Arguello

Points Arguello and Conception are rugged, desolate capes in a magnificent setting. They lie at the edge of a narrow coastal plain backed by low mountains. The Southern Pacific Railroad runs along the coast and close to Point Conception and Cojo anchorage. The seaward end of the Santa Ynez Mountains ends near Arguello. Tranquillon Mountain (2170 feet) terminates in Rocky Point, Arguello and Point Pedernales. Arguello itself is a jagged, rocky promontory that extends about 800 yards west of the coast (Lat. 34° 34′ north, Long. 120° 39′ north) (Fig. 10.2). It can be identified by an outlying rock some 200 yards inshore, Arguello is nearly separated from the land by two gullies that make the point look like two headlands when at some distance north or south of the cape.

Point Arguello is unmistakable from a long distance offshore in clear weather on account of the huge aerospace launching gantries that rise like monoliths from the brown, rocky terrain close north of the point. Vandenberg missile range is constantly in use, and you should check in advance at Morro Bay, Port San Luis, or Santa Barbara whether firing is intended at the time of your passage, and time your arrival in this area accordingly.

Point Arguello light (Gp. Fl. [2] 30 sec., 26 miles) is exhibited from a white, rectangular tower on the west end of the point, 124 feet above sea level. It has a range of 26 miles, a radio beacon, and a Loran slave station. The Loran towers show red aircraft clearance lights.

Fog is a major navigational hazard off Arguello, caused by the cool California current close offshore. Between June and October, you can have 12 to 20 days a month with visibility of less than 0.5 mile. The worst months are September and October. Arguello can be

Fig. 10.3 — *Arlight Refuge from east of the breakwater, distant 0.5 mile. Do not attempt this harbor except in grave emergency, and then only in calm weather.   (Photograph by Peter Howorth.)*

fogbound while Conception only 12 miles away is clear. Beware of sudden fog banks and keep an accurate DR plot. The 50-fathom line can be used by larger vessels as a useful navigational line when bound past Arguello and Conception.

## Arlight Refuge (Fig. 10.3)

Point Arguello Weather Station (Lat. 34° 33′ north, Long. 12° 32′ west) is located at Arlight Refuge 3.5 miles SE of the lighthouse. A tiny boat refuge harbor lies behind a curved rock breakwater built out from the north end of a small indentation in the inhospitable coast. The military maintains this harbor and a launching ramp behind the breakwater. It is possible to anchor inside the breakwater in about 10 feet (sand, kelp and rock) but you may *only* do so *in case of serious emergency,* and then only with the permission of the officer in charge. To enter the harbor, identify the conspicuous white buildings and white radio tower of the Naval facility SE of Arguello light, and steer inshore until the breakwater is spotted. You will see the white picket fence from a considerable distance. Then shape your course to pass close east of the breakwater, altering to enter between the ramp and the breakwater. Beware of the isolated rocks one-quarter to one-half mile SSW of the breakwater and of extensive kelp beds and breaking reefs 0.5 to 0.7 miles east of the harbor. Heavy swells can run in on this coast and close out the anchorage completely even in calm weather. This harbor is unlit and not recommended for entrance at night. There are no facilities for yachts.

---

*WARNING*
Arlight cannot be recommended as a refuge except in very calm weather. It is *suicidal* in rough weather.

---

Pt. Concepcion

Coxo

View, Pt. Concepcion bearing W. by S. (Compass) 3 miles

Fig. 10.4 — a. "Point Conception from NW." The 19th century navigator's profile, drawn in 1850. "A peculiar and remarkable headland... Once seen it will never be forgotten."

Arguello is a desolate and fascinating place, with an almost moon-like terrain of jagged, black rocks and stunted brown hillsides. In a curious way, the aerospace gantries seem to fit into the landscape. It is an area to be avoided in all but the calmest conditions, and even then the swell can be bumpy and unpredictable. Most yachts keep well offshore, close to the 50-fathom line. *On no account go close inshore to Arguello in foggy or rough weather if you can avoid it.* You are much safer offshore, and the approach to the emergency refuge could be a death trap to an exhausted or injured crew. Far better to stay offshore and spend the extra hours getting to Cojo, Secate or Santa Barbara.

Good anchorage can be obtained in moderate weather inside the kelp off the coast between Arlight and a conspicuous yellow-brown bluff near Jalama State Park, a good landmark.

## Point Conception

The "Cape Horn of the Pacific" stands out as a low lying pinnacle when you approach it from Arguello, 12 miles NW (Fig. 10.4). It is a bold headland with relatively low land behind it, so much so that you can mistake the point for an island from offshore (Lat. 34° 29′ north, Long. 120° 28′ west). The brown grass and yellow-brown rocks are constantly pounded by long Pacific rollers. A low, black rock, nearly awash at high water, lies 220 yards SW of the light, "upon which some of the California steamers have struck in very foggy weather," wrote Davidson in 1858. Point Conception light (Fl. 30 sec., 26 miles) is displayed from a 52-foot high white tower behind a house near the west extremity of the point. A Coast Guard station, consisting of white buildings surrounded by a white wall, lies at the top of the bluff above the light. Low, sandy cliffs 100-400 feet high recede northward from the point, where the mainland turns abruptly east. Whether approaching the point from the north or from Santa Barbara, it is advisable to give it a wide berth of not less than 0.75 mile. Low lying offshore rocks off the point are hard to see unless you are close to Conception.

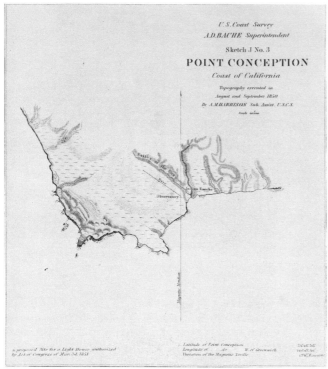

*b. Sketch of Point Conception executed in 1850, when the Coast Survey was looking for lighthouse sites. Cojo anchorage lies at the foot of the "Valley of the the Coxo."*

*a,b — Superintendent of the Coast Survey, Annual Report, 1850*

Confused swells may meet off the point, even under quiet conditions.

## Rounding Point Conception

When entering the Santa Barbara Channel from north, aim to give Point Conception a wide berth unless bound for Cojo. If you want an exhilarating sail on a clear summer's day and your ship is well found, plan to leave Morro Bay or Port San Luis early in the morning. You will probably pick up a strengthening NW wind which will carry you rapidly up to the point. Be prepared, however, for confused seas, rapidly strengthening winds, and even knockdown gusts. Stay well offshore to avoid the stronger squalls. This can be a hairy ride. We were once knocked on our beam ends when well reefed down between Arguello and Conception by a sudden canyon gust in rough seas. If you are doubtful about your equipment, or are making the passage for the first time, make the passage on a quiet, clear night. It is possible to catch Point Conception unaware and to sneak close by under full sail, as we did once on a glorious summer's evening. But only rarely can you cheat a buffeting on clear days, and the NW wind can blow for days on end in winter.

Northbound, you should plan to make the passage from Cojo to Port San Luis to Morro Bay in settled weather when night winds are minimal. Unfortunately, these conditions often coincide with thick weather and Point Conception is no place to be in dense fog. In May and June, for example, many grey days and nights follow one another with monotonous regularity. Plan to have a leisurely dinner in Cojo and two or three hours sleep before motoring around the point in the small hours. Although you may encounter some bumpy swells off Conception itself, you will be well clear of Arguello and Conception by dawn. Make sure you run an accurate DR, as the fog can thicken at sunrise. We once made this passage accompanied by a school of porpoises who gamboled about the boat all night. All you could see were their tails stirring up bioluminescent organisms as they surged around our bows, an unforgettable sight.

Point Conception is no place for an inexperienced crew, for the area can be unrelenting in its winds and swells. But with care, and careful weather planning, using broadcast forecasts and your own observations, you can round the "Cape Horn of the Pacific" in complete safety.

*c. Point Conception from south, distant 0.3 mile.*          *(Photograph by Peter Howorth)*

## Cojo Anchorage

Once around Point Conception, the coastline recedes in an easterly direction past low lying and rocky Government Point a mile east of the light. This area should be given a wide berth owing to the rocky shelves, heavy swell and kelp. The coastline now forms a series of shallow bays backed by low, sandy cliffs. Point Conception shelters this stretch of coast, and swells are much more regular. These beaches are a favorite haunt of surfers. The railroad follows the coastline east and passes close to shore most of the way to Goleta, 30 miles east.

### General Description (Fig. 10.5)

Cojo Anchorage is a well-known refuge for small

Fig. 10.5 — *Cojo anchorage, showing railroad culvert.*

craft bound up or down the coast. Named after a Chumash headman, it was visited by early Spanish expeditions and by whalers working California waters between 1870 and the late 1880s, and appeared on charts compiled as early as 1783. "This anchorage is a better one than that of Santa Barbara," wrote George Davidson in 1858, "and the kelp is not so compact. There is a large rancho . . . and it is one of the very best tracts for grazing. The beef has a finer flavor and more delicacy than any we have met with on the coast." He praised the large live oaks inland, willow logs for fuel. The water, however, "is disagreeable to the taste." Although the state has talked for years of building a refuge breakwater, nothing has yet come of it. Recently the area has been imbroiled in controversies over the siting of an LNG Plant.

**Approach**

We can describe it no better than Davidson in 1858: "After passing Point Conception from the westward, at a distance of about three-quarters of a mile, run east by north, and gradually around the bluff one mile distant from the cape, giving it a berth of half a mile; run on a NNE course for three-quarters of a mile, when the valley will open with a sand beach off it." Today, you should locate a conspicuous railway culvert beyond Government Point, where the Southern Pacific tracks pass behind the beach. Then steer inshore on a line that takes you to a point about a hundred yards west of the storm drain.

**Anchorage**

The anchorage lies under the lee of a low cliff 0.75

mile east of Government Point. The best spot is opposite a railway culvert in depths of 20-35 feet (hard sand). It is preferable to lie between the shore and the kelp. We have seen between 10 and 15 small craft anchored here, fairly well sheltered by the cliffs from moderate north, NW or west winds. You may have to navigate your way through the kelp to enter the anchorage, which should only be attempted in daylight. The unlit shore makes this a difficult spot to find at night, despite the presence of Point Conception light, a well-lit oil rig four miles east of the anchorage, and Gaviota aerobeacon 14 miles NE. Thick kelp beds can complicate a night entry even further. The strongest summer NW winds blow between noon and sunset. This anchorage is unsafe in SE and SW winds. Some people prefer to anchor immediately NW of Government Point, clear of breaking swells. Do not, however, attempt to anchor in Little Cojo 1.7 miles east of the main anchorage. It is foul with kelp and rocks.

**Facilities**

Absolutely none, not even Davidson's disagreeable water. But Cojo is an ideal place to wait for a propitious moment to round Point Conception.

*Santa Barbara Harbor from SE. Notice the extent of the sandspit, which may change dramatically according to weather conditions and dredging schedule.*

# CHAPTER *11*

# *Cojo to Santa Barbara*

This chapter describes the mainland coast between Cojo anchorage and Santa Barbara comprising the west portion of the Santa Barbara Channel (Fig. 10.1). The rugged coastline between Point Conception and Coal Oil Point just west of Goleta is less frequented by small yachts than areas to the east. There are few secure anchorages and the weather can be unpredictable. We recommend beginning sailors to stay east of Coal Oil Point until they have gained considerable experience in the Channel. With care, however, the west areas of the Channel can be navigated with comfort and safety.

## Cojo to Gaviota

The coastline trends east for 12 miles from Cojo toward Gaviota. Low, yellow-brown cliffs lie behind the beach; deep, parallel gullies extend from the low coastal shelf up to the mountains behind. A white oil storage tank lies 1.7 miles east of Cojo anchorage. Four tanker buoys lie off this tank. It is conspicuous from seaward. At present, this coastline is almost deserted except for the Southern Pacific Railroad and a dirt road. The railroad passes over trestles and bridges clearly visible offshore. At the time of writing, it seems likely that a large liquid natural gas processing facility will soon be built in this area, in which case small craft will be advised to keep far offshore.

As you approach Gaviota, a series of hills with sloping, rock strata between 600 and 800 feet high crowd in on the shoreline. Gaviota Canyon is a large gash in the Santa Ynez Mountains, that can be clearly identified even at a considerable distance. A conspicuous railroad trestle lies on the coast north of the canyon. At this point U.S. 101, the freeway between San Francisco and Los Angeles, brings traffic through Gaviota Pass and then east along the coast most of the

Fig. 11.1 — *Santa Anita anchorage from south, distant 0.75 mile.* *(Photograph by Peter Howorth)*

way to Ventura. Gaviota Pier lies immediately east of the railroad trestle.

The coastline between Point Conception and Gaviota is protected by kelp beds that extend in places up to a mile or more offshore. Oil rig *Helen* lies four miles west of Gaviota. Most yachts pass Gaviota on passage direct to Cojo or Santa Barbara, and stay well offshore. This is a pity, for there are two little-known, but pleasant anchorages that offer good shelter from NW winds, much used by fishermen and surfers.

## Santa Anita Anchorage (Fig. 11.1)

### General Description

A useful bay enclosed by reefs and kelp, which form a natural bight suitable for anchorage in calm or moderate NW weather.

### Approach

Santa Anita lies 1.0 mile SW of Secate which you should identify first (see below). Two conspicuous houses will be seen as you steer SW up the coast beyond Secate, just inside the kelp. One lies on a ridge about 1.0

mile inshore, the other above the beach on the north side of the cove. Keeping clear of the reefs that extend 0.5 mile offshore in the east side of Santa Anita, head inshore once the houses are identified, keeping your bow between them. Two conspicuous cliff bluffs lie immediately west of Santa Anita.

### Anchorage

Anchor in 25-35 feet (sand) about 300 yards offshore in a natural bight formed by the kelp and the east reefs, but well clear of the latter. If swells are moderate, this is a pleasant spot. But Secate offers more shelter.

## Secate Anchorage (Fig. 11.2)

### General Description

A spacious anchorage 4.5 miles west of Gaviota, much used by fishermen and surfers, which offers excellent NW protection even in strong winds and considerable shelter from the prevailing swell. Secate can be recommended over Cojo in rough weather.

### Approach

Approaching from deep water or along the coast

144

Fig. 11.2 — *Secate anchorage from south, distant 0.75 mile.*  *(Photograph by Peter Howorth)*

inside the kelp, identify oil platform *Helen*, close offshore, then look for two railroad embankments and Razorback Point, a prominent headland with sloping strata and a ledge of rocks extending 0.5 mile offshore from its base. The railroad embankments cross the mouth of Secate Canyon and the next arroyo west; both lie immediately SW of Razorback. Secate anchorage is an indentation in the coast, bounded by a steep, light brown cliff to the SW and by these embankments. Two railroad trestles will be seen on the coast between Secate and Gaviota, a conspicuous avocado grove lies on a hillside NW of Razorback, a wooden ranch house on a bluff SW of the bight. A long concrete sea wall lies east of Razorback. A course of about 175° M from *Helen* will take you into the middle of the anchorage.

### Anchorage

Anchor off the east embankment in 30 feet (sand and some rock), avoiding the kelp, or lie tucked behind the bluff to west of the anchorage, protected by the kelp. But look out for swells curling around the point.

Secate is a convenient anchorage for an overnight stay on the way to San Miguel or around Point Conception.

If you plan to visit Secate or Santa Anita, you are well advised to travel along the coast inside the kelp, but keeping a lookout for outlying ledges off Razorback and other headlands. You can anchor temporarily at many points along this coast, at such well-known surfing points as Ranch House Beach, where swells and strong gusts can make the anchorage uncomfortable. Many surfers and fishermen frequent this area, and have their own names for many localities.

---

### WARNING

Dangerous and unpredictable gusts can sweep down through Gaviota Canyon and the coastal arroyos between Gaviota and Conception. Be prepared for a strengthening of west winds and for strong NW gusts even on days when conditions are almost calm nearer Santa Barbara. You can tell where the gusty winds begin by keeping a close track of your position relative to *Helen* and Gaviota Pier.

---

Fig. 11.3 — *Gaviota Pier from SE, distant .5 mile.*

## Gaviota (or Alcatraz) Landing (Fig. 11.3)

### General Description
Gaviota Landing is part of the State Park system, operated by Santa Barbara County. A fine, sandy beach lies at the mouth of Nojoqui Creek. Limited park facilities lie immediately inshore of the railroad trestle and can be reached by a road from U.S. 101. Gaviota Pier extends 434 feet seaward from the bluff immediately west of the railroad trestle. It is unlit, but has an electric hoist for launching small craft (capacity 1500 pounds).

### Approach
Identify oil rig *Helen* and Gaviota Canyon, normally visible from a considerable distance in clear weather. Steer to pass well inshore of *Helen* and identify Gaviota trestle and pier, which lie immediately west of the point where U.S. 101 turns inland. A series of large, green oil storage tanks lie 1.5 miles east of the landing and provide useful markers with the trestle and pier when the cloud ceiling is low and obscures the mountains. Once the landing is identified, steer for the end of the pier, skirting kelp wherever possible. A night approach cannot be recommended, despite the red flashing aerobeacon on Gaviota Peak four miles NE of the landing.

### Anchorage
Good holding ground will be found immediately east of the pier in 25-40 feet (sand), but surge is a perennial problem. Gaviota Landing is a pleasant lunch or bathing spot, but is not recommended for an overnight stay. It can be very windy, as strong gusts sweep down from Gaviota Canyon in the late afternoon and at night. The anchorage is untenable in SE winds.

### Landing
At the pier or on the sandy beach.

### Facilities
Telephone, snack bar, camping, and toilets at state park. Limited provisions.

## Gaviota to Refugio

The coastline between Gaviota and Goleta, 20 miles east, is lined with dense kelp beds. The Santa Ynez Mountains provide an imposing backdrop to the coast

Fig. 11.4 — *Refugio Anchorage. Approach from ESE, distant 1.5 miles.*

all the way to Ventura. Rolling foothills and steep canyons slope down to the low bluffs of the coast, normally between 50 and 100 feet high. Their yellow-white cliffs are conspicuous from offshore, with sandy beaches and breaking surf below them. Thick kelp beds lie off the coastline. Southern Pacific has built trestles along this stretch of coast, clearly visible from several miles offshore. U.S. 101 runs parallel to the railroad. The constant stream of cars and trucks provide a useful landmark. The freeway traffic can be heard up to 10 miles out in the Pacific on busy days.

1.5 miles east of Gaviota Landing, an offshore oil loading terminal is conspicuous. Its green storage tanks are a useful landmark, as is a railroad trestle nearby. The terminal displays bright lights at night. Six loading buoys and pipeline markers are found off this facility, as far out as the 10-fathom line. You should avoid this area if possible. The six miles of coastline between the terminal and Refugio Landing are of little interest. Numerous small arroyos drain into the ocean between low, yellow cliffs. These coastal bluffs lead to Refugio Landing, which is formed by a small coastal indentation, where U.S. 101 and the railroad curve a short distance inland.

## Refugio (Fig. 11.4)

### General Description

Refugio was formerly the landing for the famous Ortega Ranch in the nineteenth century. Today, it is a State Park with a pleasant bathing beach. It provides a useful overnight anchorage in quiet weather, either as a weekend excursion from Santa Barbara or on passage to San Miguel or Point Conception. The Exxon deep water oil platform *Hondo* lies 4 miles south of Refugio.

### Approach

The best way to identify Refugio is to watch for the spot where U.S. 101 makes a dogleg inland to cross Refugio Canyon. The new concrete freeway bridge is conspicuous, as is a sizable red barn near a grove on the bluff immediately west of the anchorage. A bright green warehouse lies a short distance west of Refugio and can be seen some miles offshore. The anchorage is sheltered by a low, white bluff, which juts out to form the west side of the landing. A white oil storage tank situated 1.5 miles east of Refugio is a good lead-in when approaching from that direction. Once the general area of the landing is identified, steer for the freeway bridge. Inshore, sound carefully and thread your way inshore of the kelp. A night approach is not recommended.

147

### Anchorage

According to draft in 20-30 feet off the beach (sand). Tuck in behind the bluff as much as possible and lay a second anchor to counteract the swell that curves around the bluff. This is definitely a fair weather anchorage and more comfortable in settled summer weather. The bluff offers limited shelter from west to NW winds. At the first sign of deteriorating weather, you should clear out. Be warned that swell conditions can vary considerably with high and low tide.

### Landing

On the beach in calm weather.

### Facilities

Water at State Park, restrooms and showers. Limited provisions and fuel available. There is a boat launching ramp, suitable for small outboard runabouts.

## Refugio to Goleta

Between Refugio and Goleta, the coastline is generally low lying with sandy, brown-white cliffs. U.S. 101 runs just inshore along the coast. A white oil storage tank is situated 1.5 miles east of Refugio, near Las Flores

Fig. 11.5 — *Storke Tower at the University of California, Santa Barbara, from south, distant 1.25 miles. The campus is conspicuous from seaward.*

Canyon. This tank provides not only a landmark for Refugio but also for El Capitan Beach, one mile east. Four white tanker mooring buoys lie off the storage tank and should be given a wide berth. The coast indents east of the State Beach, and it is possible to lie inside the kelp in 15-30 feet off the State Beach. However, El Capitan is exposed to prevailing swells, although it can provide good protection from NW winds.

The coastline between El Capitan and Coal Oil Point 7.5 miles east is low lying, with white-brown cliffs, often with a conspicuous top layer. Five tanker mooring buoys lie off two aluminum oil storage tanks 1.0 mile west of Coal Oil Point. You will occasionally encounter tankers coming inshore to these facilities. 3.7 miles west of Coal Oil Point, a kelp-surrounded rock lies 0.9 mile offshore, depth 15 feet, another reason to maintain some distance off the coast here. Bumpy water may be encountered here even on calm days as shallow water extends some distance offshore.

Coal Oil Point marks the western extent of the Goleta-Santa Barbara urban sprawl. The Point is surrounded by dunes and a sandy cliff with a low, red-roofed building on its summit. Oil platform *Holly* lies 1.5 miles SW of Coal Oil Point, and is conspicuous from a long distance in clear weather. Extensive kelp beds front Coal Oil Point and the coastline that bounds Isla Vista and the University of California immediately to the east. Coal Oil Point acquired its name from a natural oil seep that surfaces nearby. You can smell petroleum in the air several miles to leeward. The seep has been known for centuries and does not necessarily have any connection with modern oil drilling activities in the region. George Davidson recorded how the "bitumen, floating on the water, works against the summer or northwest winds even beyond Point Conception."

You will recognize the university from a long distance offshore by its high-rise buildings and bell tower that stand out on the summit of the low cliffs that lead east to Goleta Point (Fig. 11.5). Goleta Point is a

Fig. 11.6 — *Goleta Beach anchorage from SE, distant 1.0 mile.*

low lying, sandy, 30-foot cliff that ends in semi-submerged rocks. A bed of kelp protects Isla Vista beach and the university shoreline. The ocean front apartment buildings of Isla Vista are situated on the cliff at the back of the sandy beach. It is possible to pick up messy tar from the Coal Oil Point seep on your topsides off Isla Vista, and we would advise keeping further offshore if convenient. At Goleta Point, the land turns momentarily NE in a shallow indentation that provides some shelter for small vessels. Santa Barbara Municipal Airport lies behind Goleta Beach. Jet airliners landing at the airport can be spotted offshore and provide a useful, mobile landmark on occasion. The airport beacon is 1.5 miles inland, and is easily visible at night.

## Goleta Beach (Fig. 11.6)

### General Description
Goleta Beach lies immediately east of the university, and offers sheltered anchorage in offshore winds and in calm conditions. The roadstead is completely open from east through SW, although kelp beds provide some protection. When strong winds from these directions spring up, one should clear out at once.

### Approach
Goleta Beach can be identified from a considerable distance in clear weather by the conspicuous buildings of the university campus to the west. Principal among these is Storke Tower which stands up like a slim pencil on the low lying coastline. As you close with the land, identify the west end of the anchorage, bounded by Goleta Point, a low, rocky shelf below the campus. The anchorage then curves east and is backed by a sandy beach. Past the low cliffs which bound the campus, the land dips down to almost 25 feet above sea level as you pass the end of Santa Barbara Airport's north/south runway. The cliffs rise again at the east end of the anchorage beyond Goleta Pier to a low bluff which reaches the height of about 150 feet. Two high radio masts painted red and white will be seen on the summit of this bluff 0.5 mile east of Goleta Pier. These two masts in transit are a clear sign that you have passed the anchorage.

The approach to Goleta anchorage is straightforward. There are no outlying dangers. From a mile offshore or more, identify both Storke Tower and the two radio masts. Goleta Pier lies approximately two-thirds of the way from Storke Tower to the two radio masts and is sometimes inconspicuous against the land. Groves of palm trees will be seen behind it, however. Once the radio masts and Storke Tower have been identified, steer for a position that takes you toward the lowest point of land between Storke Tower and the radio towers. This is the low ground opposite the end of Santa Barbara Airport runway. As you close the land, Goleta Pier will appear on your starboard bow. Once this has been identified, steer for the end of the pier and anchor to the west, according to draft. A thick belt of kelp lies approximately 0.5 mile offshore of Goleta Beach and extends from Goleta Point east toward Santa Barbara. This is harvested, so sometimes the kelp is thinner than normal. You can cross the kelp bed either by steering straight through it or looking for gaps which often are cut opposite the pier and near Goleta Point.

### Anchorage

Goleta Beach is smooth and sandy and shelves gradually. Approximately 0.25 mile offshore, there is 15 feet of water and a smooth, sandy bottom which, in calm conditions, is admirable for anchoring. An excellent position off the pier has the end of Goleta Pier bearing 015° M and Storke Tower bearing 215° M. More shelter from prevailing westerly swells may be obtained by moving up closer on the campus cliffs where anchor can be dropped in depths of 12-15 feet, some 200-300 yards offshore. In both of these positions, however, you should beware of swells rebounding from the beach which make the motion uncomfortable. Beware also of fouling your ground tackle on a sewer line which is often marked by kelp running perpendicular to shore near the pier.

Goleta Beach cannot be recommended as an anchorage in even moderate NE or SE winds, except perhaps for lunch. The kelp bed does provide some shelter from swells, but as an overnight anchorage, except under the calmest conditions or offshore winds, conditions are apt to be bumpy.

When canyon winds are blowing, there are sometimes strong gusts which blow over the airport and out over the anchorage. The low beach offers little shelter in these conditions.

### Landing and Facilities

You can land by dinghy on the beach or at Goleta Pier where there is a ladder. A small store sells ice cream at the head of the pier. A small park with toilets, water, and picnic facilities is maintained under a grove of palm trees at the head of the bay. Ample parking for cars and easy access to the freeway system can be obtained from the park. There is no resident warden. Goleta Beach is admirable for children or a family day sail.

## Goleta to Santa Barbara

The coast from Goleta Beach east toward Santa Barbara Harbor is of moderate height and consists of a low cliff which runs just inshore of the beach at a height of approximately 150 feet. Near Goleta Beach are groves of eucalyptus trees which give way to the flat More Mesa area, with its white cliffs. East of More Mesa more houses and trees are seen as you pass the Hope Ranch residential area and Campanil Hill. The latter can be readily identified by an arch-like monument built on its summit, which is conspicuous from seaward. Many expensive homes lie on the hillside extending up to the monument. The beach from Goleta to Santa Barbara is sandy with only occasional rocky interruptions. Approaching Santa Barbara from west, the low tower of Santa Barbara Point light is relatively inconspicuous until you are within a mile or so of the headland (Fig. 11.7a). The point itself is of moderate height, capped with trees and houses, and slopes steeply into the ocean. Santa Barbara light is built on the cliffs immediately east of the point and is sometimes difficult to see among

Fig. 11.7 — *Santa Barbara*

*a — Approach from west, showing Santa Barbara Point and light (see arrow). The harbor breakwater is coming into view east of the point.*

the houses. East of Santa Barbara light, the coast gradually declines in altitude until Santa Barbara Harbor is reached, at which point the buildings of Santa Barbara City College and the houses of the town are conspicuous behind the harbor breakwater.

There are no outlying dangers along this stretch of coast. It is possible to sail along it immediately outside the kelp bed which runs right along the coast as far as Santa Barbara Point and beyond. At intervals this kelp will extend at least 0.75 mile to seaward. There are two racing marks normally placed off Santa Barbara Point. Wide clearance should be given to yacht races which sometimes can be encountered in this vicinity. In foggy weather, this portion of the coast sometimes remains obscured when other areas are already clear. Caution should be exercised when approaching land, but you can be sure you are close to it when you encounter the kelp bed, or changes in water color. Approximately 30 feet of water will be found on the shore side of the kelp bed, at which point a close watch should be kept for breakers. Small craft, including fishing boats, move fast inshore of the kelp. A careful lookout should be kept for them in foggy conditions, also for lobster pots laid just outside the kelp.

When approaching Santa Barbara Harbor from west, care should be taken not to approach too close to Santa Barbara Point or to the beach as both areas are encumbered with kelp. Your vessel should pass offshore of the red and white striped buoys off West Beach which mark the limit of the bathing area. Be careful, also, not to pass too close to the breakwater, as there is frequently considerable water disturbance resulting from the swells breaking against the rock breakwater and then rebounding offshore.

## Santa Barbara (Fig. 11.7d)
(Large Scale Plan on Chart 18725)

### General Description (Fig. 11.7)
Santa Barbara Harbor lies 39 miles east of Point Conception and 24 miles NW of Ventura Marina. It offers complete shelter under all weather conditions. However, entrance should not be attempted in a south-easter, when it lies on a lee shore. The harbor is a friendly place, crammed with over 1000 yachts, fishing boats, and a few commercial ships. The U.S. Coast

*b — Lavigia Hill and the approach to Santa Barbara on a hazy day from ESE, distant 4 miles (arrow shows harbor entrance).*

View of the Town and Mission of Santa Barbara

*c — Profile of the mountains behind Santa Barbara, dated 1853.*

Guard maintains a cutter on station here, and there is a flourishing Naval Reserve unit. Santa Barbara itself is a well-known resort city that offers every facility for the visitor. Unfortunately, the harbor, although welcoming visiting yachts, becomes very congested during the summer months, especially during Semana Nautica Regatta (July), Old Spanish Days Fiesta, and the King Harbor Race (August). The entrance can be tricky, too, especially at low tide and when the channel has not been dredged for a while. Although a minimum depth of 15 feet is theoretically maintained, there are times, especially in the spring after winter storms, when sand build-up accelerates and the entrance shallows rapidly, to as little as six feet. Eventually it is dredged again, but sometimes there are considerable delays. Nevertheless, Santa Barbara can be strongly recommended for a leisurely visit. Every facility for yachts is available. It is an ideal place to change crews, being within easy reach of Los Angeles and San Francisco.

Santa Barbara Harbor is a recent development. In the nineteenth century, the anchorage off the town could be bumpy and dangerous. Vessels visiting the Mission anchored in the open roadstead, with their anchor cables ready to slip at a moment's notice. Thick kelp beds lay close offshore. "In winter," wrote Davidson in 1858, "vessels must anchor outside of the kelp, as the gales detach and drive in shoreward in such vast quantities that, coming across a vessel's hawse, it helps to bring home her anchors." It was not until 1929 that visiting small craft could enjoy the shelter of a breakwater.

### Approach

Again, we can hardly improve on Davidson: "Vessels coming from the westward first sight La Vigia, as upon approaching the anchorage, keep outside of the line of kelp (here nearly half a mile wide) gradually rounding the point upon which is situated the lighthouse, two miles southwesterly of the landing, keep along the kelp abreast of the town and anchor in seven fathoms; or pass through the kelp and anchor inside in 3½ fathoms, both hard bottom."

From west, Lavigia Hill, 0.6 mile NE of Santa Barbara light, reaches an altitude of 142 feet above sea level (Fig. 11.7a). It is conspicuous from both east and west, and is the primary landmark for finding the harbor. Santa Barbara Point itself is one mile east of the light, a high cliff at the SE extremity of the narrow tableland that extends from Lavigia Hill. Sandy West Beach extends from Santa Barbara Point to the west end of Santa Barbara Breakwater. The white buildings of Santa Barbara City College and La Playa Stadium, a complex of tiered seats, are conspicuous on the bluff behind the breakwater, and may be spotted before the grey breakwater itself, which tends to merge with the land. So are the stadium floodlight posts. In all probability, too, you will observe numerous yacht masts behind the breakwater before you see the 2364-foot sea wall itself. Santa Barbara Yacht Club, a wooden building with decks on pilings, stands on the beach immediately west of the breakwater. A racing start line, delineated by two marker buoys with fluorescent orange markings, extends offshore of the club and should be given a wide berth when racing is in progress. When approaching from west, identify Lavigia Hill and Santa Barbara light. Round Santa Barbara Point, keeping outside the kelp and at least 0.5 mile offshore. Then identify City College buildings, the harbor breakwater, and 2040-foot long Stearn's Wharf beyond it. Passing 0.5 mile offshore of the breakwater, there is sometimes confused water from backwash against it. Identify the black fairway bell buoy (Fl. G. 4 sec.) and aim to pass midway between the marker and the next black bell buoy that marks the beginning of the entrance channel (close west of the end of Stearn's Wharf). Once well clear of the end of the breakwater, alter course to port to leave the second bell buoy close to port and Stearn's Wharf to starboard. Do not alter course inshore too soon.

From east, your first landmark will be the Rincon oil island off Punta Gorda, 12 miles east of the harbor (its light is Fl. 5 sec.; foghorn two blasts every 15 sec.). A long wooden pier connects the artificial island with its pump and palm trees to the land. This area is known as Mussel Shoals and is a mass of oil pumping operations. Give it a good 0.5 mile berth. The conspicuous erosion contours on the side of the Rincon, two miles east, will become apparent on the starboard bow soon afterward, at the point where U.S. 101 moves inland to pass Carpinteria. A line of oil rigs extends seaward from the Rincon and your course will take you between them. Once the row of oil rigs off the Rincon is reached, on a clear day you should be able to distinguish low lying Lavigia Hill (Fig. 11.7b). The harbor lies in the dip of the land to starboard of Lavigia. In foggy weather, the course from oil rig *Heidi*, 2.75 miles off the Rincon, to Santa Barbara fairway buoy is about 280° M. At night you should be able to pick up Santa Barbara light from some distance. But it will become obscured as you pass the oil rigs and move inshore.

As you approach Santa Barbara, you will pick up the conspicuous white buildings of the Hammond estate development and the beachside tower of Coral Casino just east of the Biltmore pier. These lead you to Stearn's Wharf and the entrance 3.2 miles west. Be sure to keep outside the extensive kelp beds off the beach. Santa Barbara itself is now so built up, there are few landmarks to guide you. But some useful points of reference are:

— Montecito Country Club, a white building with a conspicuous white, square tower to the east of the city, visible above a wide expanse of green golf course.
— St. Augustine's Seminary spire NW of the harbor.
— Bekins Moving and Storage warehouse behind the harbor.
— The illuminated spire of the Arlington Theatre on State Street.

It is wiser, however, to use landmarks near the water. Some additional conspicuous features east of the harbor appear in Chapter Twelve.

Santa Barbara is difficult to pick up from offshore on hazy days as you have only the mountain tops to go by (Fig. 11.7c). When coming in from Santa Cruz Island, your best guide is a grey-colored cleft in the Santa Ynez Mountains that lies directly behind the harbor and town. A course set on this cleft will bring you safely in toward land until the important landmarks for the town emerge from the haze. These include:

— Lavigia Hill
— Santa Barbara light
— Montecito Country Club (white, square tower)
— Santa Barbara City College buildings and stadium on a bluff above the harbor
— Four oil platforms that lie 5.5 miles offshore, SSE of the harbor, in a precise line, approximately east/west

These platforms are your best guide on foggy days.

Once the major landmarks are spotted, steer for the conspicuous buildings of Santa Barbara City College which lie on a bluff above the breakwater. The red-roofed Performing Arts Center is especially prominent, isolated on a large patch of undeveloped land east of the main college campus. The squat, white structure of Santa Barbara light will be identified to port, soon afterward sandy West Beach west of the harbor. You may have some difficulty identifying the main breakwater which lies parallel to the shore. Look for the masts behind it and for surf breaking against its footings. The west end of the breakwater tends to merge with Stearn's Wharf when seen from offshore. The Bekins warehouse behind the harbor is conspicuous and is a good landmark for finding the entrance.

When approaching Santa Barbara from offshore in foggy weather, the four oil rigs that lie 5.5 miles SSE of the harbor are a useful checkpoint if you are approaching the land from east Santa Cruz or Anacapa Islands. The course from the west oil rig to the harbor entrance is 315° M. In thick weather, approach the land with great care and watch for high speed fishing boats. The foghorn on Stearn's Wharf is a useful reference mark (two blasts every 20 sec.). It is advisable to delay entrance until the weather clears, to anchor east of Stearn's Wharf instead. *Do not anchor there in SE conditions.*

## Harbor Entrance

Santa Barbara Harbor entrance is notorious for its shoaling. Many yachts have grounded on the sand bar, especially at low tide, or when the entrance is congested. Conditions in the entrance can be checked by calling the Harbormaster on VHF Channel 16, then switching to 12. Once the entrance opens up between Stearn's Wharf and the sand bar that runs NE from the breakwater and the second bell buoy (Fl. G. 3 sec.) is abeam, watch for a series of unlit black can and red nun buoys that mark the dredged limits of the entry channel. Then trend around to port, as you pass the landward end of the sand bar, and turn into the harbor proper. The buoys are often removed during dredging or severe shoaling. *Do not pass outside the marker buoys, or steer direct for the harbor after rounding the breakwater at high tide.* Strangers are advised to attempt their first entrance on the flood and at middle to high tide, in clear weather. The narrow entrance channel can become congested at weekends, and a depth sounder will save you from disaster and give you room to maneuver. Monitor depths closely at slow speeds, for the water can shoal rapidly. The deepest water is normally on the sand bar side of the dredged channel. Give the end of Stearn's Wharf a wide berth. Keep on the starboard side of the dredged channel entering.

Once safely inside the harbor, head SW up the 225-foot wide main fairway (10 feet) to the Navy pier at the head of the harbor. A Union 76 gas dock lies at the end of the pier. The sign is conspicuous. Visiting yachts should secure to the temporary mooring float that lies immediately south of the Navy pier by the Harbor-master's orange launches. The Harbormaster's office — at the head of the dock — will then assign a visitor's slip for the duration of your stay. It is inadvisable to secure to the Navy pier (16 feet), as it is busy with Coast Guard traffic, commercial boats, and unloading fishing boats.

In thick weather, you can use Santa Barbara radio beacon (294 KHz; . . .-.. . . [SB]) on the Coast Guard building to find the general area of the harbor. A foghorn sounds twice every 20 seconds from the light at the end of Stearn's Wharf. Your problem is to locate the end of the breakwater and Stearn's Wharf. Once you have located one of these landmarks, you should be able to feel your way up the channel from buoy to buoy with the depth sounder. If in doubt, however, anchor east of Stearn's Wharf until the fog clears, usually by midday.

While Santa Barbara Harbor is easy to find at night, actual entry can be confusing, owing to the bright lights of the town. Santa Barbara light (Fl. 10 sec., 142 feet) is visible for 25 miles. The harbor itself displays three lights:

On Stearn's Wharf: Fl. R. 6 sec., 25 ft., 7 miles.

On the east end of the breakwater: equal intermittent Fl. W. 6 sec., 35 ft., 9 miles.

On the south end of the north mole: QR Fl. R. The flashing green lights of the approach buoys offer a useful approach line. All the harbor lights are difficult to pick out against the mass of city illuminations. Two red flashing radio mast lights will be seen east of Stearn's Wharf, and provide a general guide.

Once you have identified the approach lights, you have to feel your way through your unlit channel buoys. Do this by using your depth sounder, keeping closer to Stearn's Wharf then to the sand bar until you pick up the first red starboard hard buoy. The best way to spot this is by bringing your head down and trying to spot the dark mass of the buoy against the shimmering water. A spotlight will help, for the buoys are marked with reflecting tape. Once you have located this mark, you should shape your course SW up the channel.

Fig. 11.8 — *A southeaster approaches Santa Barbara Harbor.*                    *(Photograph by Bob Evans)*

## WARNINGS

— Do not attempt to enter Santa Barbara Harbor during a strong SE storm, as the entrance is a dangerous lee shore, especially at low tide (Fig. 11.8).

— Beware of dredges operating in the entrance at certain times of the year. The space for navigation is then severely restricted and the entrance sometimes blocked temporarily. It is difficult to enter or leave at night under these circumstances. Consult Notices to Mariners for information on dredging activities.

— Give the sand bar a wide berth at night. Do not steer straight for the masts in the harbor, as you will go hard aground.

If in doubt about the entrance, call the Harbormaster on Channel 16.

### Mooring

Anchoring in the harbor is forbidden, indeed impossible, even if you wanted to. About 30 guest slips are available. Each berth has water and electricity. The maximum permitted stay is 14 days. Showers and heads are available, a key is obtainable against a small, refundable deposit from the Harbormaster. In the unlikely event that the harbor is full, you can anchor in sheltered conditions east of Stearn's Wharf (see below) except in SE weather. Do not try to tie up alongside the wharf (18-24 feet). The constant surge makes this an unpleasant berth. A launching ramp for trailer boats lies on the north side of the harbor. To approach it, turn starboard for the fairway when the north breakwater (Qk. Fl. R) is abeam.

### Facilities

Gasoline and diesel can be obtained from the Union 76 station on the Navy pier, water from your berth. The gas station operates a small crane on the pier for a modest charge. A small boat hoist will be found by the 30-ton TraveLift haul-out berth south of the Navy pier. Both the TraveLift and hoist are operated by Rod's Boat Yard, 200 yards behind the waterfront. The yard can undertake most small boat repair and maintenance work.

The Harbormaster's office is located at the head of the harbor above a marine hardware store and yacht brokerage. Other marine businesses, including a small fish market, fishing, diving, and radio stores, a sailmaker, yacht brokers, and another yachting hardware outlet are a few yards away. Other marine-oriented businesses are found in town, including excellent engine shops, diving stores, and a racing sailmaker.

There is much to see in Santa Barbara, including the tenth mission founded by the Franciscans, established in 1786, some fascinating old adobes, and the remains of the 1782 Royal Presidio. The Santa Barbara Museum of Art and Natural History Museum are justly famous. Discerning visitors coincide with Old Spanish Days Fiesta in August, which provides an orgy of parades, dancing, parties, and general good times. The most important sailing events of this year are Semana Nautica Regatta in July, which offers several days of keen racing for boats of all sizes, and the Santa Barbara to King Harbor Race which is rapidly becoming one of the most popular yacht races in Southern California, with over 120 entries most years.

Santa Barbara Yacht Club welcomes visiting members of reciprocal clubs, and has excellent bar, food and shower facilities. It is noted for its friendly atmosphere and keen racing programs. Santa Barbara Sailing Club has less elaborate facilities, but a very active racing program, especially for smaller craft.

## USEFUL TELEPHONE NUMBERS

*Harbormaster*
P.O. Box PP . . . . . . . . . . . . . . . . . . . . (805) 963-1737
Santa Barbara, CA 93105 . . . . . . . . . . (805) 963-1738

*U.S. Coast Guard*
Search and Rescue
    Emergencies . . . . . . . . . . . Oxnard (805) 985-9822
Santa Barbara Group Commander . . (805) 962-7430
Patrol Boat . . . . . . . . . . . . . . . . . . . . . . (805) 966-3093

*Police*
Emergency . . . . . . . . . . . . . . . . . . . . (805) 965-5151

*Sheriff*
Emergency . . . . . . . . . . . . . . . . . . . . (805) 964-9811

*Fire*
Emergency — City . . . . . . . . . . . . . . . (805) 965-5252
Emergency — County . . . . . . . . . . . . . (805) 964-9811

*Ambulance* . . . . . . . . . . . . . . . . . . . . . . (805) 964-9811

*Lifeguard Service* . . . . . . . . . . . . . . . . . . (805) 965-5734

*Chamber of Commerce*
1301 Santa Barbara Street
Santa Barbara, CA 93101 . . . . . . . . . . (805) 965-3021

*Yacht Clubs*
Santa Barbara Sailing Club
    P.O. Box 1542
    Santa Barbara, CA 93012 . . . . . . . . (805) 965-9446
Santa Barbara Yacht Club
    130 Harbor Way
    Santa Barbara, CA 93109 . . . . . . . . (805) 965-8112

*SERVICES* (Incomplete listing. For further information, consult the Yellow Pages or local officials.)

*Boatyards*
Rod's Boat Yard
The Breakwater
Santa Barbara, CA 93109 . . . . . . . . . . (805) 965-0887
(30-ton TraveLift, 2-ton small hoist.)
Hull and engine maintenance and repairs, dry storage, do-it-yourself facilities.

*Sailmakers*
Connelly Sails
    33 Parker Way
    Santa Barbara, CA 93101 . . . . . . . . (805) 965-8301
Bert Remmers Sailmaker
    The Breakwater
    Santa Barbara, CA 93109 . . . . . . . . (805) 962-5155

*Marine Engineer*
Todd Marine
35 N. Salsipuedes
Santa Barbara, CA 93101 . . . . . . . . . . (805) 965-3800
(Volva Penta)

*Fuel Dock*
Union Marine Station
The Breakwater
Santa Barbara, CA 93109 . . . . . . . . . . (805) 962-7186
(8 a.m. to 5 p.m. — Pump-out station)

*Chandleries*
Coast Chandlery
    The Breakwater
    Santa Barbara, CA 93109 . . . . . . . . (805) 962-4421
Rod's Marine Sales and Service
    29 State Street
    Santa Barbara, CA 93101 . . . . . . . . (805) 963-3604
Transpacmarine
    The Breakwater
    Santa Barbara, CA 93109 . . . . . . . . (805) 962-5700

*Fishing Stores*
(we list only the stores at the harbor)
Carter's Sportfishing
    The Breakwater
    Santa Barbara, CA 93109 . . . . . . . . (805) 962-4720
    (Licenses, bait)
Sea Landing Sportfishing
    Santa Barbara, CA 93109 . . . . . . . . (805) 963-3564
    (Bait, licenses)

*Diving Equipment*
  Diver's Den
    22 Anacapa Street
    Santa Barbara, CA 93101 ........ (805) 963-8917
    (Rentals)
  Underwater Sports
    The Breakwater
    Santa Barbara, CA 93109 ........ (805) 962-5400
    (Rentals)
*Electronic Equipment*
  Coastal Marine Electronics
    232 East Montecito Street
    Santa Barbara, CA 93101 ........ (805) 963-3915
  Hemec-Harbor Electronics
    217 West Gutierrez Street
    Santa Barbara, CA 93103 ........ (805) 963-3765
  Moright Electronics, Inc.
    2952 Glen Albyn
    Santa Barbara, CA 93102 ........ (805) 682-4212
  Ocean Aire Electronics
    7 Marine Center, The Breakwater
    Santa Barbara, CA 93109 ........ (805) 962-9385
Simple food supplies can be obtained at the Marine
Center by the breakwater, but a short cab ride to town
will take you to supermarkets.

## USEFUL COURSES

Given in degrees magnetic (1978). For reverse course,
add 180°.
*Santa Barbara* to:
  Point Conception ................. 255° 38 miles
                          (from Santa Barbara Point)
  Cuyler Harbor, San Miguel ........ 222° 39 miles
  Becher's Bay, Santa Rosa .......... 200° 30 miles
  Pelican Bay, Santa Cruz .......... 166° 23.5 miles
  San Pedro Point, Santa Cruz ........ 145° 24 miles
  Ventura Marina ................... 100° 23 miles
  Channel Islands Harbor ............ 108° 27 miles
  Arch Rock, Anacapa Island ......... 130° 28 miles

*Small craft warning displayed at
Santa Barbara Harbormaster's office.*

Fig. 12.1 — *Mainland coastline with landmarks immediately east of Santa Barbara Harbor.*

160

# CHAPTER 12

# *Santa Barbara to Ventura*

We now sail past the east mainland coastline of the Channel, from Santa Barbara to Point Mugu. This part of the coast, surprisingly, is little frequented by small boat sailors, most of whom take passage direct from Channel Islands or Ventura to Santa Barbara. When traveling east with the prevailing west winds, however, you may benefit from staying inshore. A current of 0.25 to 0.50 knot sometimes flows east close inshore, giving you extra boat speed. Although there is only one recognized calm weather anchorage between Santa Barbara and Ventura, the contrasting scenery of mountains, sandy beaches, and busy highway make this an interesting trip. Fortunately, modern sailing vessels do better than their nineteenth century counterparts. "We have known a vessel to be three days working from San Buenaventura to Santa Barbara," wrote George Davidson in 1858.

## Santa Barbara Harbor to Shark's (Fernald) Cove

A leisurely sail down to Shark's Cove off Montecito, at the east end of Santa Barbara, has long been a favorite weekend excursion for Santa Barbara sailors. The backdrop of mountains, houses, and green trees can be impressive on a fine, clear day.

Passage down the coast can be made either inside or outside the kelp bed that bounds the shore about 0.25 to 0.5 mile off the beach. There is water at least 30 feet deep just inside the kelp, but watch out for bathers and water skiers. The latter use the smooth water inside the kelp for high speed runs. It is inadvisable to close the coast nearer than 100 yards. The rocky ledges off the Santa Barbara Cemetery and immediately west of Shark's Cove should be given a wider berth.

East of Stearn's Wharf, the yellow beach is fringed with the tall palm trees of Cabrillo Boulevard (Fig. 12.1). Some yachts are anchored east of the wharf all the year round. Avoid fishing lines off Stearn's Wharf and stay clear of the landings on the wharf except in emergencies. The city sewer outfall passes south to deep water immediately east of the wharf for 1.5 miles. Its outer end is marked by an orange and white striped buoy, which is used as a racing mark by local yachts. On no account should you anchor on or near this line. A number of large mooring buoys laid by the oil companies also lie off Cabrillo Beach. They are too large for practical use by small craft. It is, however, possible to anchor east of Stearn's Wharf between the moorings and the kelp in approximately 30 feet (soft sand).

---

### WARNING
Good scope should be laid out, and you should be prepared to take shelter in the harbor if the wind swings to SE and blows with any force in this anchorage. Many boats wash ashore when they drag here.

---

A measured mile extends 6080 feet east of Stearn's Wharf on a bearing of 067° M. The limits are: diamond markers on iron posts (front), square markers on iron masts (rear). You can use this accurate distance to calibrate your log and for other similar purposes.

Palm-fringed Cabrillo Beach ends at the Cabrillo Recreation Center, a conspicuous white building with a long veranda at the back of the beach. The white tower of the Mar Monte Hotel rises immediately NE behind the Center. White buoys are sometimes laid off the Center which warn small craft to keep away from swimmers. East of the Mar Monte Hotel, the beach ends in a low cliff, which extends for the best part of a mile east. The Clark mansion, a square, grey, stone house of considerable size, stands on the west end of the cliff among low bushes and trees. The mansion grounds adjoin Santa Barbara Cemetery. As you approach the cliff from the west, Montecito Country Club with its conspicuous tower will be clearly visible inland. This important landmark can be seen far from seaward and is a useful way of identifying Santa Barbara from mid-channel. A low, house-covered ridge parallels east the shore about 1.0 mile inland from the Mar Monte Hotel. The west end bears a conspicuous vertical, white erosion streak that looks rather like a human skeleton from the ocean. This can be a useful landmark when just offshore on a foggy day.

The brown cemetery cliff slopes down to sea level as you approach the Biltmore Hotel pier. This private pier is not available for public landing, and is often tricky to approach when even moderate swells are running. There is 25 feet of water at its outer end. The white buildings of the Biltmore Hotel are to be seen immediately inshore of the pier, while the white tower of the Coral Casino lies directly east at Edgecliff Point. The Biltmore pier is unlit except for some light standards for pedestrians. Both the Coral Casino and the pier are conspicuous landmarks from all directions. So are the multi-story, white Hammond Estates condominium buildings which are a prominent landmark from the ocean. They can be seen 10 miles away on a clear day.

East of the condominiums, the tree-covered shore indents slightly north, forming a shallow bay off Miramar Beach. A row of beach houses and the blue-roofed buildings of the Miramar Hotel bound the sandy beach. It is possible to anchor off this beach for an afternoon picnic, but an overnight stay is not recommended. There is 25 feet of water 60 yards off the beach. A comfortable landing can be made on the sand, and a road into Montecito is found at the west end. The east end of the beach is low lying and backed by private houses. It ends in a rocky shelf that forms the west extremity of Shark's Cove.

Fig. 12.2 — *Approach to Shark's Cove from south, 1.0 mile offshore.*

## Shark's Cove (Fig. 12.2)

(Often called Fernald Cove.)

### General Description

A convenient day anchorage 3.7 miles east of Santa Barbara Harbor that provides a comfortable overnight anchorage in calm conditions only. An ideal day picnic anchorage.

### Approach

Shark's Cove is easy to identify from seaward, although the actual cove indentation is relatively small. Approaching from offshore, the cove is situated at the east end of the houses that form coastal Montecito. The spot can be readily located, for it lies at the precise spot where U.S. 101 climbs from sea level up Ortega Hill (250 feet) to Summerland. As soon as the last houses are identified, steer for the east house until individual structures can be discerned from outside the kelp. When about 0.25 mile outside the kelp, identify the easternmost residence, a large, two-decked, wooden house, and steer for it on a bearing of 010° M. The freeway runs at roof level behind this house. Once inside the kelp, proceed carefully inshore, altering the course east to steer for a red-roofed house that can be seen above the freeway.

Approaching from east or west, steer up the coast inside the kelp in about 30 feet. From east, pick up the wooden house and sound your way to a suitable spot. From west, give the rocky shelf at Fernald Point a good berth, and stay about 200 yards offshore until the timber house is located and anchorage selected.

### Anchorage

Sounding carefully, anchor about 250 yards offshore in about 20 feet or more (sand), depending on draft and swell conditions. At this spot, the wooden house will bear about 345° M. Beware of water skiers, surfers, and swimmers, especially close inshore. This anchorage is exposed to all southern directions, and offers only limited shelter from west. It is suitable for overnight stays only in the most favorable, calm conditions.

### Landing
Land on beach, and use path to other side of freeway or seashore to Miramar Beach. No facilities.

## Shark's Cove to Ventura

East of Shark's Cove, the cliffs rise steeply to a conspicuous 250 feet high yellow bluff known as Ortega Hill, where the Southern Pacific Railroad tracks pass. The bluff is crisscrossed with highway and railroad units which render it conspicuous from seaward. Ortega Hill descends into the buildings of Summerland, a small village fronted by a sandy beach that runs eastward to Carpinteria. A bed of kelp lies offshore of the beach in 30-35 feet. Navigating close inshore is often hampered by its dense growth. The

Fig. 12.3 — *Oil platforms in haze. Do not approach closer than 200 feet.*

wooded, yellow-brown cliffs of Loon Point are easily identified both from offshore and when passing Summerland near the kelp. This stretch of coast has a backdrop of steep mountains. The coast soon gives way to the foothills. U.S. 101 passes close inshore of the beach most of the way between Shark's Cove and Ventura, except at Carpinteria where it passes through the town. The lights of passing traffic can be seen at night, and trucks can be heard far offshore in still conditions.

Oil platform *Hilda* lies 1.7 miles SSW of Loon Point. It is lit at night and sounds a foghorn in thick conditions. Platform *Hazel* is situated 1.5 miles east of *Hilda.*

On its east side, Loon Point trends NE. The coast is low lying from this yellow bluff as far east as the Rincon, low cliffs giving way to a sandy beach and the conspicuous white buildings of Santa Claus Lane, and, less conspicuously, 1.7 miles east of Carpinteria. The structures at Santa Claus Lane can be seen far offshore, and are a useful landmark when approaching the coast in thick weather.

Carpinteria claims it owns the "world's safest beach," protected as it is by a kelp bed, in 30-50 feet. It is possible to anchor off the beach for bathing in quiet weather, but not overnight.

Four oil platforms — *Heidi, Hope, Hogan and Houchin* — lie SE of Carpinteria, on an approximate SW bearing from shore. *Heidi* is 2.7 miles SSW of the Rincon and the closest inshore. Each of the platforms is lit and sounds a foghorn in thick weather. They should not be approached closer than 200 feet and can be associated with unlit mooring buoys (Fig. 12.3). A complex of white mooring buoys and an oil pier lie 1.6 miles east of Sand Point, a small headland with off lying shoal just west of Carpinteria. This point should be given a berth of at least 0.75 mile because of an exposed rock 550 yards offshore. You should avoid anchoring off the oil pier as pipelines run offshore from shore facilities and storage tanks to the platforms at this point. Keep a sharp eye for launch traffic between the

Fig. 12.4 — *Rincon Island and associated structures from south. Altitude 3000 feet.*

pier and the platforms at all hours of the day and night. The green oil tanks behind the pier are conspicuous.

The coastline remains low lying east of Carpinteria, the beach being bounded by low, brown cliffs that end in sandy Rincon Point. Behind lie the yellow-brown slopes of Rincon Mountains. The Rincon is conspicuous for these yellow-brown slopes and large scale anti-erosion works that stand out as straight lines for a long distance. U.S. 101 rejoins the coast east of the Rincon. The coast mountains now press on the coast, leaving only a narrow strip of land for the freeway and Southern Pacific, with 2000-foot peaks behind them. An obvious fold in the mountains lies immediately behind the Rincon itself. It is possible to anchor on the east side of the Rincon (sand), but it is at best a temporary anchorage. Keep a sharp lookout for surfers when maneuvering inshore in this vicinity. The surf can come up rapidly here.

The shoreline at the foot of the mountains now forms a series of shallow bays that run between the Rincon and Ventura. Punta Gorda is prominent because of a long pier that runs from its extremity to an artificial oil pumping island 0.50 mile offshore (Fig. 12.4). Rincon Island is adorned with oil pumps and some straggly palm trees. At night it displays a white light (Fl. 5 sec.), sounding a horn in thick weather. Three other pumping piers are seen closer inshore just east of Rincon Island. You should keep well clear of these facilities, but can anchor in the lee of the artificial island with good shelter from west/NW winds.

The kelp-lined coastline has few noticeable landmarks between Punta Gorda and Ventura. Houses of Seacliff Village can be seen 1.5 miles east of the Rincon. Some conspicuous oil storage tanks lie on a ridge above Rincon Island. These oil facilities are brilliantly lit at night, an isolated patch of brilliance that provides a

Fig. 12.5 — *Conspicuous freeway trestle and erosion contours on hillside immediately west of Ventura River, from SSE, distant 1.25 miles.*

Fig. 12.6 — *Pierpoint Bay, Ventura, with landmarks for finding harbor entrance indicated, from south, altitude 2000 feet.*

useful landmark. Keep well offshore this stretch of coastline until you approach Ventura, and certainly outside the kelp. Pitas Point, 5.5 miles NW of Ventura, is conspicuous, a low spit running seaward from a steep slope. A deep arroyo appears west of the point.

The coastal mountains fall away into the Ventura River Valley. The isolated buildings and beach houses of the rock wall-faced shoreline give way to the dry estuary of the Ventura River and the urban spread of Ventura itself. An easily identifiable concrete freeway bridge and a contoured freeway cutting lie on the coast approximately four miles west of Ventura Marina, and are your first landmarks when looking for the harbor. The coastline of the Santa Barbara Channel now begins to trend SE toward Point Hueneme and the eastern entrance of the Channel. The harbor lies close to two green oil tanks and a silver one on the coast ahead.

## Ventura Marina    (Fig. 12.7)
(Large Scale Plan on Chart 18725)

Ventura Marina is less used by visiting small craft than Channel Islands or Santa Barbara, although it is an attractive and friendly harbor. Unfortunately, the entrance to Ventura Marina is notorious for its dangerous wave conditions in strong west conditions. There is talk of making improvements to the entrance, and the situation may improve in the future. In calm weather, Ventura provides a safe berth with all reasonable facilities for small craft. An attractive development named Ventura Keys with waterfront homes (least depth nine feet) lies NE of the main harbor, with an access channel leading into the marina.

### Approach
*From west:* The mouth of the Ventura River lies immediately east of the coastal mountains, which comes down to sea level west of the city. You should be able to identify this point from a long distance on clear days. A large concrete freeway bridge at the foot of the

mountains is also prominent, also the erosion contours on the slope behind the highway (Fig. 12.5).

The buildings of Ventura should now be clearly visible (Fig. 12.6). Look for the grey, highrise Holiday Inn building on the shore. You can normally spot this conspicuous structure from some distance. This useful checkpoint lies 0.5 mile east of the green- and yellow-roofed buildings of Ventura County Fairgrounds near the coast. A conspicuous microwave tower on top of a hill overlooks Ventura 1.8 miles NE of Ventura Pier and can sometimes be spotted above a mantle of coastal fog and haze. Padre Junipero Serra's cross can be seen at the summit of a 350-foot hill NE of Ventura, when lit at night. Once the Holiday Inn has been identified, it should be possible to make out the landmarks that mark the final approach to Ventura Harbor. These are:

— A fishing pier that extends 1.960 feet seaward just east of the Holiday Inn into Pierpoint Bay. Six white tanker mooring buoys (and sometimes a tanker) lie off the pier. A privately maintained red buoy (Fl. 10 sec.) is 0.8 mile SSW of the pier and marks the moorings. This pier is 1.8 miles NW of Ventura Harbor entrance and has 19 feet at the outer end.

— The SE end of a row of conspicuous trees that grow along the coast behind Ventura Marina are a useful background to the harbor entrance.

— Three oil tanks, two green, one silver colored, lie behind the breakwater.

— A red bell buoy "2VU," Fl. 4 sec. lying about one mile SSE of the mooring buoys off the pier. This marks the position of five large mooring buoys lying about 0.5 mile from the breakwater.

Once the pier is abeam, you should be able to see Ventura Marina breakwater 1.8 miles SE (Fig. 12.7). The breakwater lies parallel to the land and tends to merge against the shore, especially in foggy conditions. You should, however, be able to spot the white mooring buoys near "2VU," the buoy itself, and Ventura Marina

Fig. 12.7 — *Ventura Marina from west. Aerial shot showing major landmarks and channels.*

lighted whistle buoy, known as No. 2, which is painted red and is Fl. W 2½ sec. This marks the entrance of the harbor.

The outer breakwater is detached from land, and is lit:

— At the northern end by a light Fl. west 4 sec., 7 miles.

— At the southern extremity by Fl. G. 2½ sec., 5 miles.

Steer for the southern extremity of the detached breakwater and pass between 2VG and the Ventura Marina whistle buoy, which lies 0.8 mile SW of the entrance. Maintain your course until the entrance of the harbor behind the detached breakwater is clearly visible, then shape your course to pass between the detached breakwater and the south jetty of the harbor itself. Stay well clear of the small, sandy beach on the south side of the entrance inside the breakwater.

---

## WARNINGS

— Do not attempt Ventura entrance when high swells are running or strong NW or west winds blowing. Extensive shoaling makes the entrance extremely hazardous. Several vessels have been lost trying to make the harbor in bumpy conditions. *Under these circumstances, divert to Channel Islands.*

— Approach Ventura Marina with caution at night. Both the harbor and its lights are difficult to locate against the bright lights of the mainland. When entering at night, keep a close check on your position, watch for unlit mooring buoys, and *never attempt the entrance in marginal conditions.*

— Do not enter Ventura Marina from the north end of the detached breakwater. There are least depths of three feet in this entrance and often broken water.

*If in doubt about conditions at the entrance, call Ventura Harbormaster's office on VHF Channel 16.*

---

*Approach from south:* Locate the conspicuous red and white smoke stack of the Edison Power Plant three miles SW of Ventura Marina. Follow the coastline NW, staying at least 0.5 to 0.75 mile offshore until Ventura Marina buoy and the breakwater are located. The conspicuous trees and green storage tanks behind the harbor are also useful landmarks. The approach lights can be very confusing against the mainland at night, and you must approach the entrance with care.

### Entrance (Fig. 12.7)

Two jetties that enclose the harbor entrance are at an angle to the detached breakwater. You should approach the entrance around the SE end of the detached breakwater, keeping a close lookout for breaking water in the entrance. Leave the small red buoy that marks the west edge of the sand shoal in the entrance to starboard as you enter. This shoal, with a reported least depth of four feet, extends into the entrance channel and can create dangerous conditions in rough weather.

Once abeam of the south jetty, alter course to starboard and proceed up the dredged channel (20 feet) through the 300-foot wide entrance (Fig. 11.8). Leave the red channel buoys to starboard, the black to port. Once beyond a rock groyne that extends from the sandspit on the NE side of the channel, the harbor itself will open up before you. Pierpont Basin (least depth 10 feet) lies to port, reached between two Channel buoys. The dredged channel to Ventura Keys residential development with its waterside homes leads NE off Pierpont Basin, least depth 10 feet. There is eight feet in the Keys channels. The main harbor lies to starboard of the entrance channel and is dredged to 10-14 feet in most places. Small boat hoists, a fuel dock, and launching ramps lie east of the Harbormaster's office and National Park Service facilities at the head of the entrance channel. The marina itself lies in A and South Basins, and is reached by a dredged channel marked with a mid-channel marker. Ventura Yacht Club lies to starboard just as you enter South Basin. Visiting yachts from other clubs sometimes may find a slip berth there.

South Basin is a major marina development, but Basin A is still not yet completely reconstructed after a disastrous flood that swept through the slips in 1969. You can expect, however, to find new development in this area in the future.

**Berths**

Ventura Isle Marina, on the south side of South Basin, has guest slips. You should apply to the Dockmaster (805) 644-5858. There are showers, laundry and pump-out facilities and electricity. A launching ramp is operated by the Port District on the NE side of the marina. Anchoring in Ventura Marina is not recommended. You can anchor in Pierpont Bay outside the harbor, but this is only recommended on a very temporary basis. In the words of George Davidson in 1858, "There is excellent holding ground off Buenaventura in 10 fathoms, but the landing is not good." Vancouver spent a day recovering a fouled anchor here.

**Facilities**

A Union fuel dock lies just east of the Harbormaster's office. A full service shipyard can lift out yachts up to 25 tons and carry out most work. Dry storage ashore is also available. There are marine hardware stores and yacht brokerages in the marina area. All normal city services are within an easy cab ride. There is plenty to see and do in Ventura. The Ventura County Fair is a popular annual event, while Mission San Buenaventura, the Ortega and Olivas adobes, and the Padre Serra Cross are worth visiting.

## USEFUL TELEPHONE NUMBERS

Harbormaster
1603 Anchors Way Drive
Box 1107
Ventura, CA 93001 . . . . . . . . . . . . . . . (805) 642-8535
Ventura Isle Marina
1363 Spinnaker Drive
Ventura, CA 93003 . . . . . . . . . . . . . . . (805) 644-5858
(Pump-out station)
*U.S. Coast Guard*
Search and Rescue
Emergencies . . . . . . . . . . . . Oxnard (805) 965-9822
*Police*
Emergency . . . . . . . . . . . . . . . . . . . . . (805) 643-2121
*Sheriff*
Emergency . . . . . . . . . . . . . . . . . . . . . (805) 648-3311
*Fire*
Emergency: City . . . . . . . . . . . . . . . . . (805) 643-6121
Emergency: County . . . . . . . . . . . . . . (805) 648-7711
*Ambulance* . . . . . . . . . . . . . . . . . . . . . . . . (805) 648-3311
Chamber of Commerce
785 South Seaward Avenue
Ventura, CA 93003 . . . . . . . . . . . . . . . (805) 648-2875
*National Park Service*
1699 Anchors Way Drive
Ventura, CA 93003 . . . . . . . . . . . . . . . (805) 644-8157
*Yacht Clubs*
Pierpont Bay Yacht Club
1363 Spinnaker Drive
Ventura, CA 93003 . . . . . . . . . . . . . . (805) 644-6672
Ventura Yacht Club
1755 Shoreline Drive
Ventura, CA 93003 . . . . . . . . . . . . . . (805) 642-0426

*SERVICES* (Incomplete listing. For further information, consult the Yellow Pages or local officials.)

*Boatyards*
Anchors Way Marine
1644 Anchors Way Drive........... (805) 642-6755
Ventura, CA 93003 ................ (805) 485-4771
(50-ton TraveLift, 2½-ton hoist.)
Hull, electronic, and engine maintenance and repairs, dry storage, do-it-yourself facilities.

*Sailmakers*
Svenson Sails
2065 Sperry Drive
Ventura, CA 93003 ................ (805) 644-5612

*Marine Engineers*
Dick Core Marine
5895 Valentine Road
Box 3716
Ventura, CA 93003 .............. (805) 644-1722
Stanton Marine
3940 East Main Street
(Box 3477)
Ventura, CA 93003 .............. (805) 644-5545
Wright Marine Sales
935 East Front Street
(Box 1060)
Ventura, CA 93001 .............. (805) 648-2511

*Fuel Dock*
Union Fuel Dock
1404 Anchors Way Drive
Ventura, CA 93003 ................ (805) 644-6776
(7 a.m. to 6 p.m. in summer, early mornings and late afternoons in winter)

*Chandleries*
B and B Marine
2411 East Main
Ventura, CA 93003 ................ (805) 659-1810

*Fishing Gear* (at marina only)
Ventura Sportfishing Landing
1500 Anchors Way Drive
Ventura, CA 93001 ................ (805) 642-1323
(Bait, licenses, also tackle rental)

*Diving Equipment*
Ventura County Skin and Scuba Schools
2805 Palmer Drive
Ventura, CA 93003 ................ (805) 647-0167
(Rentals)

*Electronic Equipment*
Buddy Sales
2445 East Harbor Boulevard
Ventura, CA 93003 ................ (805) 644-1823

The nearest shopping center is Marina Village, adjoining Ventura Keys.

## USEFUL COURSES

Given in degrees magnetic (1978). For reverse courses, add 180°.

*Ventura* to:
Santa Barbara .................... 280°, 23 miles
Pelican Bay, Santa Cruz .......... 224°, 25 miles
San Pedro Point, Santa Cruz ....... 209°, 18 miles
Arch Rock, Anacapa Island ....... 183°, 14.5 miles
Channel Islands Harbor ............ 140°, 6 miles

Fig. 13.3 — *Channel Islands Harbor from west, altitude 3000 feet. An aerial shot showing entrance channels and major landmarks.*

# CHAPTER 13

# *Ventura to Point Mugu*

---

### IMPORTANT WARNING
A passage to Los Angeles along the coastline east of Point Hueneme will take you across the Pacific Missile Range. Call (805) 982-8841 before departing or call "Plead Control" on Channel 16 to avoid delay. *Also consult Local Notices.*

---

A low lying, sandy beach stretches SE to Port Hueneme and then east to Point Mugu. Oxnard and Port Hueneme occupy much of the Santa Clara plain behind the sandy shoreline. Point Mugu Air Base lies east of Oxnard, its main runway extending south to the coastline west of Point Mugu itself. The Pacific Missile Range extends offshore across the eastern entrance to the Santa Barbara Channel. All in all, the coastline is tedious, considerably developed, and exposed to dangerous swell during winter storms. We are fortunate to have a comfortable, all-weather, small boat harbor at Channel Islands, which offers a secure refuge in all conditions.

## Ventura to Channel Islands

The five miles of low lying coastline between Ventura Marina and Channel Islands Harbor consists of low sand dunes and a yellow, sandy beach, with few features of interest inshore. A highway between Ventura Marina and Oxnard follows the coast about 0.5 mile inland. It is advisable to stay at least 1.0 to 1.75 miles offshore, especially if a moderate or heavy swell is running.

A line of trees extends SE from Ventura Marina. A group of oil storage tanks stand at the end of the trees. Another row of trees can be seen immediately south of the most conspicuous landmark on the coast, the Mandalay Beach electrical generating plant three miles

SE of Ventura Marina (Fig. 13.1). This plant, with a *single* red and white striped chimney 220 feet high, can be identified from a considerable distance. Indeed, when approaching Channel Islands from west, you may sight the plant long before the low lying coast comes into view. Note that this power station has only *one* smoke stack, lit at night by a flashing red light. Seven mooring buoys lie off the generating plant, marked by buoy "2MB," 1.0 mile offshore that is Fl. 4 sec. at night. The plant is brightly illuminated and provides a useful landmark for a nocturnal approach. Six oil storage tanks lie immediately SE, behind the plant.

The low lying beach extends three miles SE to Channel Islands Harbor. A row of beach houses marks the outskirts of Oxnard and Channel Islands. The built-up area extends all the way to Port Hueneme. In clear weather, the Santa Monica Mountains behind the coastal Santa Clara plain provide an admirable landmark for locating Channel Islands from as far away as Santa Barbara.

Beyond Channel Islands Harbor, the coastline continues without major change to Port Hueneme 1.0 mile east. Point Hueneme itself is low and sandy. The land turns abruptly east at the point, lit by a 52-foot

Fig. 13.1 — *Mandalay Beach Generating Station. Note that this has ONE smoke stack. Photographed from west, distant 1.0 mile.*

high light (and fog signal) (Fl. 5 sec., 20 miles). This foghorn can be confused with that on the south jetty at Channel Islands, which seems, however, to have a higher pitch.

East of Point Hueneme, the coastline remains low and sandy as far as rocky Point Mugu, which can be located from a long distance west. Ormond Beach electrical powerplant lies on the coast 2.4 miles SE of Port Hueneme Harbor (Fig. 13.2). In contrast to the Mandalay Bay plant, Ormond Beach has *two* red and white striped smoke stacks. They display red flashing lights at night. The runway of the Point Mugu Air Base ends at the seafront east of the powerplant. Low-flying jets sometimes give you quite a shock as they pass overhead. A lagoon lies inshore of the beach south of the air base. A rifle range is situated at the east end of this long beach about 1.0 mile west of Point Mugu. Red flags are displayed, and a depressing sign reads: DANGER LIVE FIRING. They mean it!

You should keep about 1.0 mile off this desolate coast, and 2.0 miles off the rifle range to avoid unnecessary surge and strong richochets when firings are in progress. A launch patrols the fire path of the Pacific Missile Range south of the beach. You may be asked to wait for a missile to be fired. Information on firings can be obtained by telephoning the Range officer at (805) 982-7209. Information on actual firings are broadcast on 2638 KHz and 2738 KHz at 0900 and 1200 Monday through Friday.

Point Mugu is the seaward end of the Santa Monica Mountains. Highway 1 passes through a blasted roadway through the point, leaving an isolated rock as the outer extremity of the headland. Two aluminum colored tanks 1.5 miles NW of Point Mugu and radar warning installations on the peak behind the headland are conspicuous, and a useful lead to the position of the point in thick weather. The tanks are marked by flashing red lights.

You can encounter windy conditions off Point Mugu and west to Point Hueneme, especially in late afternoon. The west wind can give you a bumpy ride to

Fig. 13.2 — *Ormond Beach Generating Station from south, distant 1.5 miles. Note that this has TWO smoke stacks.*

windward as you tack toward Channel Islands along the sandy wastes of the Santa Clara Valley to starboard.

## Channel Islands Harbor (Fig. 13.3)
(Large Scale Plan on Chart 18725)

### General Description (Fig. 13.3)

A magnificent, modern yacht harbor that offers every possible facility and complete shelter to visiting small craft. The entrance is safe in all but the roughest weather, and has ample space for visiting yachts. Channel Islands is an ideal stopping-off point for visiting the islands or Santa Barbara, and is a comfortable day's sail from Santa Cruz Island, or Marina del Rey. Catalina Island is also within easy cruising reach.

### Approach

Channel Islands Harbor is protected by a detached breakwater, lit at both its northern and southern extremities. The lights are mounted on metal brackets. A marker radio beacon (308 KHz -.-./ . . [Cl] is mounted on the extremity of the south jetty that lies inside the detached breakwater. Both this and the north jetty are also lit. Like Ventura, the detached breakwater lies parallel to the low lying mainland and is difficult to locate from offshore, especially in thick weather. Remember that the higher pitched foghorn on the south jetty may be confused with that on Point Hueneme.

*Approach from SE:* Once around Point Hueneme, steer NW parallel to the shore 0.75 mile offshore until the detached breakwater and south jetty are located ahead. Then shape your course for the entrance, keeping a safe distance offshore from the breakers.

*Approach from south through NW:* Your best long distance landmark is the Mandalay Bay Power Plant with its prominent *single* red and white striped smoke stack. Approaching from Anacapa Island in clear weather, you should be able to obtain an accurate fix from this powerplant and the Ormond Beach plant with its *twin* stacks. Both facilities are marked on Chart 18725.

As you approach the shore between Channel Islands and Ventura, leave the Mandalay Power Plant well on the port bow and look for the north end of the row of beach houses that extends from Point Hueneme toward Ventura. Channel Islands breakwater lies about one mile SE of the first houses. You should be able to locate Point Hueneme and the detached breakwater one mile NW once you are within two miles of shore in clear weather. Once the 2300-foot long detached breakwater is located, alter course for the south extremity. A foghorn (15 sec.) is located on the south jetty inside the detached breakwater. Unfortunately, there are no conspicuous landmarks behind the harbor to aid your daylight approach, except for some water towers. Regular visitors develop their own from experience.

---

### WARNING
Do not attempt to pass between the north end of the detached breakwater and the beach in rough weather. This entrance can shoal rapidly and is inadvisable without local knowledge.

---

A night approach from offshore is complicated by the confusing mass of lights behind the flashing harbor beacon. As you approach the land, identify:

— The brilliant lights of Mandalay Bay Power Plant to port.
— Point Hueneme light (Fl. west 5 sec. 20 miles) to starboard.

Fix your position from these points of reference, then approach land cautiously and identify the detached breakwater lights:

— North end — Fl. R 4 sec., 5 miles
— South end — Fl. west 6 sec., 9 miles

Then shape your course to pass to starboard of the south extremity of the breakwater.

The two harbor jetties bear the following lights at the outer ends:

— North jetty — Fl. F 4 sec.
— South jetty — Fl. R 2½ sec.

*If you doubt your exact position at night or in thick weather, steer for Mandalay Bay Power Plant or Point Hueneme.* Once you have identified one of these two landmarks, alter course parallel to the shore 0.75 mile offshore and proceed until you sight the breakwater.

---

### WARNING
Approach Channel Islands with caution in rough westerly weather. A heavy swell can make conditions in the entrance bumpy and potentially hazardous. Strong NE winds can blow down the Santa Clara Valley on occasion and also cause problems for small vessels. Sudden currents can be experienced inside the detached breakwater in rough weather, and ample engine power is advised.

---

**Entrance**

Channel Islands harbor entrance lies between two rock jetties 300 feet apart. The 1650-foot entrance channel is dredged to a least depth of 13-20 feet. 9.5 feet will be found in most of the harbor. When entering, leave the south extremity of the detached breakwater to port, head north midway between the former and the south jetty, leaving the red buoy off the latter well to starboard. Then turn NE as the entrance opens up. Keep just to starboard of the middle of the channel when entering or leaving. After 0.5 mile, the channel trends north and the Harbormaster's office and Coast Guard docks will be seen on the starboard bow. Make sure you keep in the middle of the channel as you start to turn north. A shoal extends from the north shore of the channel immediately to seaward of the Fl. G light marked on the chart. The outer extremity of this shoal is marked by a small red and white buoy, and you should give it a wide berth.

Do not use the northern entrance channel between the shore and the detached breakwater unless you have local knowledge. It is said, however, the deepest water lies near the breakwater.

As you approach the Harbormaster's office area, you will open up the main harbor basin, bounded to the west by extensive marina developments (Fig. 13.3). The basin bifurcates at the north end of the harbor, the right hand fork leading to Kettenburg Marina (with its large, yellow crane) and the new Fishermen's Wharf development. The left hand channel passes the Casa Serena Marina Hotel, a conspicuous building, and heads past Anacapa Island Marina, under a road bridge (clearance 29.5 feet) to the waterside Mandalay Bay and Leeward Marina residential development. A lowerable mast is necessary to pass under this road bridge.

The following are conspicuous landmarks as you proceed up the harbor:

*To starboard*
— The Harbormaster's office and Coast Guard facility.
— Nearby, an Arco fuel station.
— Channel Islands Sport Fishing Center.
— Quarterdeck Restaurant.
— Anacapa Yacht Club clubhouse.
— Kettenburg Marine and Boatyards.

*To port*
— Channel Islands Yacht Club clubhouse.
— Whale's Tail Restaurant.

*Straight ahead*
— Lobster Trap Restaurant and Casa Serena Marina Hotel. These lead, via the port channel, to Anacapa Island Marina, surrounded by condominium developments.

— To starboard, the lighthouse tower and buildings of Fishermen's Wharf development.

*Night entrance*
Once the detached breakwater is to port, identify the two jetty lights:

— North jetty: Fl. G 4 sec., 6 miles
— South jetty: Fl R 2½ sec., 6 miles

Once you are in the channel, identify two channel lights 0.5 mile inside the jetties, situated on either shore:

— Fl. G 4 sec., 25 feet
— Fl. R 4 sec., 25 feet

Keep midway between these lights until the brightly illuminated harbor basin opens up to port. These lights may be difficult to spot from a distance owing to bright lights ashore.

**Berth**

The Harbormaster's office will allocate you a guest slip. Thirty-five are available. Channel 16 is monitored on a 24-hour basis. Guest berths are also available at Channel Islands Marina on the west side of the harbor. Anacapa Isle Marina also has some temporary slips. So does Peninsula Yacht Anchorage, next to the Lobster Trap Restaurant. All these marina developments offer excellent facilities, including showers, electricity and water. Anacapa Isle Marina also boasts of a fine clubhouse. Bahia Cabrillo Apartments on the west side of the harbor offer apartments with slips, Casa Serena Marina Hotel rooms with slips.

Anchoring in the harbor is impossible.

Trailer boat owners can launch their vessels at the county ramp on the east side of the harbor. The ramp is open 24 hours a day, seven lanes, free.

**Facilities**

Gasoline and diesel are available from the Arco fuel

dock (Channel Islands Marine Services) in daylight hours. Three boatyards can haul your boat. Kettenburg Marine has a 40-ton TraveLift and offer every service to small vessels, as well as do-it-yourself facilities. They also build new boats. Anacapa Marine Services offer haul out for yachts up to 30 tons and complete boatyard facilities, including engine work. They accommodate people wishing to work on their own yachts. Channel Islands Landing has a four-ton hoist and dry storage. All marine services, including sailmakers and diesel mechanics, can be found near the harbor. Port Hueneme and Oxnard are a 2½-mile cab ride away, with all normal urban facilities. You can fly to Santa Barbara or Los Angeles from Ventura County Airport on Golden West Airlines.

## USEFUL TELEPHONE NUMBERS

*Harbormaster*
  3900 Pelican Way
  Oxnard, CA 93030 ....... (805) 487-7711, ext. 4288
*U.S. Coast Guard*
  Search and Rescue
    Emergencies ................... (805) 985-9822
*Police*
  Emergency ..................... (805) 486-1663
*Sheriff*
  Emergency ..................... (805) 648-3311
*Fire*
  Emergency ..................... (805) 487-6311
*Ambulance* ........................ (805) 648-3311
*Chamber of Commerce*
  2800 Roosevelt Boulevard
  Oxnard, CA 93030 ............... (805) 985-2244
*Yacht Clubs*
  Anacapa Yacht Club
    3821 Victoria Avenue
    Oxnard, CA 93030 ............. (805) 985-6003
  Channel Islands Yacht Club
    P.O. Box 942
    4100 Harbor Boulevard
    Oxnard, CA 93032 ............. (805) 985-6091
*SERVICES* (Incomplete listing. For further information, consult the Yellow Pages, or local officials.)
*Marinas* (we omit hotels and apartment complexes)
  Anacapa Isle Marina
    3001 Peninsula Road
    Oxnard, CA 93030 ............. (805) 985-6035
  Channel Islands Marina
    3850 Harbor Boulevard
    Oxnard, CA 93030 ............. (805) 985-7558
  Peninsula Yacht Anchorage
    3700 Peninsula Road
    Oxnard, CA 93030 ............. (805) 985-6400

*Boatyards*
Anacapa Marine Services
3800 Curlew Way
P.O. Box 68
Oxnard, CA 93032 ............... (805) 985-1818
30-ton haul out possible. Hull and engine maintenance and repairs. Do-it-yourself facilities. Marine hardware.
Channel Islands Landing
3821 Victoria Avenue
Oxnard, CA 93030 ............. (805) 985-6059
(4-ton hoists, dry storage)
Kettenburg Marine
3615 Victoria Avenue
Oxnard, CA 93030 ............. (805) 985-5000
40-ton TraveLift and 10-ton crane, full service boatyard with comprehensive facilities. Do-it-yourself facilities. Marine hardware and electronics. Also a yacht builder.
*Sailmakers*
Windward Custom Sails
3600 Cabezone Way
Oxnard, CA 93030 ............... (805) 985-1852
*Marine Engineers* (in addition to boatyards)
Marine Engines Ltd.
3600 Cabezon Way
Oxnard, CA 93030 ............... (805) 985-0144
*Fuel Dock*
Channel Islands Marine Services
3855 Pelican Way
Oxnard, CA 93030 ............. (805) 985-6058
(8 a.m. to 5 p.m. summer weekdays,
7 a.m. to 5 p.m. weekends,
8 a.m. to 5 p.m. all winter)
*Chandleries*
Captain's Locker
3735 West Hemlock
Oxnard, CA 93030 ............. (805) 985-3322
Cliff's Marine Store
465 West Channel Islands Boulevard
Port Hueneme, CA 93041 ........ (805) 985-3603
(Also electronics service and
compass repairs)

Coast Chandlery
3600 Cabezon Way ............. (805) 985-0801
Oxnard, CA 93030 ............. (805) 985-0541
(Also electronics service and
rigging work)
*Fishing Gear* (near marinas only)
Channel Islands Sportfishing Center
3825 Pelican Way
Oxnard, CA 93030 ............... (805) 985-8511
*Diving Equipment*
Seafarer Dive Shop
3600 Cabezon Way
Oxnard, CA 93030 ............... (805) 985-6022
(Rentals)
*Electronic Equipment*
Beacon Electronics
3735 West Hemlock
Oxnard, CA 93030 ............... (805) 985-9828
Simple food supplies can be obtained close to Channel Islands Harbor, but an easy cab ride takes you to major supermarkets.

## USEFUL COURSES
Given in degrees magnetic (1978). For reverse courses, add 180°.
*Channel Islands* to:
Santa Barbara .................... 288°, 27 miles
Pelican Bay, Santa Cruz ........... 237°, 25 miles
San Pedro Point, Santa Cruz ....... 227°, 16 miles
Arch Rock, Anacapa Island ........ 202°, 11 miles
Santa Barbara Island ............. 151°, 42 miles

## Port Hueneme

(Large Scale Plan on Chart 18725)

### General Description

Port Hueneme is a commercial harbor approximately one mile SE of Channel Islands Marina. This deep-water port is maintained and operated by the U.S. Navy and the Oxnard Harbor District. Large commercial vessels, Naval craft, and oil boats use this harbor day and night. Since Channel Islands Harbor is so close, little provision is made for small craft. *You are strongly advised to use Channel Islands except in conditions of grave emergency* or when the entrance of the former is unsafe in heavy weather. The following general notes are for emergency use only, and should be used in conjunction with Chart 18725, where a plan of the entrance will be found.

### Approach and Entrance

Port Hueneme lies at the extreme east end of the Santa Barbara Channel. To approach the harbor, identify the Mandalay Bay and Ormond Beach power stations with their conspicuous smoke stacks and fix your position. Then lay a course for Point Hueneme, which is low lying and inconspicuous. As you approach the land, you should be able to identify the two rock jetties that enclose the entrance channel. A red bell buoy (Fl. R 4 sec.) lies 800 yards SW of the east jetty. There is 36 feet in the entrance channel, 31 feet inside the harbor. Other useful landmarks are:

— A large yellow building 500 yards east of the entrance.

— Two red and white checkered elevated water tanks, one 0.8 mile, the other 1.3 miles north of the entrance.

— A silver elevated water tank 1.0 mile east of the entrance.

Night entrance is straightforward, with Point Hueneme light (Fl. 5 sec.) and Oxnard aerobeacon (Rot. W and G) conspicuous. Two red range lights on 022° M lead up the fairway, visible 4° either side of the range line.

When entering Port Hueneme, watch out for large ships in the fairway and keep a close lookout for instructions from the shore. Note that regulations surrounding shipping traffic lanes apply.

### Berths and Facilities

There are no facilities for yachts, as this is a commercial port. Berth temporarily at Wharf 1 and request instructions from the berthing master at the root of the dock. Leave for Channel Islands as soon as conditions permit.

We repeat, Port Hueneme is NOT recommended for yachts. One can anchor outside the harbor east of the entrance in 35 feet (sand and shale), but this berth is bumpy and little more than a temporary stopping place.


USEFUL TELEPHONE NUMBERS

*Port Hueneme*
   Naval Construction
      Battalion Center . . . . . . . . . . . . . . . (805) 982-4711
      (Base Information Officer)
   Officer of the Day . . . . . . . . . . . . . . . (805) 982-4571
   Ship and Weather Information . . . . . (805) 982-3123
   Port Services Department . . . . . . . . . (805) 982-5202
*Point Mugu*
   Naval Weapons Test Center
      Headquarters . . . . . . . . . . . . . . . . . . (805) 982-7209
      (Officer of the Day)
*Yacht Club*
   Channel Island Naval Sailing Association
   P.O. Box 4395 N.C.B.C.
   Port Hueneme, CA 93043

# Part IV:

# Sailing Directions-Eastern Offshore Islands

Fig. 14.1a — *Santa Barbara Island from south, with Sutil Island.*

# CHAPTER *14*

# *Santa Barbara Island*

A visit to Santa Barbara Island can be somewhat of an adventure, for this small and desolate landmass lies 42 miles SW of Los Angeles Harbor, and on the outer approaches to the Santa Barbara Channel. Even from Santa Cruz, you have a 40-mile passage over open water in front of you.

Santa Barbara Island is only 1.5 nautical miles long and about 1.0 mile wide. The National Park Service administers the island (and Anacapa) as part of the Channel Islands National Monument. From a distance, the island appears as two landmasses, for the two peaks are 635 and 562 feet high, with the higher of them to the south. These peaks can be seen from over 25 miles away on clear winter days. The island is waterless, devoid of trees, but covered with succulents and interesting shrubs, which flower in brilliant colors during the spring. The flora includes the giant coreopsis which blooms yellow in the spring, and can reach a height of eight feet. Santa Barbara Island is famous for its sea lion colonies, and for occasional sea elephants, as well as thousands of sea birds. The fishing grounds around its shores are celebrated for abalone and lobsters.

*General Sailing Directions* (Fig. 14.1)

When making a passage from the Santa Barbara Channel, check with the Range Officer at Point Mugu before setting out, to avoid a time when missile firing is in progress (805) 982-8841. Your course will take you across the range, and it is always disconcerting to be turned back by an aircraft with a colossal loud hailer ordering you to return to port. This happened to us one fine summer's day, when an interesting cruise had to be aborted on short notice. Such restrictions don't apply when bound from Catalina or the Los Angeles area. When on passage from the mainland to Santa Barbara Island, keep a sharp lookout for shipping as you cross major shipping lanes into San Pedro and Long Beach.

As Santa Barbara Island is a relatively small target after a 40-mile passage, you should lay a compass course, even in clear weather. Your first sight of the island will probably be of one or two prominent peaks. The lower portions of Santa Barbara Island will come into sight when you are less than 10 miles out. In thick weather, you should approach the island with great care as soundings shoal rapidly from 60 feet into shallow water. The island is, however, surrounded by dense kelp beds, which give warning of land. The kelp extends out as far as the 10-fathom line in many places, on the west side of the island for more than a mile.

A night approach is simple, for Santa Barbara Island light acts as a signpost for commercial shipping bound for Los Angeles. Situated at the NE corner of the island, on Arch Point, the light is 195 feet high (Fl. 2½ sec., 6 miles). But, be warned — the light is obscured from 342° to 053° M by high ground. The main island lies 700 yards west of the light. Be careful when navigating close to shore at night. There are numerous, unlit, off lying dangers.

Cliffs of Santa Barbara Island are steep, dark-colored and bold. Arch Point, the NE corner, is low lying and steep cliffs on the east side of the island merge with dry slopes of the higher ground that drains into the ocean. The main anchorage at Santa Barbara Island lies off these cliffs.

## Santa Barbara Island Anchorage

### General Description

An open roadstead, which extends from Arch Point to the middle of the east shore of the island, the main landing and anchorage, is little more than an indentation in the shoreline that offers limited shelter from the prevailing westerlies. The kelp beds off Arch Point provide some protection from the surge, but the anchorage can be quite bumpy.

### Approach

From north, east or SE, identify Arch Point and shape

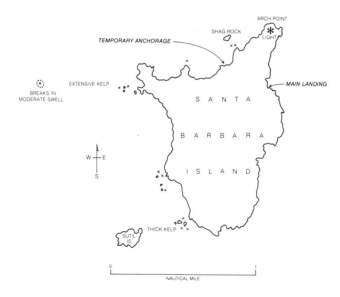

Fig. 14.1b — *Santa Barbara Island anchorages.*

*(Adapted from U.S. Government chart 18756)*

your course to the headland until just outside the kelp beds. Then look for the Park Service quonset huts on the top of the cliffs. The main anchorage lies north of the huts and the landing spot below it. Sometimes a gap in the kelp will be found, otherwise you'll have to thread your way through the seaweed growth.

### Anchorage

Anchor according to available room, draft, and swell conditions, in 25-35 feet (hard sand). To avoid disturbance from backwash, do not anchor too close to the cliffs. Most people use only a single, well-dug-in anchor for there is ample room to swing.

### Landing and Facilities

By dinghy, on the flat rocks east of the landing platform. Take care when stepping onto the rocks and judge the moment so that the dinghy is on the crest of a wave. No facilities on the island, but you may camp ashore, bringing your water with you! Sea lion rookeries are on the NW corner of the island, also about 0.5 mile SE of the landing. Keep well clear of the herds, for they are easily scared and have been known to bite humans.

---

### WARNING

Santa Barbara Island can be very windy. Should a strong NE wind fill in, *get out immediately*. The anchorage becomes a suicidal lee shore. W/NW winds occur mostly in fall and winter, when the anchorage is very gusty.

---

The south half of the island slopes steeply into the ocean, the 250-foot contour high above the ocean. Extensive kelp beds mantle this portion of the shore. Sutil Island, 300 feet high, lies 0.4 mile west of the southernmost point of the main island. This islet is surrounded by dense kelp. Although some bold ocean racers do it, we suggest that you resist the temptation to pass between Sutil and the main shoreline. The passage is congested with kelp. Although there is 20 feet in the channel, isolated subsurface rocks make navigation hazardous. The west coastline is very precipitous with high, dark cliffs. Again, dense kelp mantles the shore. You should keep well offshore at the NW corner to avoid both kelp and rocks off the point. But beware of an unmarked rock 0.7 mile west of this corner. Swell breaks on this rock in moderate weather, but you can easily come on it without warning in a calm. Shay Rock, 145 feet high, lies 200 yards off the NE coast, 0.2 mile west of the light. Keep clear of the rock and kelp beds around it.

You can anchor in calm weather off the north coast in 30-35 feet (sand). The anchorage is kelp-free, lies below the highest cliff on the north coast. When moving into this temporary anchorage, leave Shay Rock well to port and maneuver through the kelp, sounding carefully. High cliffs provide considerable shelter in SE weather, but this should never be regarded as an overnight anchorage, even if it is a good base for rowing close to sea lions playing in the water.

In calm weather, you can have an energetic day exploring the island's fascinating coastline by dinghy. The north and west shores can be alive with sea lions, gregarious and companionable, pausing to peer up at your dinghy.

Further information on Santa Barbara Island and its fascinating wildlife can be obtained from the Superintendent, Channel Islands National Monument, 1699 Anchors Way Drive, Ventura, California 93003, telephone (805) 644-8157. Rangers inspect the island regularly and sometimes reside there for short periods.

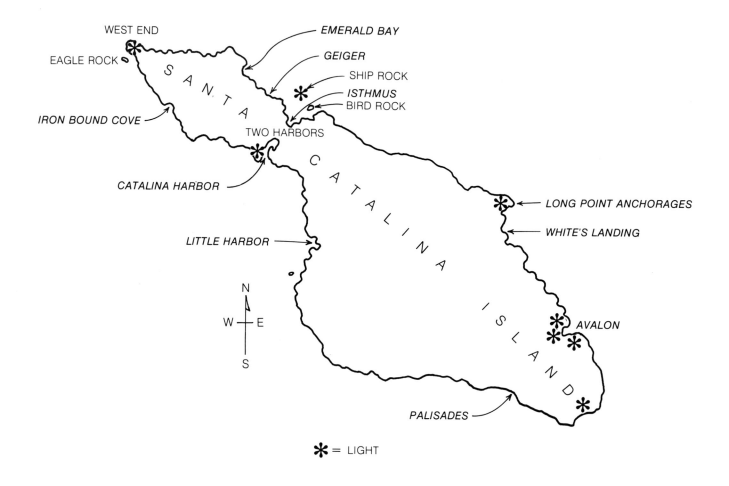

WEST END

EAGLE ROCK

EMERALD BAY

GEIGER

SHIP ROCK

ISTHMUS

BIRD ROCK

S A N T A

IRON BOUND COVE

TWO HARBORS

CATALINA HARBOR

C A T A L I N A

LITTLE HARBOR

LONG POINT ANCHORAGES

WHITE'S LANDING

I S L A N D

N

W — E

S

AVALON

PALISADES

✳ = LIGHT

Fig. 15.1 — *Santa Catalina Island anchorages described in the text.*

**186**

# Santa Catalina, San Nicholas, and San Clemente

Three offshore islands, one well-known and frequently visited, the other two largely off limits to small craft, lie off the south approaches to the Santa Barbara Channel. Many people will combine a visit to the Channel with a cruise to Santa Catalina and perhaps a night in an anchorage at San Nicolas or San Clemente Islands. The harbors and coves of Santa Catalina Island are relatively straightforward to cruise, many of them filled with private mooring buoys owned by individuals or Southern California yacht clubs. The military control access to San Clemente and San Nicolas, so public use of these outlying islands is severely restricted. This chapter summarizes some of the better anchorages and interesting features of the three islands, in the belief that more complete descriptions are unnecessary.

## Santa Catalina (Fig. 15.1)

Fig. 15.2 — *Catalina landmarks: Avalon harbor and town, with circular casino building to west.*

Emerald Bay and Howlands Landing. An annual card costs $35, contact Catalina Cove and Camp Agency, P.O. Box 1566, Avalon, CA 90704, (213) 832-4531. The remainder of the island is not covered by this permit, at the time of going to press the situation is uncertain.

Moorings at Catalina are privately owned, however, you can pick up a vacant mooring without charge on the understanding that the owner can ask you to leave at anytime. There are certain summer restrictions in this regard. Check locally for details.

---

### (Chart 18757)

Catalina lies 18 miles south of Point Fermin, 21 miles SE of Santa Barbara Island, a comfortable day's sail across the San Pedro Channel from the many marinas in the Los Angeles area. The island was first visited by Cabrillo in 1542, received its name from Sebastian Vizcaino in the seventeenth century. The flourishing Indian population of Catalina was soon decimated by Spanish missionary efforts, by foreign diseases, and seal hunters. The survivors evacuated to the mainland in the eighteenth century. Mexican Governor Pio Pico granted the island to Tomas Robbins, a sea captain, in 1846. Robbins sold Catalina for $10,000 after the island became part of California two years later. The present owner is the Santa Catalina Island Conservancy which controls most of the island except the incorporated city of Avalon at the east end.

Catalina is 18.5 nautical miles long NW/SE, and seven miles across at its widest point. Rugged peaks of the highest points of the island can be seen from a long distance on a clear day, reaching their greatest elevation of 2125 feet near the middle of the east portion of the island. Catalina is nearly severed by a deep canyon about six miles from West End light. Two coves, forming the Two Harbors area, almost sever the island, their bights being only 0.5 mile apart. This area is one of the most popular with small craft, for it offers excellent shelter in almost all conditions.

As you approach Catalina, the shoreline appears precipitous, with steep hillsides and inaccessible canyons falling into the ocean. The coast is steep-to, there are few outlying dangers. You should, however, keep a sharp lookout for offshore rocks off Isthmus Cove. The following are useful landmarks when approaching Catalina from the mainland:

— West End light, a white, pyramidical structure at the NW end of the island (Fl. 6 sec. 76 ft. 7 miles). This light is often faint, and you may be quite close to Catalina before you sight it.

— The low, Isthmus Cove area, visible from a long distance seaward on account of its low topography. Several conspicuous buildings lie behind the anchorage. Ship Rock, 1.0 mile offshore, is prominent, shaped, as the U.S. Pilot rather aptly remarks, like a haystack with a white summit. Ship Rock is lit at night (Fl. 4 sec. 6 miles).

— A prominent quarry 1.0 mile SE of Isthmus Cove.

— The city of Avalon, with its huddle of buildings and circular casino building at the root of the west breakwater. The harbor breakwaters are lit at night.

— The Carillon, an illuminated, white, concrete tower, 0.2 mile SW of Casino Point.

— Another conspicuous rock quarry 1.5 miles east of Avalon Bay.

— KBIG Radio tower on Blackjack Peak midway between Long Point and Avalon. A flashing red light on the tower can be seen for a long distance on a clear night. (The station's AM signal [740 KHz] is a useful signpost on thick days.)

— Long Point light on the NE side of the island, exhibited from a white, pyramidical structure (Fl. 2½ sec. 71 ft. 6 miles).

— The SE light, exhibited from a white, pyramidical structure (Fl. 6 sec. 212 ft. 7 miles).

The NE coast of Catalina is generally free of kelp, but the SW shore is protected by a narrow zone of seaweed.

A passage to Catalina, even at night, is straightforward, except after the passage of a front, in Santa Ana conditions, or in dense fog. Both Avalon and the Isthmus are well lit and visible from some distance. When approaching Catalina from the Santa Barbara Channel, you will sight the high peaks at the west end of the island first. Shape your course to leave West End at least 0.7 mile to port or starboard depending on your destination, especially at night when West End light may not appear until you are within two or three miles of the island. Keep a close lookout for shipping in the San Pedro Channel, especially in foggy weather.

---

*WARNING*
Avoid Santa Catalina Island in Santa Ana conditions. Both Avalon and Isthmus Cove can be extremely hazardous in these strong east/NE winds (page 18).

---

## Santa Catalina Anchorages

There are numerous anchorages at Catalina, many of them congested with private moorings. Here's a selection of the more important coves. More complete information will be found in the *Sea Guide* and the *Pacific Boating Almanac*.

## Two Harbors

## Isthmus Cove (Fig. 15.3)

### Approach

When approaching from seaward, identify the following landmarks:

— Ship Rock (66 feet), lies 1.0 mile offshore north of the cove. A reef extends 120 yards south of the rock. Its extremity uncovers three feet.

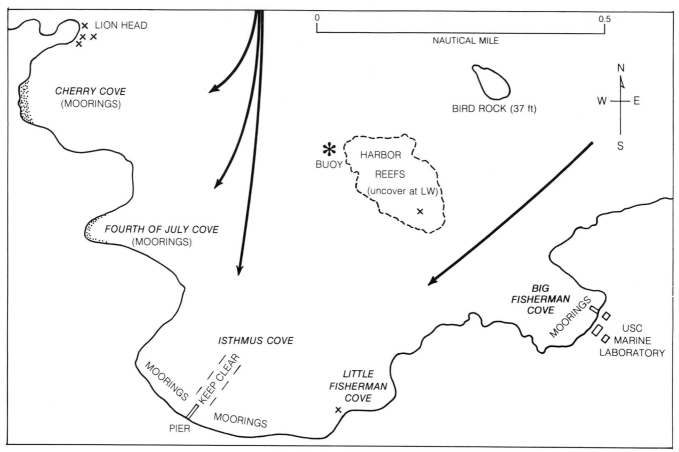

Fig. 15.3 — a. *Plan of Isthmus Cove and nearby anchorages.*

— Bird Rock (37 feet), a rounded, white-topped outcrop 150 yards long, is located SE of Ship Rock, some 500 yards off the east shore of Isthmus Cove. A kelp bed and Harbor Reefs, a large, rocky patch, lies awash at low tide, extend south of Bird Rock and should be given a wide berth. Two buoys mark the SE and west sides of Harbor Reefs.

The SE red buoy is lit (Fl. R 4 sec.), the black west marker unlit.

— Isthmus Pier extending from the center of the pier 300 feet seaward. A least depth of 12 feet will be found at the outer end. The pier is lit by shore lights.

*b. Ship Rock from NNE.*

— An unlighted red buoy ("No. 2") one mile SW of Ship Rock and 0.5 mile NW of Lion Head, marking Eagle Reef, least depth three feet, 0.25 mile offshore.
— USC Marine Laboratory buildings, conspicuous ashore SE of Bird Rock.

Once sufficient landmarks are identified, steer to enter Isthmus Cove itself. Leaving Bird Rock and Harbor Reefs well to port, and steering for the pier, head until your precise destination within the Isthmus is identified.

You can pass on either side of Ship Rock or between Eagle Rock and the shore in a least depth of 110 feet.

When entering the Isthmus from east, make sure you leave the red buoy that marks the SE side of Harbor Reefs well to starboard.

Entering the Isthmus at night is straightforward. Identify Ship Rock light, pass 400 yards to port or starboard, then move inshore, steering for the lighted buildings at the head of the cove. Steer on a course that keeps you well clear of Harbor Reefs and Bird Rock. Keep a sharp lookout for unlit mooring buoys.

## Isthmus Anchorages

### Isthmus Cove

The area off the pier is laid out with rows of private moorings. The Harbormaster's office at the foot of the pier will allocate you a vacant mooring or direct you to anchorage. Otherwise, anchor outside the 239 moorings in 60 feet or less, few facing SW if you lay too anchors. Isthmus Cove anchorage can be uncomfortable in strong west to NW winds, is dangerous in NE winds. About 100 vessels can anchor here, in addition to moored yachts. No lights are required on boats under 65 feet. The Harbormaster monitors Channel 11.

## 4th of July Cove

### Cherry Cove

Both coves lie NW of Isthmus Cove and are congested with private moorings. Both are well sheltered from west. The 42 moorings in 4th of July Cove are owned by the Fourth of July Yacht Club. Keep clear of the kelp beds off the headlands, separating these coves. A shore boat to the Isthmus is available during the summer. Hail a passing boat, or sound your horn three times.

## Little Fisherman Cove

The SE portion of this cove is leased to King Harbor Yacht Club, SW to the Channel Cruising Club.

## Big Fisherman Cove

The entire cove, including the waters contained by the two headlands, is leased by the USC Marine Science

Center. Three moorings SW of the dock can be picked up if not in use, but is better to inquire ashore first. You can anchor in 25 feet except when anchorage is prohibited. Big Fisherman is, however, one of the few berths on the north coast sheltered from NE to SE winds.

### Facilities

A fuel dock will be found at the head of Isthmus pier, also small boat docking facilities. Engine repairs and some boat maintenance work can be arranged at the Isthmus, there is a general store, an inn and a restaurant. Catalina Harbor, on the other side of the Isthmus is but a short walk across the narrow spit of land behind the pier. The Isthmus is the headquarters of the Cove and Camp Agency that maintains and leases moorings and collects landing fees for all the island except Avalon.

## Catalina Harbor (Fig. 15.4)

### Approach

Catalina Harbor lies on the south side of the Isthmus, a narrow, well-sheltered inlet that provides protection in all weather (Fig. 15.4b). Eighty moorings have been laid in the harbor, but there is plenty of space for up to 300 boats, most lying at anchor. Approaching Catalina Harbor from west, identify Eagle Rock, 300 yards offshore, 0.4 mile south of West End light. Incidentally, look out for steep swells off West End if any breeze is blowing or ocean surge running. Then follow the coast SE 6.5 miles to the deep coastal indentation that marks the entrance to Catalina Harbor, and the Isthmus. You can safely approach the shore to within 400 yards as you near the 800-yard wide entrance between two steep headlands. Approaching from east, follow the outer edge of the kelp beds as you round China Point, then identify the Isthmus area and the indentation that marks Catalina Harbor entrance.

Fig. 15.4 — *a, b* — *"Reconnaissance of Catalina Harbor" and "View of Catalina Harbor" by Lieutenant James Alden, 1852.*

Enter Catalina Harbor midway between the two headlands, keeping at least 150 yards off either side (Fig. 15.4). Identify Pin Rock, 100 yards offshore just inside the east point and give it a wide berth. Sounding your way toward the head of the cove, select your anchorage spot, clear of moorings.

Catalina Harbor light (Fl. 4 sec. 11 miles) has a higher intensity beam on a bearing of 030°, is obscured by hills from 104° to 208°.

### Anchorage

Anchor according to draft and available space in 24-30 feet (mud and soft sand) opposite low lying

c. *Catalina Harbor approach from the air, 1977.*

Ballast Point on the east side of the harbor. The head of Catalina Harbor is shallow, and you should anchor clear of the 80 moorings. There are two piers. A second anchor is advisable. Up to 300 vessels have been known to anchor here at one time. Beware of anchoring in the seaplane fairway.

**Facilities**

See Isthmus Cove.

## Avalon Harbor (Fig. 15.5)

Avalon Harbor is a popular port of call for yachts, and is usually congested with visitors. A winter visit is perhaps preferable, to avoid the summer crowds. The town itself is attractive and well worth a leisurely visit.

### Approach

Identify the following landmarks:

— Buildings of the town, the only major cluster of houses on Catalina.

— Water-edge rock quarry 1.5 miles east of the town, with its fresh cliff scars.

— Wrigley Mansion, high above the east side of the harbor. This large house with many windows is often floodlit at night.

Fig. 15.5 — a.  *Avalon Harbor from NW, 1977.*
b.  *Avalon Harbor in the aftermath of a Santa Ana.*

— Circular casino building at the root of Casino Point breakwater.

— Two harbor breakwaters, at the SE and SW edges of the bay.

Once these landmarks have been identified, steer to enter the harbor midway between the breakwaters. Keep a close lookout for ferries and seaplanes taking off and landing. The latter have the right of way.

Avalon Harbor can be entered at night by using the two harbor lights (Fl. W 2½ sec. on Cabrillo Breakwater; Fl. R 4 sec. on Casino Mole). They are visible about six miles out. A radio beacon (307 KHz .-/. . .- [AV]) is located on Casino Point.

### Anchorage and Moorings

The Harbormaster (VHF 16, then Channel 12) allocates visitor moorings when available. A harbor boat will meet you as you arrive and escort you to a mooring. Anchorage inside the harbor is impossible, but you can lie in Descanso Bay NW of Casino Point in 65-85 feet (sand and rock) clear of the moorings, a bumpy spot in even moderate west conditions. Anchor lights are required. The pier at the head of the harbor is used for a variety of commercial purposes.

### Facilities and Landing

A shore boat and garbage service operate in Avalon Harbor. The Standard Oil fuel dock lies close to the casino. Avalon Marine Service provides engine and underwater repairs, while normal provisions and marine hardware can be purchased near the harbor. Place your garbage on the stern for collection. Toilet treatment systems are mandatory.

*Useful phone number:* Harbormaster, Avalon 535; Chamber of Commerce, (213) 831-8822.

## Other Anchorages

The following anchorages are often used by small craft, but do not merit further description here (from West End, clockwise).

*Emerald Bay.* A popular skin diving anchorage, with 97 moorings. The 5-10 boat anchorage area is limited (sand). A 200-yard fairway with depths of 12-24 feet between the moorings leads into the bay. Many small outboard boats use this bay, which should be used in settled conditions only.

*Big Geiger Cove.* A 10-boat anchorage with shore area leased to Blue Water Cruising Club (no moorings). Little Geiger nearby is leased to the Offshore Cruising Club, holds one anchored boat and has three moorings. Both offer limited shelter from west.

*Buttonshell Beach, Hen Rock, Moonstone Beach.* Three anchorages under the west lee of Long Point. Buttonshell is a useful refuge in strong west winds. Anchor in 30 feet (sand). Only seven moorings, anchorage for 10 boats. Hen Rock Cove is leased to Balboa Yacht Club, Moonstone to Newport Harbor Yacht Club. Both contain moorings.

*White's Landing.* Another western refuge 3.5 miles NW of Avalon that accommodates up to 16 yachts or more anchored in 30-60 feet (sand). The Balboa Yacht Club leases part of the beach, Angeles Girl Scout Council the rest. Only 17 moorings.

*Palisades.* Three miles west of East End light on the south side of the island, Palisades consists of a small bight at the foot of high, conspicuous cliffs. This anchorage provides shelter from Santa Ana winds.

*Little Harbor.* 3.0 miles SE of Catalina Harbor, this anchorage is relatively sheltered in east conditions, is congested with moorings. The small anchorage is open to west and is partially protected by a series of rocks and reefs extending 300 yards south from the north side of the cove. Keep on the south side of the entrance when entering, sounding carefully. Kelp sometimes mantles the shoreline. Use plenty of scope, the bottom is rock and gravel. Up to 10-15 boats can anchor here, in 15 feet or more water.

*Iron Bound Cove* (sometimes called West End Santana Anchorage). This deep water anchorage, 3.0 miles south of West End, provides shelter in a Santa

Fig. 15.6 — *West end, Catalina Island from west, with Eagle Rock and Ribbon Point in far background.* *(Photo by Elyse Mintey)*

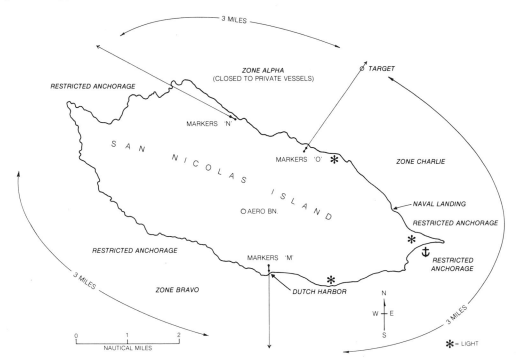

Fig. 15.7 — *San Nicolas Island anchorages described in the text.*

Ana in 30-50 feet. Many fishing boats use this berth in east winds. The anchorage is located SE of Eagle Rock opposite a conspicuous saddle in the land that terminates in a high, almost white colored cliff (Fig. 15.6). Anchor as far inshore as you can, clear of the kelp, to gain maximum shelter. At night, this will take you inside the obscured zone of West End light.

Our list of Catalina anchorages is by no means complete, and you should consult *Sea Guide*, the *Pacific Boating Almanac*, or *Sea* magazine, July 1976, for more information for details of Howlands, Willow and other spots.

## San Nicolas Island (Fig. 15.7)

San Nicolas (Chart 18755) is located 54 miles west of Port Hueneme, and 24 miles SW of Santa Barbara Island. The outermost of the California islands, San Nicolas was discovered by Juan Cabrillo in the sixteenth century. Although some enterprising sheep ranchers attempted to graze their herds on the island in the early years of this century, San Nicolas remained almost deserted after the Spanish removed its Indian inhabitants to the mainland. The U.S. Navy took over the island in the 1930s, and it is now closed to the public. Few yachts venture to San Nicolas, which is, in any case, off limits to the public, serving as part of the Pacific Missile Range.

From a distance, eight-mile long San Nicolas has a gently rounded profile, rising to 905 feet at its highest point. The middle of the island is visible from a long distance, especially at night, when an aerobeacon (Alt. Gp. Fl. W[2] G[1] 10 sec.) flashes brightly. Once you close the land, the west end of the island is mantled with drifting sand. An airstrip has been built at the east end of San Nicolas. Naval buildings are concentrated in this area. Deep arroyos cut into the high ground of San Nicolas. The entire island is surrounded with dense kelp beds, up to three miles offshore at the west end.

You should give this extremity of San Nicolas a wide berth, for there are dangerous reefs under the kelp beds. Begg Rock, a 15-foot off lying rock, rises abruptly from deep water of 300 feet eight miles NW of the west end of San Nicolas. It is named after the ship *John Begg* which struck a reef nearby on September 20, 1834. Reefs associated with the rock extend 100 yards north and south. You can come on this danger without warning in thick weather, missing the red whistle buoy (Fl. 4 sec.) 500 yards 330° M from Begg Rock. A lighted target ship is located 6.5 miles NW of Begg Rock, and exhibits Fl. W lights at bow and stern and a Fl. R at the masthead. A bell on board sounds 24 hours a day. The target is sometimes removed for repair, in which case a bell buoy (Fl. W) marks the spot. Another target is normally anchored two miles north of the middle of the north coast of San Nicolas, and is marked by a lighted bell buoy.

San Nicolas is lit by three major lights:

— North Side light, on the north shore, Fl. 6 sec. 8 miles, 33 feet (visible from 102° to 293° M),

— South Side light, on the south shore, Fl. 6 sec. 11 miles, 50 feet (visible from 247° to 086° M),

— East End light, on a point at the eastern extremity, Fl. G 4 sec. 6 miles, 55 feet (visible from 140° to 355° M),

— The aerobeacon already mentioned is the best long distance signpost at night.

This remote island is usually a very windy place. The prevailing NW winds sweep around both shores and over the summit of the island, especially in spring and when the Catalina Eddy is blowing. However, if you leave the mainland in the evening, you should have a calm passage, reaching San Nicolas in the morning.

San Nicolas is a Naval Restricted Area. You are only allowed in certain designated areas of the coastline. Specific written permission from the Commander of the Pacific Missile Range at Point Mugu is needed to land. The waters off San Nicolas have been divided into three zones, designated by lines of onshore markers, pairs of triangular RW beacons on 80-foot poles 100 yards apart. Zones "Alpha," "Bravo" and "Charlie" are marked on Fig. 15 and extend three miles offshore. Only official craft may use zone Alpha, while privately owned vessels can enter the other two zones unless Naval operations are in progress. Call (805) 982-7567 before leaving for the island to check whether the zones are open.

### Anchorages

The restricted anchorages at San Nicolas are clearly shown on Chart 18755. You may anchor in these berths only with written permission, or, in a grave emergency, with the authority of the senior officer on the island. These areas are sometimes under bombardment. If you attempt to enter them, you will be told to leave. Here, however, are the main anchorages:

— On the south side of a 0.6 mile sandspit at the east end of the island, 30-50 feet (hard sand). Anchor about 200 yards off the sandspit and about the same distance off the mainland, in the protection of the kelp. This can be an uncomfortable spot as the west swell breaks on the sandspit with great force. If you anchor too far inshore, ground swells can be dangerous. Strong land breezes can sweep over the anchorage. In rough weather, Santa Barbara Island is to be preferred.

— Dutch Harbor, on the south side of the island, one mile west of South Side light. A long, open bay foul with rocks and kelp that is entered through a gap in the kelp. Anchor in 30 feet (hard sand) as far in as possible. *This anchorage is available by permission only.*

Other possible anchorages exist (see Arthur R. Sanger's article, "How to Land on San Nicolas Island," *Sea*, October 1951) but local knowledge is essential to use them.

### Facilities

No facilities are available on San Nicolas except in the gravest emergency.

San Nicolas Island is best avoided by small craft. There is little to see or do here, except for the fishing.

## SAN CLEMENTE (CHARTS 18762, 18763) (Fig. 15.8)

Like San Nicolas, San Clemente is off limits to the public. The island, owned by the Federal Government since 1848, lies 43 miles SSW of Point Fermin, 19 miles beyond Santa Catalina Island across the outer Santa Barbara Channel. San Clemente is 18 nautical miles long NW to SE, four miles wide at its widest point, and 1965 feet high. From a distance, San Clemente looks like a table mountain. The NE coast is bold and precipitous. A conspicuous white radar dome is located on the highest part of the island and can be seen from both sides of San Clemente. The SW shore is more irregular and has more gentle slopes. Kelp beds extend out to the 60-foot line, masking outlying rocks for several hundred yards offshore. George Davidson was unenthusiastic about San Clemente: "Very few trees were found, and the aspect is sterile."

Approaching San Clemente is straightforward, for its bold topography is visible from a considerable distance even in restricted visibility. The island is well lit:

— West shore, south of Wilson Cove, two lights;
— Fl. G 6 sec., 8 miles 125 feet (visible 140° to 302° M);
— Fl. W 2½ sec. 7 miles, 140 feet (visible 305° to 135° M).
— Pyramid Head, Fl. G 6 sec., 6 miles, 235 feet (visible from 132° to 080° M). Pyramid Head is 900 feet high, jagged and conspicuous.
— China Point, Fl. W 4 sec., 6 miles, 112 feet (visible from 245° to 113° M).

A flashing red light (4 sec.) is exhibited at a height of 886 feet at the south end of San Clemente.

### Anchorages

Here are details of some San Clemente anchorages: *NW* Harbor (Chart 18763) lies at the NW corner of the

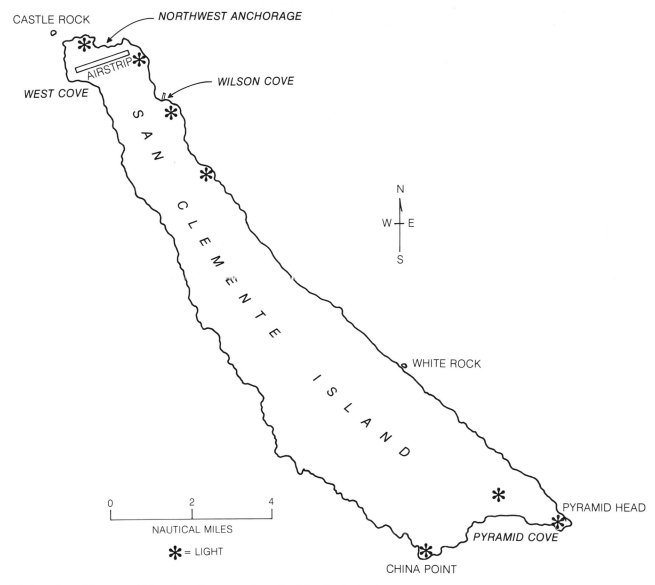

CASTLE ROCK

NORTHWEST ANCHORAGE

AIRSTRIP

WEST COVE

WILSON COVE

SAN CLEMENTE ISLAND

N
W — E
S

WHITE ROCK

0   2   4
NAUTICAL MILES

✳ = LIGHT

PYRAMID HEAD

PYRAMID COVE

CHINA POINT

Fig. 15.8 — *San Clemente Island anchorages described in the text.*

island, provides shelter from south and west winds. The anchorage is protected by a low islet and dense kelp beds to the north. A military pier extends from the head of the cove. You can anchor close to the west shore just outside the kelp in 18-30 feet (sand). The south side is less sheltered.

NW Harbor is dangerous in strong NW winds.

---

### WARNINGS

A danger area for live firing extends 300 yards around Castle Rock, at the extreme NW corner of the island, near this anchorage.

The Navy controls the waters within 300 yards of the island shores.

---

*Wilson Cove* (Plan on Chart 18763) lies 2.0 miles SE of NW Harbor, is the major military anchorage on the island. You can anchor here if military activity is not in progress. A 550-foot Navy pier extends seaward from the center of the cove. The buildings on the hill above the pier are conspicuous from offshore, and provide a useful landmark. Approach Wilson Cove from NE, as there are numerous military buoys north and south of the cove. The best anchorages for small craft is up to a mile NW of the pier in the lee of the kelp in 30 feet or more (sand). This berth provides some shelter from west winds, but the surge can be uncomfortable and strong. Winds may blow downslope in the afternoon. *You may not land at Wilson Cove except by official permission.*

Wilson Cove can be approached at night by identifying:

— Wilson Cove North End light (Fl. W 6 sec. 60 feet, 7 miles) visible from 124° to 315° M. The white pyramidical structure can be seen for some distance offshore by day. A large sand dune can be seen behind the light.

— Wilson Cove light (Fl. G 6 sec., 125 feet, 8 miles) is visible from 140° to 302° M. A huge radar dish lies behind this light

— Navy Anchorage South End light (Fl. . 2½ sec., 140 feet, 7 miles) is visible from 305° to 135° M, and is exhibited two miles south of Wilson Cove.

Once these lights are identified, look for the two range lights for the Navy pier:

— Two Fl. R lights on a bearing of 183° M from seaward. These lights are exhibited from two small houses 27 and 40 feet above sea level respectively.

*Pyramid Cove* lies at the extreme SE end of San Clemente, provides shelter from NW winds. When approaching the cove, identify Pyramid Head, a jagged headland 900 feet high, and China Point, lower lying with several detached rocks close offshore. Give China Point a wide berth to avoid off lying kelp and submerged rocks. The approaches are lit:

— Pyramid Head light (Fl. G 6 sec., 226 feet, 6 miles) visible from 132° to 080° M.

— Pyramid Cove anchorage light (Fl. R 4 sec., 0 miles, 886 feet), visible from 113° to 205° M.

— China Point light (Fl. W 4 sec., 6 miles, 112 feet), visible from 245° to 113° M.

Give Pyramid Point a wide miss, to avoid off lying dangers and kelp close inshore, and steer for the head of the cove. Keep a lookout for patches of kelp which may hide shallow dangers. Anchor at the west end of the cove under the cliffs and away from the beach in 25-40 feet. Numerous fishing boats use this anchorage. The best shelter is found by careful observation of wind patterns and local currents.

The Commandant of the 11th Naval District writes: "Any unoccupied anchorage can be used in Pyramid Cove except during periods when shore bombardment exercises are scheduled. To determine when these exercises are scheduled, you can call Commander, Amphibious Force, Pacific Fleet, at the Naval Amphibious Base, Coronado (714) 437-2231."

*West Cove* lies 1.5 miles SE of Cattle Rock (3 feet) at the NW corner of the island and provides some shelter from Santa Anas. Extensive sand dunes lie behind the anchorage, which is entered through a gap in the kelp. Anchor in 30 feet (rock and sand) inside the kelp.

---

### WARNING
A danger area extends 1.5 miles offshore and 3.5 miles south of this anchorage, due to live firing during military exercises.

---

This by no means exhausts the possibilities of San Clemente Island. We hope one day the island will be reopened to the public, and people will be able to explore more freely.

**Facilities**

No facilities are available on San Clemente Island except in the gravest emergency.

For information on restricted anchorages, contact The Commander, Amphibious Force, Pacific Fleet, Naval Amphibious Base, Coronado, California, (714) 437-2231, or 11th U.S. Coast Guard District, Heartwell Building, 19 Pine Avenue, Long Beach, California 90802.

---

### WARNING
*It is vital that you get up-to-date information on military activities before visiting either San Nicolas or San Clemente.* You should avoid the restricted areas at all times. If you do stray into one, obey the orders of patrolling boats or aircraft at once.

---

# INDEX OF PORTS, ANCHORAGES AND HAZARDS

BRIAN FAGAN was born in England and has been cruising since he was eight. He is a Professor of Anthropology at the University of California and a well-known teacher of archaeology. His books on archaeology include several textbooks and the widely acclaimed *The Rape of the Nile* and *Elusive Treasure,* histories of archaeological discovery in Egypt and in the Americas. Fagan's sailing experience is widespread and includes extensive cruising in Europe, from Finland to Greece. He and his wife Judy sail for three months in Europe each year in their 41-foot cutter. Research for the *Cruising Guide* has been a ten year project, begun in 1967 when he first started sailing in California. This involved thousands of miles of sailing, repeated channel crossings, and long hours of delving into archives and old official Pilot Books. Most of the research was carried out from the deck of a 31-foot sloop, which the Fagans own in partnership with two Santa Barbara friends. The project was nearly aborted when their house and library was destroyed in the 1977 Sycamore Canyon fire. Brian and Judy are cat lovers and won the Cruising Association's Hanson Cup in 1975, for a cruise from England to Finland and back.

GRAHAM POMEROY was born in London and received his first ocean experience at age five when he crossed the Atlantic on the *Queen Mary*. Since the age of sixteen he has assisted in the delivery and running of many types and sizes of vessel and has sailed extensively off the Southern California coast. He has also cruised in Canada and Europe and has recently returned from a 2500 mile cruise along the coast of Baja California. Combined with his love of sailing and the ocean is his interest in people and their ships. Graham has worked in the photographic business for ten years and has extensive marine photography experience. For the past two years he has taught photography (both color and "black and white") in the Recreation Program at the University of California, Santa Barbara.

Brian and Graham met in an Adult Education class on navigation in Santa Barbara and have subsequently sailed many miles together in the research for this book and just for fun.

# NAUTI-NOTES

*NAUTI-NOTES*

# NAUTI-NOTES

NAUTI-NOTES

*NAUTI-NOTES*

# NAUTI-NOTES